THE BIG 50

DETROIT TIGERS

The Men and Moments that Made the Detroit Tigers

Tom Gage

TRIUMPH
BOOKS

This book is available in quantity at special discounts for your group or organization. For further information, contact:

Triumph Books LLC
814 North Franklin Street
Chicago, Illinois 60610
(312) 337-0747
www.triumphbooks.com

Library of Congress Cataloging-in-Publication Data

Names: Gage, Tom, author.
Title: The big 50 Detroit Tigers : the men and moments that made the Detroit
  Tigers / Tom Gage.
Other titles: Big fifty Detroit Tigers
Description: Chicago, Illinois : Triumph Books, 2017.
Identifiers: LCCN 2016041163 | ISBN 9781629373218 (paperback)
Subjects: LCSH: Detroit Tigers (Baseball team)—Biography. | Detroit Tigers
  (Baseball team)—History. | BISAC: SPORTS & RECREATION / Baseball /
  General. | SPORTS & RECREATION / Baseball / History.
Classification: LCC GV875.D6 G34 2017 | DDC 796.357/640977434—dc23 LC
record available at https://lccn.loc.gov/2016041163

Printed in U.S.A.
ISBN: 978-1-62937-321-8

Design by Andy Hansen

*To Sarge and Bear, who slept—and
sometimes barked—while I wrote*

[Contents]

[Foreword]

by Alan Trammell

After an exhibition game the Tigers had just played at Marchant Stadium in Lakeland, Florida, Tom Gage, a baseball writer I've known for 30 years—maybe more—mentioned he was writing a book about the Tigers, so we started talking about the chapters that were going to be included.

One, he said, was going to be about Al Kaline, a man I respect so much, someone who long ago became my friend. Another chapter was going to be about the home run Kirk Gibson hit off Goose Gossage in the 1984 World Series. Watching Gibby's home run at Tiger Stadium was one of the great thrills of my career.

I loved the sound of the book. I loved the history it was going to cover. The more we talked about the Tigers that day in Lakeland, the more I was reminded about the long and really fascinating story of the team for which I played 20 years.

I played next to Lou Whitaker for 19 of those years. Tom said there would be a chapter about Lou. We broke in together, Lou and I. He got three hits in his first game; I got two. We had won the Double A championship on a Wednesday night and then flew up to Detroit the next morning. We went up to the front office together, signed our contracts together but then didn't play in the game that day. After that we flew to Boston for a Friday doubleheader and we started the second game. Then our manager Ralph Houk told us we were going to start *The Game of the Week* on national television the next day. What a way it was for our careers in the majors to start.

I played 17 seasons for Sparky Anderson, a man who I owe so much to because of how much I learned from him. I was told there would be a chapter about Sparky, too, and there is.

Now that I've been a coach and a manager, as well as a player, I better appreciate everything he went through.

I'm glad to see there's a chapter on Ernie Harwell because his kindness was so genuine.

Frank Tanana's wonderful game against the Toronto Blue Jays in 1987, Jack Morris' no-hitter against the Chicago White Sox in 1984, Dave Bergman's memorable at-bat against Roy Lee Jackson—they are all part of this book.

It's great to see that Willie Hernandez is also included because he was the last piece of our puzzle in 1984. What control he had, and to pitch multiple innings as a closer? You just don't see that anymore.

I was part of those stories because that was my era. They were part of me. They're still part of me. You don't play for as long as I did for the Tigers without realizing just how great a history the team has. And because I played at Tiger Stadium, I played in the ballpark where so many generations of great players were the Tigers of their day. That old dugout I sat in when I played, and had to duck not to hit my head, was the same dugout where Hank Greenberg and Charlie Gehringer, among many others, sat before me.

I'm very happy I played in the era of baseball in which I did. I wouldn't change that for anything. But to me, baseball is interesting to talk about, read about, and learn about in all its eras. I've always felt I've been sort of a student of baseball. So when Tom asked me if I'd be interested in writing the foreword for his book, I said I would be, in part because I'm eager to learn more Tigers history from it.

But it's also because I knew Tom would treat that history the right way. I was pleased to be asked—and am honored to help. Tom covered many of the moments and many of the players you're going to be reading about, including me. Much of what you will read took place during my career. Some of it occurred after I played, and a lot of it occurred before. I hope you have as much fun exploring these pages as I did.

KIRK GIBSON'S GAME 5 HOME RUN

In the colorfully long history of the Detroit Tigers—with its great players and defining moments—there have never been words more memorable than: "He don't want to walk you."

That, of course, is what Sparky Anderson repeatedly shouted to Kirk Gibson as Gibson waited to see if Goose Gossage would pitch to him with first base open during the 1984 World Series.

The footage of the video seems grainy now because it no longer happened yesterday. But almost as if it did, there's Sparky—as he was that October day—watching from the Tigers' dugout while his San Diego counterpart, Dick Williams, saunters to the mound to speak with Gossage. It's Game 5 at Tiger Stadium. The Tigers are looking like the better team—as they would prove to be. But they've not yet put away the pesky Padres. Gibson is at the plate in the eighth inning; two runners are on. It is center-stage time. But he embraces it. With the Tigers up by two games and leading by a run, the city is poised to celebrate.

In the first inning, Gibson had hit his first home run of the series off left-hander Mark Thurmond. Through the first four games, it hadn't been an impactful World Series for him—just a few contributions here and there. He singled in a run in the first inning of Game 2, which the Tigers lost. In Game 3 he was hit by a pitch with the bases loaded, giving the Tigers a four-run lead in the third inning en route to a 5–2 victory.

But he had not done anything in the way of late thunder. Then again, no one had. Through the first four

games, there'd been only two runs scored after the fifth inning—both by the Padres. Neither had come close to deciding an outcome. But the buildup would merely be an appetizer to the entrée of one showdown, one decision, and to the immortality of Sparky's words to Gibson: "He don't want to walk you."

The Tigers scored three runs in the first inning of Game 5, two of them on Gibson's home run. It took three singles, along with Lance Parrish's steal of second, to add a third run, which was enough to knock Thurmond out of the game after just one out. By the fourth inning, though, the Tigers' lead was gone. So was their starter, Dan Petry.

And when Alan Trammell flied out to center to leave the bases loaded in the bottom of the fourth, the Padres were clearly encouraged by the problems they were causing. "We thought they were going to roll over," Gibson said, "but they came back."

Then came a huge play, the most important of the series so far—a pop-up to shallow right. With the game tied, the bases loaded, and one out in the fifth, Rusty Kuntz was called upon to pinch-hit for Johnny Grubb. It was a lefty-righty percentage move, but it surprised the kindly Kuntz all the same.

"I was down at the end of the bench, cheering on the boys and thinking, *There's no way I'm ever getting into this game*," he said years later to *The Kansas City Star*. "Thank God, I didn't say it out loud, but I remember thinking to myself, when my name was called, *why?*"

A .286 hitter in 140 at-bats for the Tigers during the regular season, Kuntz had struck out as a pinch-hitter in Game 2 against the same pitcher he was about to face, lefty Craig Lefferts.

Making contact, though, was essential this time. Knowing he couldn't afford to strike out, Kuntz went up to the plate dead set on swinging at a first-pitch fastball. "And what did I get?" he said. "A change-up. I barely made contact."

But, such as it was, he did, lofting a sickly little pop-up to no man's land between second and right. "I always kid him about it being a deep fly ball," Gibson said. Kuntz still thinks of it as a "dying quail."

Coming in from right, Tony Gwynn lost sight of the ball. It was his play to make, but he didn't know where the ball was. Desperate to help, second baseman Alan Wiggins made a good play to catch it.

Normally the runners wouldn't have advanced. "But we had this going for us," Kuntz said. "Gibby was on third, and he was going to run through anybody who got in his way."

Or as Gibson put it, "I could always run the catcher over if I had to." In any case, as soon as the ball was hit, he thought about scoring. "I was taught not to predetermine the outcome of a play," Gibson said, "always be ready for an opportunity. That's what I did. But I was always one to push the issue. That was one of my strengths."

Tagging up, Gibson beat the throw home. He had scored on a sacrifice fly to second base, giving the Tigers a 4–3 lead. They increased it to two runs with Parrish's solo shot that greeted Gossage in the seventh. "It was a huge home run for the 'Big Wheel,'" Gibson said. "What a great teammate Lance was, but we were all close on that team. There was pressure to get it done because of the [35–5] start, and we wanted it bad."

If Parrish's home run meant that Gossage was going to be hittable that day, the last to realize it was Gossage himself—because in the most pivotal showdown of the series, his stubborn self-confidence became a pivotal factor. Hanging tough, the Padres were just a run down at 5–4 after Kurt Bevacqua's solo home run off Willie Hernandez in the eighth. As Vin Scully said on the telecast, "We have a game again."

But with faltering command of his fastball, Gossage walked Marty Castillo on a full-count pitch to start the bottom of the eighth. Lou Whitaker was up next. Off the field, it had already been a memorable day for Whitaker. His daughter, Sara, was born that morning. But it was about to be a good day for him on the field as well.

After swinging away on the first pitch, Whitaker bunted the ball to third, but when Graig Nettles' throw went to second base for the start of a possible double play, shortstop Garry Templeton was standing in front of the bag instead of on it. Templeton thought the throw would be going to first base, so Castillo was ruled safe at second, while Whitaker was retired at first on a sacrifice. "I can't believe what's happening," said broadcaster Joe Garagiola. "Gremlins have hit the field. Templeton can't believe he did that."

After Trammell bunted the runners to second and third, Scully speculated—logically so—that the Padres would walk Gibson

intentionally with first base open. Thinking the same thing, catcher
Terry Kennedy put up four fingers to indicate an intentional pass. But in
a meeting at the mound, Williams decided not to walk Gibson. Rather,
Gossage decided not to walk him. Miked in the dugout, Anderson can
be heard saying, "If he changes his mind, I can't believe it."

It's what happened, though. "I have a distinct feeling," Scully
said on the air, "that Goose Gossage talked Dick Williams out of an
intentional walk."

And understandably so. Gossage had struck out Gibson the first
six times he ever faced him. At the time of the showdown, Gibson
was 1-for-10 with seven strikeouts against him. Goose also had easily
retired Gibson on a pop-up in Game 4. He owned Gibson.

And both of them knew it. "I remember the first time I faced him,"
Gibson said of Gossage. "It was my first big league at-bat in 1979. The
Yankees had just taken the lead, so Goose was coming in to pitch. As
soon as he got to the mound, I noticed all the extra guys suddenly had
to take a pee. They disappeared.

I walked down to the bat rack, grabbed my bat, and started
clanking it around, so Sparky could see I wanted to hit. Then he said
to me, 'what do you want, big boy?' I said, 'I want him [meaning
Gossage].' With a runner on base later in the inning, Sparky said, 'Go
get him, he's yours.' So in my first major league at-bat, I'm going up
against the best [f---ing] closer in the game."

It did not last long. "He fires the first pitch, I swing and foul it
back," Gibson said. "Goose didn't look in for signs back then. He just
threw. He quickly threw the second pitch, and I fouled that one back,
too. The third one was on the black, and just like that, I'm out. The ball
hissed as it went by me. I'd never seen anything that hard. It was like a
15-second at-bat."

No wonder Gossage, a future Hall of Famer, felt confident he could
get Gibson out again in the eighth inning of Game 5. But Gibson was
mentally preparing himself for the showdown, feeling ready because
of what he'd gone through in 1983. "I got into it with Sparky that year,"
Gibson recalled. "He told me at the beginning of that season, 'I'm
either going to make you or ruin you. You'll either handle it or you will
go crying home to your mama's lap. When the easy pitchers are out

there, the cake-eaters, you'll be sitting next to me learning the game. But when the big boys are pitching, you'll be out there.'"

Gibson hit only .227 in 1983, but by the time 1984 rolled around, he not only knew the game, he was ready to face the so-called big boys. Gossage was one of the big boys.

"The key was 1983," Gibson said. "It forced me to my knees. But Sparky did it for the right reasons. Then the next thing I know, I'm in the World Series facing Goose with a chance to put it away. The thought that wanted to come into my mind at the time was that this guy owned me, but all of a sudden, I'm staring at the upper deck in right and thinking to myself, *You love it when people challenge you. That's when you perform even better.* So I looked into the dugout at Sparky and flashed five fingers at him twice."

"Taking him up, 10 bucks," was the message. It was Gibson's way of betting Sparky $10 he would take Gossage upstairs. Sparky grinned but kept shouting, "He don't want to walk you."

"I knew I wasn't going to be walked," Gibson said. "I just wanted to be prepared. I was getting my mind comfortable with the situation—instead of with Goose dominating me. The count went to 1-0, then I smoked it. I can still see it. I can still feel it."

So can some of his teammates. "It's a joy to watch even now," Trammell said, "and always will be."

During the ball's majestic flight, Sparky kept yelling, "Get outta here. No, don't walk him. Don't walk him."

The home run wasn't an immediate game-winner but might as well have been. "The joy of the moment was that we knew it was all but over," Gibson said. "They were done."

Years later he would sign two dozen baseballs and send them to Gossage. On them Gibson wrote, ".133 average, 2-for-15, 1 HR," signifying what he'd done against the Goose in his career. Good-naturedly, Gossage signed them and sent the balls back with this inscription: "I should have walked him."

But if he had, the most magical Tigers' moment never would have happened.

2

TY COBB

Is it unanimous? Of course it is. There's no denying that Ty Cobb was a great baseball player, the most dynamic ever to play for the Tigers. No other Tiger, for instance, ever won 12 batting titles, including nine in a row. No other Tiger hit .400 three times, the third coming in 1922 when he was 35. To finish it off, Cobb hit .524 (22-for-42) in his last 13 games.

An argument can be made—and likely won—that he was not the best of teammates, and that his talent, by itself, could not transform the Tigers into a championship club. The truth is that Cobb never played on a World Series-winning team. Three of his teams lost the series, and his postseason batting average for the three series in which he participated was an ordinary .262.

Cobb, however, was not an ordinary player nor an ordinary individual. Indeed, he was as far from being ordinary as anyone who ever played the game. Part of that can be attributed to a personality for which the list of applicable adjectives would require the rest of this chapter.

One, however, seems to say it all: complex. Finishing a close second: difficult. Not far behind: tormented. How about mean? Was Cobb a mean person? By many accounts he was. To be sure, he was capable of being mean.

It was absurdly mean in 1912, for instance, for him to pummel a disabled heckler at Hilltop Park in New York, an incident that led to a 10-day suspension for Cobb and a one-day players' strike by the Tigers. In a game that they lost 24–2 with inept substitutes, one of the Tigers' temporary outfielders got hit on the head with a fly ball.

But to say that meanness was Cobb's dominant trait would be to undermine the good he sought to do as a philanthropist after his playing days, which included a donation to build a hospital in his hometown of Royston, Georgia, in 1950.

Was he a racist? Again, there have been numerous such accusations, but in his book, *Ty Cobb: A Terrible Beauty*, Charles Leehrsen wrote that several of the black men Cobb with whom he allegedly fought "were actually white." Leerhsen also discovered that Cobb was descended "from a long line of abolitionists" and that his grandfather refused to fight for the Confederacy in the Civil War "because of the slavery issue." So if Cobb was racially motivated at times, it was not because his family had been incorrigibly bigoted. Whether it was against white men or black, opposing players or teammates, Cobb was a fierce combatant. He didn't always win his fights—nor did he always start them—but he often found trouble.

And trouble often found him.

To understand Cobb as a high-performance player, he must also be understood as a high-strung individual. There is always this caveat about Cobb, however: trying to understand him rarely translates into doing so. He was that complex. And because he was, there often were ramifications involving his team.

It's true, for instance, that in the spring of 1907—the year in which Cobb began to mature into the electrifying performer who became the first player elected to baseball's Hall of Fame—he fought with both a groundskeeper and the keeper's wife in Meridian, Mississippi, during the closing days of spring training. Cobb reportedly took exception to the groundskeeper's impertinent familiarity that was influenced by the possibility the so-called culprit was inebriated. That incident led to a series of altercations with Charles "Boss" Schmidt, the Tigers' burly catcher who knocked Cobb unconscious in one such skirmish.

There also was an incident that took place in Cleveland while the Tigers were trying to win their third consecutive American League pennant in September 1909. Unlike the raw 20-year-old who was pummeled by Schmidt before his first full season in the majors, Cobb was nearing his third consecutive batting title when he had a run-in with an elevator operator and a security guard at the Tigers' hotel. Because the guard was injured—and with Cobb allegedly threatening to kill him—a warrant was issued for the outfielder's arrest. The charge was "assault with the intent to kill."

The matter still hadn't been resolved by the time the World Series between the Tigers and the Pittsburgh Pirates was about to begin, making it necessary for Cobb to avoid traveling through Ohio when the team journeyed from Detroit to Pittsburgh. But in the hours after the incident in Cleveland, the immediate problem was how to get Cobb out of town before the police detained him. The escape, according to the *Detroit Free Press*, required "the cunning" of manager Hughie Jennings.

While the local constable concentrated on nabbing Cobb as he boarded the Tigers' scheduled transportation to the train station, Jennings "steered Cobb out through a rear entrance and down several side streets" to a waiting car. Cobb got on board "just as the train was pulling out." The matter was settled two months later when Cobb pleaded guilty to assault and battery. But he was required to pay only a fine and costs.

To say that all players despised Cobb is incorrect. He certainly had detractors, including his earliest Tigers teammates, who taunted, teased, and hazed him. Some say that such treatment merely sharpened his focus on becoming the best. Cobb was emotionally fragile, which didn't help his state of mind when word came from home in 1905 that his mother had accidentally killed his father, whose message of "Don't come home a failure" had become Cobb's earliest mantra. Young Ty, just 18 at the time and in his first year with the Tigers, had wanted to make his father proud.

One great player who liked Cobb the instant he met him was Pittsburgh's Honus Wagner, who hadn't known him before the 1909 World Series, which the Pirates won in seven games.

The two got along so well, in fact, that Cobb invited Wagner down to Georgia for a hunting trip after the season. Wagner took him up on the offer, only to return home three days later, according to *The New York Times*. "Cobb is one of the most genial gentlemen I ever met," said Wagner, who also was part of the first Hall of Fame class, "but there are two things we will never agree on."

One of them was baseball. The other was the quality of hunting in Georgia. Wagner had gone there because Cobb bragged about it, but he came away empty-handed. "I could have had a crack at a squirrel

A WILD BRAWL

Do yourself a favor. Check it out on YouTube if you've never seen it before because it's one of the most amazing moments in Tigers history. In the seventh inning of the second game of the 1972 American League Championship Series, the Tigers' Lerrin LaGrow hit Oakland's Bert Campaneris on the ankle with a pitch—and Campaneris of the A's responded by throwing his bat at him.

It wasn't a soft toss. "Campy" heaved it with everything he had. He didn't hit LaGrow; the bat sailed over his head. But the Tigers reacted with rage, especially fiery manager Billy Martin, who had to be restrained by the umpires.

Campaneris, of course, was ejected. Not only that, he was suspended for the rest of the series. "I don't know what that idiot was thinking," Martin said about the incident that emptied the Tigers' bench, "but if there's ever another fight, I'm going to find him and beat the shit out of him."

Of the A's, who were relatively docile in the aftermath of the incident, Martin said, "They didn't want to fight us. They would have gotten their heads knocked off."

Martin never met a fight he'd shy away from, and it was with his spirited leadership that the Tigers nearly snarled their way into the World Series that year. Because of a players' strike, the Tigers and Boston Red Sox didn't play the same number of games, so it was possible to win the American League East by half a game, which the Tigers did with a record of 86–70.

Hugely important for them down the stretch was Woodie Fryman, a Kentucky tobacco farmer who'd been claimed off waivers from the Philadelphia Phillies. In 14 starts over the final two months, Fryman went 10–3 with a 2.22 ERA. He also won the game against Boston that clinched the division title.

The Tigers came up short, three games to two, in the ALCS, though. Fryman allowed only one earned run in Game 5, but the Tigers lost 2–1 all the same. The difference was Reggie Jackson's steal of home in the second inning, a play on which he tore a hamstring. The injury forced Jackson to miss the World Series.

But check that out, too. After you watch Campaneris heave his bat at LaGrow on YouTube, you can relive Reggie's steal of home. If you care to, that is.

or two," Wagner told *The Times*, "and perhaps a barnyard chicken, but as for hunting, Georgia won't do. No more of it for 'Baby Hans.'"

It's true, though, that Wagner had called Cobb genial, which must have come as a surprise to those who had formed an impression of Cobb as a snarling, angry, combustible individual. He was capable of being all three, especially combustible. But he could also be the opposite of all three.

He was constantly complex, though, and often difficult. With his tragic family situation, Cobb spent his early years in the majors with a certain degree of torment churning within. Therefore, he came across as a combative, ultra-competitive southern punk who let nothing stand in his way. But he was also talented, smart, and confident.

Nothing conveys Cobb's self-confidence in better fashion than the way he did whatever he chose to do on a baseball field.

He could even change himself as a hitter, which he did to prove a point in 1925 by hitting five home runs in two days against the St. Louis Browns just to show he could have been "that kind of hitter." Cobb would voice regrets later that he hadn't been more of a power hitter during his career.

He was better known for the way he owned the base paths. Four times in his career—equaled only by Wagner—Cobb stole second, third, and home in the same inning. In 1911 he did it on three consecutive pitches against the Philadelphia Athletics. In the same week, he won a game by scoring from first on a routine single to right. When the catcher went to apply the tag, it was written that "All he touched was thin air." Such plays made Cobb a thrilling player to watch. He loved utilizing his speed because he thrived on outthinking those who felt they could get the better of him.

Leading the American League in stolen bases six times, he had a reputation as a dirty base runner, one who would go in with his spikes high. But a Washington Senators infielder of the era, Bob Unglaub, defended him. "It may look to some folks that Cobb was a dirty player," Unglaub said in a 1909 *Free Press* story, "but it is my honest opinion that he never thinks of putting spikes to one who thinks to block him. He thinks only of getting to the bag. He takes 10 chances to the average player's one, runs like the wind, and slides with such terrific force and speed that anyone who tries to stop him is likely to get into trouble. The man who gets in front of Cobb's spikes has no one to blame but himself if he gets cut."

That's the kind of player Cobb was. He had enemies but equally strong defenders. No one ever completely understood him. Decades after his death, however, it's still worthwhile to try.

3

MICKEY LOLICH'S HEROICS IN THE 1968 WORLD SERIES

With the ball in the air, the improbable was a blink away from happening. From actually, unbelievably, wonderfully, happening. Bill Freehan camped under Tim McCarver's pop-up. Eager to make sure the final out was caught, Norm Cash had initially charged in from first base, but he began to back off. Directing traffic, Mickey Lolich was yelling, "Bill, Bill, Bill!"

Were the Tigers really going to come all the way back from the brink of losing the 1968 World Series to win it? Were they really going to beat the unbeatable Bob Gibson with it all on the line? They were. And was Lolich about to go for a triumphant ride in Freehan's arms as the Tigers celebrated? He was. "I figured it was better to jump on him than to have him jumping on me," Lolich said.

Whether it happens with a fly ball, a ground ball, or a spectacular play, the last out of a World Series for the winning team becomes a snapshot—forever stored in the album of the mind.

The last out in 1968 looked like a routine little pop-up near the plate. "I just remember thinking, *Freehan's got it. This is over,*" Lolich said.

Considering what it took to arrive at the magnificent moment, however, the pop-up wasn't routine. The 1968 World Series had been one of twists and turning points, including Mayo Smith's decision to play Mickey Stanley at short, Willie Horton's throw home in Game 5, and Jim Northrup's triple in Game 7. Not to mention Lolich's pitching and even his hitting.

With a decision that never got the attention it deserved—partly because its success neutralized whatever second-guessing it would have generated had it failed—Smith proved in Game 5 just how golden his Midas touch was. Down three games to one and with the Tigers trailing by a run with one out in the bottom of the seventh—eight outs to go, in other words, with the World Series on the line, Smith elected not to pinch-hit for Lolich.

It's true that the Tigers starter had hit the first home run of his career in Game 2 off Nelson Briles, the pitcher he was about to face. But it's also true that Briles already had struck him out twice that day. And what's truer than true is that Lolich was thoroughly stunned by Smith's decision. "It's standard procedure when it's your time to bat," Lolich said, "that if the manager doesn't make an immediate decision, you're supposed to go out to the on-deck circle. So that's what I did with Don Wert batting. When Wert struck out, I looked back at the dugout, right at Mayo, and he was looking at me. But no one was coming out of the dugout."

In anticipation of pinch-hitting for Lolich, Gates Brown already had a bat in his hands.

"Gates later told me he'd gotten ready when the inning began," Lolich said.

Broadcaster George Kell theorized that Smith thought the Tigers still had time to get the runs they needed in the final two innings and couldn't afford to take out the dependable Lolich.

Even so, Lolich could not believe he was hitting in that situation. He checked two more times, gazing into the dugout once before the first pitch to him and once after. "Mayo was motioning for me to stay where I was," Lolich said, "so I thought to myself, *Well, I guess I'm supposed to be here.*"

Did Mickey strike out a third time against Briles? Not exactly. "I hit a flare to right field," Lolich said, "and as I was running to first base, I kept yelling at the ball to 'Get down, you son of a bitch, get down.'" Following orders, it got down. With Lolich at first base, the problem now became one of speed. The tortoise of the Tigers had just singled.

But just as there'd been no pinch-hitter, no pinch-runner emerged from the dugout.

At that point the Cardinals replaced Briles with relief pitcher Joe Hoerner. Unlike Smith's strategy, the move failed. Al Kaline eventually got the inning's big hit, a two-run single that drove in both Lolich and Dick McAuliffe to put the Tigers in front. Cash's single made it 5–3 Tigers.

After a harmless eighth, the Cardinals put two runners on base in the ninth, but Lolich worked out of the jam, in part with a strikeout of Roger Maris. "I don't remember if it was Maris [whom he struck out 11 of the last 20 times he faced him]," Lolich said, "but I was glad to see a left-hander coming up in that situation."

With hope renewed by their Game 5 victory, the Tigers tied the series with a 13–1 rout in Game 6. And with Lolich becoming Freehan's passenger after the final out, they completed their incredible comeback in Game 7. For winning three games, Lolich was named the World Series' Most Valuable Player. "Although it's just a plaque," he said, "it's the item from my career that I treasure the most."

Without question, acclaim had arrived for the chubby chucker, who would have been content being a mailman instead—and was late to spring training one year because of a test to become one. By his own admission, Lolich had a much better major league career than what he called his "very, very bad" time in the minors. In fact, after signing in 1958, the amount of time Lolich allotted himself to become successful had nearly expired.

Fortunately, Lolich received a game-changing tip in 1962, a difficult year during which he told the Tigers that he was quitting. "The first batter I faced that season, Bobby Boyd, hit a one-bounce liner that hit me in the face and went down to the right-field corner for a stand-up triple," said Lolich, who opened the season at Triple A Denver. "My left eye closed on me completely. The ball only cracked my cheekbone, but I pitched the next four games not being able to see out of my left eye. I was totally blind out of it, which meant that when I followed through, I couldn't see the hitter. So the Tigers tried to send me down to [Double A] Knoxville, but I didn't want to go because of the manager there [Frank Carswell]. I had pitched for him the year before, including a game in which I felt a twinge in my elbow, which I told him about. But because the temperature was something like 105 degrees that day, Carswell thought I was trying to get out of the game, so he said, 'Get your ass back out there and pitch the next inning.' Well, I felt more twinges and some severe pain, so I told him about it, and he ordered me again to 'Get back out there.' After the game he closed the clubhouse doors and called me everything in the book, including gutless, in front of the team. It was a total embarrassment to me."

Meanwhile, there proved to be a medical reason for Lolich's elbow pain: "Three bone chips, which I still have," he said. "But I learned to

WAIT 'TIL NEXT YEAR

The 1967 Tigers proved that sometimes it's worth the wait. After seeing their pennant aspirations abruptly vanish, the Tigers not only waited 'til next year, they won it all next year.

It was an exciting, to-the-wire pennant race in 1967. In their last 27 games, the Tigers never trailed by more than one and a half games, nor did they lead by more than a game. But with all their hopes on the line, they had to play consecutive doubleheaders on the final weekend.

Despite blowing a four-run lead in the eighth inning to lose the nightcap on Saturday, the Tigers would have forced a playoff against the Boston Red Sox if they had won both games on Sunday against the California Angels. Detroit won the opener, but Dick McAuliffe—representing the tying run with one out in the bottom of the ninth inning—hit a double-play grounder to second, ending the Tigers' season.

Instead of tying the Red Sox, they finished one game out. "They went down battling like champions," manager Mayo Smith said about his Tigers, knowing it wasn't much consolation at the time. The Tigers waited because they had to wait. But it made 1968 all the sweeter.

pitch with them." No wonder he didn't want to go back to Knoxville. "I just declined to do it," he said. "When the Tigers tried to order me to go, I told them I was retiring and was now out of baseball."

Lolich went home to Portland, Oregon, where a deal was worked out to pitch for the Portland Beavers of the Pacific Coast League. The direction of his career changed forever at Portland. "The best piece of pitching advice I ever received was from Gerry Staley, the pitching coach in Portland," Lolich said.

Staley had just retired from a fine career in which he averaged 18 wins from 1951 to 1953 for the St. Louis Cardinals. He also played a prominent relief role for the Chicago White Sox when they won the American League pennant in 1959. His last stop was with the Tigers in 1961. "Back then," Lolich said, "I could throw a ball through a brick wall but not hit the brick wall. I'd hardly met the guy, but Staley went to the manager in Portland and said he wanted to work with me. What he did was to teach me how to throw a sinking fastball. It didn't come easily, God no, but it changed my whole career. All of sudden, I could paint the outside corner all day long."

Staley taught Lolich to throw off the smooth part of the ball instead of its seams. "Some of my early pitches traveled 56 or 57 feet, and others went four feet over the catcher's head, but I eventually learned," Lolich said.

And with that, any chance of Mickey becoming a mailman ended. Instead he was headed for a major league career that would be known for its durability and his 1968 World Series performance. It also should be known for the four games that Lolich won for the Tigers in relief in 1968—another of Smith's decisions that worked wonders.

Slumping as a starter in late July, Lolich was assigned to the bullpen and responded with 15 scoreless innings and four wins in the Tigers' next 10 games, including a five-inning stint that helped turn around the first game of a doubleheader against the Boston Red Sox. Blessed with an arm that never bothered him, except for those bone chips, Lolich's durability still amazes those who have grown up knowing only a five-man rotation.

From 1971 to 1974, he averaged 330 innings, 24 complete games, 42 starts, and a 20–16 record. But despite retiring with the most strikeouts ever by a left-handed pitcher, he never received more than a third of the required 75 percent of the vote for Hall of Fame induction.

"As time goes by," Lolich said, "you just fade away. I wondered why I wasn't getting a shot at it, considering I had a better record than some who are in it, but I sort of got over it."

Of his own career, Lolich said, "I did okay." He was better than okay. He even hit a World Series home run. "The thing about that home run is that I never saw where the ball went," Lolich said. "I'd usually hit the ball to right if I hit it at all, but the home run was to left. So when I got to first base, I stepped over the bag because I thought I was out, and there was always the chance of getting hurt if you stepped on the bag. When Wally Moses, the coach at first, said, 'It's outta here,' I turned around and asked him, 'What did you just say?'"

"You just hit a home run," Moses replied.

So Lolich touched first—and around the bases he trotted, deservedly savoring yet another highlight of his distinguished career.

AL KALINE

H e was the flawless Tiger. Al Kaline could hit, run, and throw. In short, he did everything well. He won a batting title when he was 20, got his 3,000th hit just short of turning 40, and was a first-ballot Hall of Fame inductee in 1980. He was an 18-time All-Star, a 10-time Gold Glove winner, and he hit .379 in his lone World Series appearance. His list of accomplishments was virtually endless. He led the American League one year with 200 hits, led it another year with 41 doubles, and yet another with a .530 slugging percentage.

After playing 22 years for the Tigers—and only for the Tigers—his baseball home was in their television broadcast booth with George Kell for the next 28 seasons. George and Al, they made a great team. Since then Kaline has been a special assistant in the front office. For more than 60 years he's been associated with the Tigers and with the city of Detroit.

Fittingly, there is a statue of him at Comerica Park. His uniform number (6) has been retired, and if you mention "Mr. Tiger," people all over Michigan know without hesitation to whom you are referring. If Kaline wasn't the greatest Tiger, he was certainly the most respected. He would be on the team's Mount Rushmore with Ty Cobb, Hank Greenberg, and Charlie Gehringer in all likelihood.

His Tigers career started in 1953 when he was a gangly young man loaded with potential. Kaline had just graduated from Southern High School in Baltimore. There was no baseball draft back then. If you were a prospect, you not only listened to what teams had to say, but also to what they were offering.

Several clubs were interested in Kaline. Some offered more than the Tigers. But it wasn't a case of the highest bidder wins. "I remember we were sitting at the kitchen table at my house in Baltimore, talking with [Tigers scout] Ed Katalinas," Kaline said. "I nearly fell off my chair when my father asked him, 'So, who are the best outfielders you have in the minors?'"

When Katalinas started listing them, he mentioned that one of the prospects was hitting .280. To which, Kaline's father, Nicholas, quickly replied, "My son can hit .280."

Not being impertinent, just making sure his father didn't go too far in praising him, Kaline replied, 'Wait a minute, Dad, they're talking about the major leagues."

But it had been a shrewd inquiry all the same. "A smart question," Kaline would recall, "because he wanted to know who'd be blocking my playing time."

There were not as many promising young outfielders in the Tigers' organization as in others it turned out, which decided the matter. "I turned down more money from other teams," Kaline said, "because I didn't want to sit and watch."

Reporting immediately to the big leagues as a bonus baby, however, had its drawbacks.

When Kaline arrived in Philadelphia to join the Tigers, a resentful veteran player "grabbed me by the shirt, and asked 'What the (bleep) are you doing here?'"

Kaline's presence meant that someone on the team would be losing his job. So he understood the anger. "It was a dog-eat-dog world back then among players," he said. "When I first joined the Tigers, I was looked down on because I was an 18-year-old kid taking a veteran's job away from him. A lot of guys were thinking, *what the hell is going on here?* It's true. I had a guy grab me my first day in uniform, saying he didn't want me around."

In his major league debut on June 25, 1953—with a crowd of only 2,368 on hand at Connie Mack Stadium—Kaline batted in the ninth inning after replacing center fielder Jim Delsing. He flied out to shallow center on the first pitch thrown to him by Harry Byrd.

Playing sparingly, Kaline got his first hit, a single, on July 8 in Chicago, but he wouldn't be given his first start until September 16 in Boston, a game in which he got three hits.

In more ways than one, some of them the hard way, Kaline learned several lessons his first year. "It's not like today when the veterans take care of the younger players. A lot was different back then," he said. "Players weren't treated the same. For instance, there was no postgame spread. We were given chicken broth and carrots. If you ate an ice cream bar, you had to mark your name down as owing for it."

Kaline, though, was luckier than some. He got into 30 games his first year and played regularly his second. Tom Qualters, a pitcher who was a bonus baby with the Philadelphia Phillies at the same time, got into just one game in two years. And Bob Miller, a bonus baby pitcher on the Tigers at the same time as Kaline, saw action in only 13 games in 1953.

Miller would last four years with the Tigers, ending up with a 4–6 record. His career ended with the 1962 New York Mets.

The Tigers knew they had something special, though, when Kaline hit .315 during the second half of the 1954 season, including .416 in August. He would win the A.L. batting title the next season with a .340 average. Despite never leading the league in hitting again, Kaline remained an offensive force throughout his career. When he retired after the 1974 season, he was 11th on the all-time, major league list in total bases with 4,852. For all Kaline achieved, however, there was an offensive yardstick he fell short of reaching. He never hit 30 home runs in a season. But he assuredly would have reached the mark had it not been for a tumble he took while making a game-ending catch at Yankee Stadium.

One of Kaline's best seasons was 1962. At the same time, it was also the biggest "what could have been" year of his career. Nearing the end of May, it appeared that Kaline not only would hit for a high average but was headed for his highest home run and RBI totals as well.

In fact, he was on a pace to hit at least 40 home runs and drive in at least 130 runs.

No wonder the Tigers were encouraged about contending deep into the season again. Coming off 101 victories in 1961, they went into 1962 not just with optimism but with confidence.

Their pitching staff, though, suffered an early setback. A knee injury to Frank Lary on Opening Day in Detroit eventually affected his arm. Losing command of his fastball, he was never the same again. Kaline, meanwhile, was rolling with 13 home runs and 38 RBIs in his first 34 games—and finally getting some consistent pitching after Lary's injury, the Tigers welcomed a chance to play the Yankees. But in their first visit to New York in 1962—after their previous season had crumbled following a sweep at Yankee Stadium in September—disaster struck again.

Playing in deep right while the Tigers were protecting a 2–1 lead in the bottom of the ninth on a Saturday after they had won the first game of the series, Kaline charged Elston Howard's shallow fly ball. He caught it for the game's final out, but on his dive to make the play, he broke his right collarbone. "You better get the trainer," Kaline told Norm Cash, who'd come out to congratulate him for the catch. "I think I'm hurt."

He would miss the next 57 games. With his arm in a cast, there wasn't much Kaline could do except nap and watch television. "I watch it all the time," he said. "Tennessee Ernie Ford, *American Bandstand*, old movies." When asked if he worried that he wouldn't be the same when he returned, Kaline answered honestly. "Yes, I think about it," he said.

Not able to satisfactorily replace Kaline, the Tigers lost whatever momentum they'd been building. The team's record while he was injured was 26–31. Three games out of first place when Kaline got hurt, they were 10½ out when he returned and would get no closer than nine the rest of the way. Hoping it wasn't too late to help, Kaline picked up in late July where he had left off. It took him five games (in which he went 3-for-20) to shake off the rust, but in his final 59 games he hit .297 with 16 home runs and 52 RBIs.

In many ways it was his most impressive season. The only problem was that he missed 35 percent of it. Kaline ended the year with 29 home runs and 94 RBIs in 398 at-bats. Projecting the same ratio in 560 at-bats—his average number of at-bats from the previous eight years—Kaline would have hit 40 home runs, far more than he had hit in any season of his career. Using the same formula, he also would have had 132 RBIs. But we'll never know, will we? We can only crunch the numbers. It could have been his best year, certainly his most productive. And for sure—if he hadn't missed such a large chunk of games—he would have finished his career with more than 400 home runs instead of falling one short at 399.

So if anyone ever tells you that Kaline was a great player but never had a season of super slugging, you can now reply: "You're wrong. He did." Had he just not gotten hurt.

MAGGLIO'S HOMER
TO WIN THE
2006 ALCS

We remember the sheer joy of his home run trot. Except that, initially, it wasn't a trot at all. Watching the ball head for the seats in left field, Magglio Ordonez slowly took a couple of steps toward first base as the reality of the moment sunk in. He'd done it, he really had done it.

As soon as the ball came down, pandemonium broke loose—a level of it that had never been seen at Comerica Park, which was in its seventh season in 2006. Ernie Harwell's famous description of the Tigers clinching the American League pennant in 1968 had been, "Let's listen to the bedlam," and decades later it was blissful bedlam erupting again following Ordonez's home run. The kind, in fact, that the Tigers hadn't experienced in a generation—not since Kirk Gibson's blast off Goose Gossage in 1984 at Tiger Stadium.

But instead of taking place in the World Series, as Gibson's had, Ordonez's home run was the Tigers' ticket back to it for the first time in 22 years. Occurring with Craig Monroe and Placido Polanco on base and two outs in the bottom of the ninth, it was the hit that completed a four-game sweep of the Oakland A's in the American League Championship Series.

But it was also a vehicle that brought the Tigers back from the depths of the baseball world.

Just three years before, they'd been a laughingstock, avoiding the record for the most major league losses in a season by sweeping the Minnesota Twins in the final series of the season. "Their reversal was essential to bring out in my call of Magglio's home run," said radio broadcaster Dan Dickerson. "I wanted to encapsulate how far they'd come."

Dickerson's was an emotionally explosive call, almost as if he was trying to bellow the ball over the fence. At the same time, it was heartfelt and fully equal to the moment. "I just wanted to get it right," he said.

Here was Dickerson's call, which occurred while his WXYT broadcast partner, Jim Price, can be heard saying, "Wow!" in the background: "Monroe edges off of second...the 1-0...a swing and fly ball to left field, it's DEEP. It's WAY BACK!...THE TIGERS ARE GOING TO THE WORLD SERIES! ...A THREE-RUN WALK-OFF HOME RUN!... OH, MAN! ...ORDONEZ AROUND THIRD, HE'S INTO A MOB SCENE AT HOME!"

Dickerson labeled the turnaround "one of the greatest in baseball history." The Tigers suddenly were relevant again following years of obscurity and of gathering the dust of decades. Even in their last years of Tiger Stadium, they'd been a forlorn franchise, losing a generation of fans because of an inability to contend. They weren't always boring, just seldom competitive.

The malaise carried over from the old to the new ballpark with its far fences instead of short porches. At the start of one season—just six games into 2002, in fact—the Tigers dismissed both their manager and general manager because they already looked lost. After going 71–91 in 2005 and hiring Jim Leyland to replace Alan Trammell as their manager in an attempt to return to the ranks of the respected, the Tigers still had not finished over .500 since 1993.

But the early returns in 2006 were promising. Opening on the road, they won their first five games. But possibly overimpressed with themselves, the Tigers had a 2–5 homestand, after which Leyland yelled at them for looking like they were already on the plane to Oakland. Maintaining their focus would not be a problem again.

The Tigers had been a team without stars before 2004. But that's not how owner Mike Ilitch ran his hockey team, the Detroit Red Wings. Ilitch not only liked having big-name players on the Wings, he associated them with leadership. So with a "why not?" attitude after the Tigers lost 119 games in 2003, he pursued Ivan "Pudge" Rodriguez as a free agent. To the surprise of many, Ilitch signed him. To the surprise of more, the Tigers also took a chance on Ordonez in 2005 after he'd played in just 52 games for the Chicago White Sox the season before due to calf and knee injuries.

With the commitment Ilitch showed toward improving the team, fans began to return. Although the Tigers dropped to 71 wins in 2005 after 72 in 2004, they drew more than 2 million in attendance for the first time since Comerica Park opened in 2000. Aside from the years in which they were either opening or closing a ballpark, it was the first time the Tigers had topped 2 million since 1988.

Ilitch's star power was paying off at the gate. Unfortunately for Ordonez, a sports hernia kept him out for most of the first three months of the 2005 season. But he hit .312 in his final 79 games. Make no mistake, Magglio was a fine hitter throughout his career and would silence any remaining doubters by winning the A.L. batting title with a .363 batting average in 2007, the first such title for a Tiger since Norm Cash in 1961.

But he was streaky in 2006 with his production proving unusually tame for long stretches. For instance, he hit just .252 with four home runs and 29 RBIs in a 56-game stretch ending September 7. "For us to do well, it's simple," Leyland said. "We need Magglio to hit."

Later in September, Ordonez belted five home runs in a seven-game stretch, so by the time the postseason arrived, he had found his missing punch. The Tigers, though, stumbled into the playoffs as a wild-card team after losing their last five games. Tied for the division lead on the final day, they blew an early six-run lead en route to a 10–8 loss in 12 innings to the Kansas City Royals.

Minnesota, meanwhile, downed the White Sox 5–1 to win the American League Central by one game. But the Twins were swept in their division series against Oakland. Beginning the playoffs the way they ended the regular season, the Tigers lost their division series opener to the New York Yankees but won the next three games. Ordonez demonstrated some power with a home run in Game 4.

By the fourth game of the ALCS against Oakland, the Tigers had extended their postseason winning streak to six. After a masterpiece by Kenny Rogers in Game 3 of the ALCS, the Tigers—and their fans—felt good about the series but weren't counting out the scrappy A's.

What gets forgotten in the context of the heroics that took place in the ninth inning of Game 4 is that Ordonez also hit the home run that tied the score in the sixth, a liner to left off Dan Haren. With the A's becoming wary of him after that, Ordonez walked to load the bases in the seventh inning—only to have Carlos Guillen end the threat

Magglio Ordonez pumps his fist after launching a three-run, walk-off home run in the 2006 ALCS to send the Tigers back to the World Series for the first time in 22 years. (AP Images)

with a double-play grounder off right-hander Huston Street, who would still be on the mound in the ninth to face Magglio. "Once the Tigers got two runners on base with two outs in the ninth," Dickerson said, "I'm thinking that if Magglio was going to come through, it would be with a single to right. He was so good at doing that to get a runner in. It was like his signature hit. So what you hear in my voice with what he does next is surprise. I mean, suddenly all these emotions came spilling out of me. Thankfully, it was a no-doubter, not a 'might be, could be.' That was part of the fun of it all. It was such a bomb."

Years later, fans still approach Dickerson to say, "I loved your Magglio call."

On the field after Ordonez connected, the Tigers rushed from the dugout. Calmly, though, Leyland climbed the dugout steps and pointed to his family in the crowd, not betraying the excitement he was feeling within. But it was definitely there. "It was just total relief, even though we'd been in pretty good shape, up three games," Leyland said. "But in a series like that, where anything can happen, you want to get it done as quickly as you can. I certainly hope that's one of the great moments in Tigers' history. I think it is. To see the fans so happy was one of my most memorable days in baseball, no question."

A man of few words, Ordonez's happiness was visual, painting a lasting memory as he rounded the bases with his hands raised while Monroe and Polanco pranced home ahead of him.

What a joyous night it was.

But Ordonez's home run was the high-water mark of the 2006 postseason for the Tigers. Making too many mistakes, they lost the World Series in five games to the St. Louis Cardinals.

They'll always have a magical moment to flash back to, though, the memory of that chilly Saturday night in October when Magglio swung at a pitch in the ninth. And there it went. "Deep...way back...oh man!"

"I'm going back in. We're in trouble, and there's only one thing to do—return to the service."

—Hank Greenberg, December 9, 1941

He was a true star. He hit home runs. He drove in runs. He was friendly, handsome, and articulate. In today's world Hammerin' Hank Greenberg would have been a multimedia, social media, and—any type of media—darling. And although he was a target of slurs for his Jewish heritage—baseball being the hotbed of prejudice that it was—he became a hero. Not just to fellow Jews, but to all baseball fans who appreciated his dignity, as well as the class with which he conducted himself. "I don't recall anyone I ever played with or against having a bad word for him," Hall of Fame pitcher Hal Newhouser once said about him.

What was the greatest achievement of Greenberg's career? There is no shortage of choices. It might have been the home run he hit for the Tigers in his first game back from World War II. He hadn't played in a major league game since 1941, but in the eighth inning of his return on July 1, 1945, he connected with the bases empty.

Or it could have been the grand slam he hit to clinch the American League pennant for the Tigers on the final day of that same season. Greenberg was hitting just .219 after 29 games into his return from military service when he suddenly caught fire and hit .547 in his next 15 games. By the time the Tigers were down to needing just one more victory, his batting average was .309. It was a soggy Sunday afternoon in St. Louis for the opener of a possible doubleheader against the Browns. The Tigers led the Washington Senators by one game, but the Senators had no games remaining. If the Tigers had lost to the Browns, they would have had to play again. Weeklong rains had made a swamp of Sportsman's Park, so it was in the mud, and with only 5,582 on hand, that the Tigers trailed 3–2 in the top of the ninth when Greenberg—after an intentional walk to Doc Cramer loaded the bases—hit the dramatic slam that clinched the A.L. pennant. The next day the *Detroit Free Press* called it "the most thrilling home run in the history of baseball."

After that the Tigers downed the Chicago Cubs in seven games to win the World Series. Greenberg hit the Tigers' only home runs, knocking two out of the park. The choices for his greatest achievement, however, don't end there. There were the 184 runs he drove in during the 1937 season. Then again, it might have been when he was named the A.L.'s Most Valuable Player in 1935 or the second time he won the award in 1940.

Likely, though, his most significant achievement had nothing at all to do with baseball.

It almost certainly was Greenberg's unwavering sense of duty to his country. The year was 1941, the month was April, more than seven months before Pearl Harbor. With war raging in Europe, President Franklin D. Roosevelt had signed the Selective Training and Service Act the year before, meaning that conscription was back.

Baseball players were suddenly eligible to be drafted, even if they had several major league seasons under their belts, Greenberg had made himself an immediate candidate to be drafted when he became the first A.L. player to register. The future Hall of Famer had flat feet, a condition that looked as if it might make him exempt. But when he passed a second exam, the probability of being drafted became a reality. Local speculation ran rampant about when it might occur. Sooner rather than later, it turned out. After hitting two home runs on May 6, Greenberg reported for military service the next morning. "Uncle Sam is the only boss I know now," he said.

The constant publicity about the draft process had been difficult on him. When the day finally arrived, he welcomed it. "It will be a relief to get in the army and have all this bother over with," he told the *Detroit Free Press*.

The two home runs he hit in his final game before reporting did not surprise anyone familiar with his career. Greenberg was a prodigious slugger. He threatened Babe Ruth's record of 60 home runs in 1938 before falling short with 58. He also could have eclipsed 500 career home runs if military service had not intervened.

Power defined him as a hitter; honor defined him as a person. Sometimes the two elements meshed. In the September pennant race of 1934, Greenberg didn't play on the Jewish holy day of Yom Kippur (Day of Atonement) but had earlier changed his mind about playing on Rosh Hashanah (the Jewish New Year). He responded by hitting two home runs in a 2–1 victory against the Boston Red Sox. By playing on one holiday, but not the other, he was true to his faith as well as to his profession.

Comfortable on baseball's biggest stage, Greenberg also hit five home runs in the 23 World Series games in which he played. In 12 major league seasons, he hit at least 25 home runs eight times and more than 35 home runs five times. Whenever he fell short of his normal numbers, there was a legitimate reason. In 1933, for instance, he hit only 12 home runs, but he was a 22-year-old rookie that year. Despite hitting .301, neither he nor his power had fully matured. In 1936 Greenberg was limited to 12 games—and to one home run—because of a broken left wrist sustained in a collision at first base. The initial prognosis was that he would miss a month to six weeks, but he ended up sitting out the rest of the season.

Not yet accepting the injury's severity, Hank thought he was recovering "faster than expected" in late May, only to hear from New York Yankees manager Joe McCarthy that "these wrist injuries are bad," which was why McCarthy doubted from the time it happened that Greenberg would be of much help the rest of the year. However, the hope of playing again kept teasing the Tigers' big first baseman. In June it was thought Greenberg would return on July 1, but he didn't. Saying he had suffered through the "tortures of the damned" by not being able to play, one target date for his return followed another. But his wrist didn't fully heal until October. Except for 55 plate appearances in April, he lost the entire 1936 season.

Such a setback was minor, however, compared to the challenge Greenberg faced five years later when the slugger became a soldier. He reported for duty in May, but the attack on Pearl Harbor occurred two days after his honorable discharge in December, 1941, so he went right back into the army. By that time, Hank had long since become a role model. "Among Jews he was really a pathfinder," remembered Al Rosen, both a major league player and executive during his career. "Coming through the minors, I'm sure he encountered a lot of anti-Semitism. I guess if you want to draw an analogy, it would be the equivalent of what Jackie Robinson went through."

Opposing fans were rough on Greenberg after he reached the majors. The New York City native often heard himself being called "that dirty Jew."

But he was so highly regarded for the way he conducted himself that the *Free Press*, when Greenberg was drafted, wrote an editorial calling him "an honor to the game, an honor to your people, and to your country. All Detroit wishes you the best in the new game of life you are about to undertake. We know you will give it all you have."

There was never a question about Greenberg giving it his all. His commitment to being a soldier was no less complete than it had been to becoming the best hitter he could be. But his playing days were possibly over. In May of 1942, Greenberg told the *New York World-Telegram*, "I'm through with baseball. I'm not kidding myself about this war; I'm going to be in a long time—four or five years, maybe. What I'm going to do when I come out, I don't know, don't really care much at the moment. But I know I am through as a ballplayer."

Greenberg was certainly wrong about his future. He wasn't through as a ballplayer. He went on to become an honored soldier as well as an honored player who led the A.L. in 1946 in both home runs (44) and RBIs (127). Such a season might have been his finest moment—if his finest hadn't already taken place by so quickly going back in.

THE MARK
FIDRYCH
PHENOMENON

he Bird was the word. For some he always will be. Mention the 1976 season to any Tigers fan—or to any baseball fan old enough to remember the world before cable television—and they will smile while recalling the star who burned so brightly that year. But only for that year.

Mark Fidrych was the rookie pitcher who manicured the mound and spoke to the baseball, the curly-haired kid who emerged from obscurity to become the talk of baseball. Within weeks of his first start, he had become everyone's favorite player. Even other teams would make arrangements for him to sign autographs when Detroit came to town. For the Tigers he was more than an excellent pitcher. He was an attraction unlike any they'd had in a long time—maybe ever. "Seriously, he might have been the most popular player ever to play in Detroit," said Al Kaline, himself a candidate for that honor.

After Opening Day the Tigers drew 13 crowds that season of more than 32,000. Fidrych started all but one of those games. The one he didn't start was a jacket giveaway day. "He brought people to the ballpark," Willie Horton said. "He brought families back to the game. What he did in a short amount of time was amazing."

To say that Fidrych came from nowhere is an understatement. A month into the season, he had barely pitched at all for the Tigers, throwing only one inning in two relief appearances. "It took forever for [manager Ralph Houk] to use him," said John Wockenfuss, a catcher on that Tigers team.

So where did his road to stardom begin? When the Tigers invited Fidrych to spring training as a non-roster pitcher in 1976, they couldn't have known he would pitch well enough to earn a spot on the roster. But he did, winning the last spot on the pitching staff in a decision that newspaper headlines labeled a surprise. The Tigers, though, didn't start him. In their first six games that season, Fidrych didn't pitch at all despite the team's recurring bullpen issues.

In the Tigers' third game, John Hiller allowed a game-tying single with two outs in the bottom of the ninth inning to pinch-hitter Andy Etchebarren, who would win it for the California Angels in the 11th inning with another single off Steve Grilli. Three days later, the Tigers again surrendered a one-run lead in the bottom of the ninth to the Oakland A's and would lose in the 10th inning on Phil Garner's single off Hiller following a pair of walks. The resilient Hiller would go on to have a fine season with a 12–8 record, a 2.38 ERA, and 13 saves, but before settling down, he stumbled a few times. So when the Tigers had a late lead yet again against the A's—only to have the first two Oakland batters get on base in the ninth—they turned to left-hander Jim Crawford for help in a save situation. When Crawford blew the lead, they finally called for Fidrych as a last resort. Making his first major league appearance, he quickly allowed the game-winning single to Don Baylor.

After that, Fidrych didn't pitch again for more than a week. If anything, his roster spot was in jeopardy. Pitching once in the first 15 games and only twice in the first 23, he seemed to be someone the Tigers neither needed, nor were eager to use. According to *Detroit Free Press* columnist Charlie Vincent, Fidrych's lack of work meant just one thing: Houk didn't trust him. Not yet anyway.

To give Fidrych some needed work, though, the Tigers started him in their annual benefit game against the Cincinnati Reds. It didn't go well. Fidrych allowed five runs on eight hits in five innings against the Reds. There still wasn't a sign he was anything special. One reporter wrote, "If he was talking to the ball as he says he does, it wasn't listening."

There still wasn't a sign he was anything special, but there soon would be.

Only because the Tigers couldn't allow him to keep gathering dust, Fidrych started on May 15 against the Cleveland Indians. That night their starless season suddenly came to life.

Fidrych not only retired the first 14 Cleveland batters he faced in his first major league start, but he also took a no-hitter into the seventh inning before Buddy Bell led off with a single.

The Indians would score a run in the seventh and threaten to get another, but Fidrych ended up with a complete-game two-hitter for his first major league victory. "What impressed me," Houk said after the 2–1 outcome, "was that he was just as strong at the end as he was at the beginning."

With that, Houk's lack of confidence in his young starter vanished to the extent that Fidrych later pitched 94⅓ innings in a 10-start stretch. He was a rookie who became a workhorse. Three of his first 13 starts were won with 11-inning, complete-game performances.

In those 13 starts, Fidrych went 11–2 with a 1.72 ERA. One of the victories was against the Texas Rangers, a game in which Fidrych and future Hall of Famer Bert Blyleven matched skills for 11 innings. "I loved watching 'the Bird' pitch," Blyleven recalled. "He had pinpoint control.

The always eccentric Mark "the Bird" Fidrych talks to the baseball before throwing a pitch. (AP Images)

Talk about someone who could hit the corner down and away. But I not only admired him when he was pitching, I admired him when he wasn't. He had a lot of energy. He was great for baseball."

Fidrych also gained the respect of the hitters he faced. "A lot of people call it flaky, a lot of people call it loony," Milwaukee Brewers slugger George Scott said after witnessing Fidrych's routine on the mound, which included telling the ball where he wanted it to go. "But I like it. The ball really moved. It exploded. That's confidence."

Some hitters had fun with Fidrych. When he pitched in New York, for instance, the Yankees fed him birdseed. After Graig Nettles dropped sunflower seeds on the mound for him, Fidrych responded by eating them. The Bird would get the last laugh. The first time he pitched in Yankee Stadium, he lost. The second time, he shut out the Yankees.

The sadness of Fidrych's career, of course, was that he got hurt in his second season and never was the same again. He hurt his knee shagging fly balls in spring training, had surgery, came back for a while, but eventually a shoulder injury ended his career. He didn't know what the specific injury was until 1985 when Dr. James Andrews diagnosed it as a torn rotator cuff. Fidrych went 19-9 with a 2.34 ERA in his one big year but just 10-10 with a 4.28 ERA in four seasons after that.

The sadness of his life was that he died far too young, the victim of an accident while working under his truck in 2009 at age 54. Decades after his special season, friends, former teammates, and all of baseball mourned his loss. "He was a special person, such a giving human being," Horton said. "When my daughter needed a lung transplant, the Bird came back to Detroit to give her the proceeds from a signing session because he thought of us as family. 'Anything for you, big man,' he said to me. 'Anything for you.'"

The legacy Fidrych left for baseball was the golden memory of that glorious 1976 season.

Maybe you remember him for the way he spoke to the baseball. Or maybe for the way he threw it—such as the way he threw it one night when a veteran hitter, trying to slow him down, decided to make him wait between pitches.

SCHOOLBOY ROWE

If only it had lasted.

He developed a sore arm, so Lynwood Thomas "Schoolboy" Rowe is remembered more for the promise of greatness and for being one of the mainstays of a Tigers team that lost a World Series in 1934 but finally won one in 1935, the franchise's first championship, than he is for being the Hall of Fame pitcher he might otherwise have been.

Rowe, Tommy Bridges, and Elden Auker were the three best starting pitchers on those Tigers teams. But the folk hero of the three was Schoolboy. He was gregarious. He was quirky because of his good luck charms. He was the fans' favorite and when he made a name for himself by asking his future wife on the radio, "how'm I doin', Edna?" he became a sudden celebrity.

From 1934 to 1936, Rowe's record was 62-31. That doesn't mean he dominated other teams—just that he beat them, including a record-tying stretch of 16 consecutive victories in 1934. Three of them came in relief.

He was such an iconic figure that reporters were assigned specifically to cover him. Sportswriter Charles P. Ward said he'd been "marked for stardom." Another sportswriter wrote, "He won his games by combining control with guile."

Schoolboy won so regularly, though, that it looked like he was going to be an excellent pitcher for several more years. But his arm became chronically sore, and his only other good season for the Tigers was when he went 16-3 for the 1940 pennant winners.

Rowe was sold to the Brooklyn Dodgers in 1942 and enjoyed some later success for the Philadelphia Phillies, but he had lost all semblance of velocity. Even after he held the Chicago White Sox to two unearned runs for eight and one-third innings in April of 1942, Sox manager Jimmie Dykes said, "Rowe wasn't 1/10th as fast as he was eight years ago. I don't see how he got us out."

Although he never replicated what he accomplished early as a Tiger, it was a sad moment when he left. Wrote columnist Dale Stafford of the *Detroit Free Press*, "No Tiger ever had more heart than the Schoolboy, and no man ever lived who was more genuine. Few people ever received the praise accorded Rowe—and succeeded in continuing to be an unchanged person. We shall miss him, and we know you will, too."

It was July 16, a Friday night at Tiger Stadium with the A's in town. Sporting a 9–2 record, Fidrych had long since been fully embraced by Tigers fans, so a crowd of 45,905 was on hand. The Bird was being himself, smoothing down the dirt on the mound, fluttering around, telling the ball what he wanted it to do. And working quickly, of course. Fidrych was a rapid worker on the mound. Some hitters didn't like it.

To slow his tempo, or simply to disrupt him in the eighth inning of a scoreless game, A's hitter Claudell Washington took extra time between pitches before stepping back into the batter's box. He adjusted this. He adjusted that—once, twice, a full 40 seconds between pitches while Fidrych squatted down on the mound, biding his time. When the A's outfielder finally indicated he was ready for the next pitch to be thrown, Fidrych let him know how he felt about the delay by throwing a fastball at Washington's knees, backing him out of the box.

Without ever saying so, it was the Bird's signal that he—not Washington—controlled the pace of the game, a big league moment for a kid who'd grown up and become a star in two months. Washington reacted angrily to the pitch. He huffed and puffed, and both benches emptied but only half-heartedly. "I told him if he wanted to do something about it," Fidrych said, "he could come and get me. It wasn't that far inside."

Oh, but it was. "Two feet inside," said Washington, who expressed confusion about what happened next. "I didn't know if he was talking to me or to the ball." But when the dust settled, Washington was more impressed than irked. "I don't have anything against him," he said. "He's a hell of a pitcher."

Indeed he was. Unruffled, Fidrych went on to strike out Washington and win 1–0, when Horton singled in the winning run in the bottom of the 11th inning.

The vintage showdown, though, had been flash-frozen in time, sending the message to all that the Bird was in charge. If it is your favorite Bird moment with all its elements, you have chosen wisely. If it isn't, you might even be wiser because he gave us so many memories from which to choose.

CHARLIE GEHRINGER

"Charles Leonard Gehringer, get back here. Your chores aren't done."

"Coming, Ma."

He had good intentions. But there was always something better to do. And farm work? Well, he didn't enjoy that either. From the first time he picked up a glove, bat, and ball at his boyhood home in Fowlerville, Michigan, what young Charlie preferred was to play baseball. His mother once said that as a little boy he would even risk a spanking to play. Anything for the game.

His father was the one who said that Charlie wasn't cut out for the farm. But everyone could see he was definitely cut out for baseball—and to play it well.

He just didn't talk about it much or about anything else for that matter. This could have been the quietest Tiger of them all. Gehringer was friendly and popular with his teammates but never had a lot to say. A great second baseman, hitter, and ballplayer, he was so efficiently smooth in all aspects of the game that he was called "The Mechanical Man." But he was silent to the point of being shy. In fact, it wasn't until Gehringer took a sales job during the offseason at Hudson's, a downtown Detroit department store, that any kind of personality began to emerge. Being a sales clerk made him more outgoing.

In all likelihood a player as talented as Gehringer eventually would have created his own path to playing time, but it helped in 1926 when Frank O'Rourke, the Tigers' incumbent second baseman, came down with the measles. It also helped a year later when Marty McManus, a veteran infielder whose presence might have bumped Gehringer to third on a full-time basis, was knocked out of the lineup after getting spiked.

An opening suddenly was created for Gehringer to take over at second base full time in 1927, and that's exactly what he did. He took over. The Tigers didn't have to worry about filling the position again until he left for military service during World War II in 1942.

Gehringer didn't make the best first impression, though, at least according to one account. "A bungling play on the defensive by [Charlie] Gehringer, who was making his first start as a major leaguer, and an inability to hit with runners on, were chiefly responsible for Detroit's downfall," read a report of a Tigers' loss in the *Detroit Free Press* in 1926. And it got worse. "Gehringer seemed to be laboring under the impression that he was making his debut as a circus performer. Twice in the late stages, the recruit second baseman hit the dirt, only to come up without the ball—each of his dives figuring in Chicago's scoring."

Gehringer didn't play like a circus performer for long. He quickly established his consistency while reinforcing his reticence. Mickey Cochrane, both his teammate and his manager, used to joke that Gehringer would "say hello on Opening Day, good-bye on closing day, and in between he would hit .350."

But more than just in between, Gehringer also proved to be a quality individual. He was both a gentleman and a devoted son. In order to take care of his diabetic mother, who lived until 1946, he didn't get married until he was 46 because he felt it would be unfair for a bride to share the responsibility of his mother's care.

After his mother died, Gehringer married Josephine Stillen, a secretary who worked for the Chrysler Corporation. His wedding coincided with his Hall of Fame induction, so he missed his induction. Said J. Robert Quinn, the director of the Hall of Fame, "Knowing Charlie as I do, I can't believe he ever popped the question in the first place."

For a man of few words, there have been countless words of praise bestowed upon Gehringer over the years. Hal Newhouser, his Hall of Fame teammate, had the highest regard for Gehringer, saying he was "so fluid" in the field and "a gentleman all the way through." It wasn't a case of seldom hearing a disparaging word about Charlie. There was never a disparaging word about him. "He was even the best ever at being the best ever," *Free Press* columnist Bob Talbert once wrote. "He was honestly humble and modest to a fault."

Being quiet, though, didn't endear Gehringer to everyone. Ty Cobb thought he should show more "pepper" on the field, and when he suggested to Gehringer that he should be noisier, Charlie's reaction created a permanent distance between the two. Indebted to Cobb earlier in his career for taking him under his wing and being "super" to him, Gehringer came to know Cobb as a "hateful person."

But it was rare for Gehringer to be critical of anyone, especially his teammates and superiors. As a player he did not criticize his manager, and as the Tigers' general manager after his playing days—a job he did not like—Gehringer was never publicly critical when owner Spike Briggs took the lead in trade talks.

For instance, when Gehringer attended the winter meetings with Briggs after the 1952 season but was unable to prevent the impulsive owner from considering trades he shouldn't, Gehringer bit his lip. He'd been warned to keep Briggs away from St. Louis Browns' owner Bill Veeck in particular because Veeck would try to pick the Tigers' pocket in a deal. But there was never any on-the-record evidence that Briggs' meddling annoyed Gehringer.

Other than his dislike of Cobb, though, there's no evidence of anything ever annoying Gehringer—including when, for the *sixth* time in his Tigers' career, it was rumored he'd been killed in an automobile accident. In 1937 the *Free Press* ran a story saying, "for what he believes is the sixth successive year, the Tigers' second baseman was forced to deny that he'd met with death or serious injury in a crash."

As silly as it sounds, Gehringer was asked if he had been killed, an awkward question to which, true to his quiet character, he simply said, "No." The fact that such reports had become an annual occurrence did not anger him—as it no doubt would have other players. Gehringer, though, wasn't like others. He was more cordial than most, and because he was nice to others, including players on other teams, they often tried to be nice to him. But Charlie didn't always trust reciprocal kindness.

Bill Dickey of the New York Yankees, one of the best catchers of his time, used to tell the story that because the Yankees and Tigers were out of the pennant race and because his friend Gehringer was trying to win a batting title, he tipped off pitches to Charlie while he was at the plate. But Gehringer didn't believe him, expecting something other than the pitch that Dickey told him would be thrown. If Dickey said it would be a fastball, Gehringer looked for a curve instead. Despite Dickey's intentions as a friend—ethically surprising though they were—Gehringer went 0-for-5, and Dickey never attempted to "help" him again.

The fact is, of course, that Gehringer didn't need help. Yes, Cobb had given him some pointers early in his career when Cobb managed the Tigers, but Gehringer was as natural a hitter—and as natural a ballplayer—as there was. Ten years after giving way to Gehringer as the Tigers' second baseman, McManus called him the greatest infielder and greatest batter "the major leagues ever had." He was quoted as saying, "Ty Cobb himself often wished he could hit and play ball like Gehringer."

McManus was no slouch as a ballplayer himself. He was traded by the St. Louis Browns to become the Tigers' second baseman in 1927. The plan was for Gehringer to move to third base after just one full year in the majors. But it was the colorful McManus who ended up moving to third and staying there until the Tigers traded him to Boston in 1931.

McManus, who hit .320 for the Tigers in 1930, could recognize talent when he saw it. "[Gehringer] could do things without an effort that other baseball stars had to sweat and practice to do," McManus said.

Gehringer's career accomplishments were many. He exceeded 200 hits seven times, including five seasons in a row from 1933 to 1937. The Tigers lost the World Series in 1934 and again in 1940 but won it in 1935, and in 1937 Gehringer was the American League's Most Valuable Player.

He had as many as 60 doubles in a season, as many as 19 triples, and also had 100-plus RBIs seven times. Maybe his most remarkable stat, however, was that in his career Gehringer averaged just one strikeout per 27.5 plate appearances. That's just one K per week. Cobb struck out more often than that. So did Sam Crawford and Harry Heilmann. They were great Tigers, too. But they weren't as quietly efficient as the Mechanical Man. Then again, it can be argued that no one was.

GOOSE GOSLIN'S WORLD SERIES-WINNING SINGLE

He was serious when he said it. Goose Goslin, the hero of the 1935 World Series champion Detroit Tigers, believed that he would have been a substantially better hitter—throughout a career in which he was an excellent hitter anyway—had it not been for one obstacle. "This here nose of mine," he once said.

Indeed, Goslin's "schnozzle," as newspapers sometimes referred to it, was large—and to a great extent—he overcame it.

But not entirely.

In Ira L. Smith's 1954 book *Outfielders*, Goslin, a left-handed hitter, was quoted as saying, "When I was up there at the plate, my left eye was pretty well blocked off from seeing the pitcher and the ball. [It] seemed like I was seeing pitches with only one eye most of the time." Then he joked, "If my left eye had been able to see what was going on, what's wrong with thinking I would have doubled my batting average?"

Goslin was a .316 career hitter who drove in 100 or more runs 12 times and who won the American League batting title with the Washington Senators in 1928 with a .379 average.

An eventual Hall of Famer, Goslin spent most of his career with the Senators. But his most dramatic hit occurred with the Tigers, to whom he'd been traded for outfielder Johnny Stone after the 1933 season. "The Goose is the kind of player who can win a pennant for you and the World Series after you win the pennant," Tigers manager Mickey Cochrane said of the trade. "I want him. He's a money player."

It was no small deal when it was made. Goslin wasn't a young player anymore. He would be 33 for the entirety of his first season as a Tiger. There'd been signs of him slowing down with Washington, but the trade to Detroit rejuvenated him. For the first three of his four years with Detroit, Goslin hit .303 and averaged 112 RBIs. Stone, meanwhile, never made it onto anyone's list of all-time greats, but he had been a solid player for the Tigers. From 1928 to 1932, he hit .310. Better than that, he hit .325 with the Senators in the first four years following the trade before tuberculosis abruptly ended his career at age 32 in 1938.

Both teams, though, were happy with the trade. The Tigers had been willing to take on Goslin's age in order to add his productivity. The Senators were enamored with Stone's potential despite the fact he was coming off an abnormally lackluster season. His departure did not come as a surprise to Tigers fans, according to the *Detroit Free Press*: "Last year he slipped woefully and seemed to lose interest. In addition to this, John seemed at times downright lazy. Perhaps a change of scenery is what he needs."

The analysis became a prophecy.

Goslin would have been a designated hitter had he played in the DH era. Although he was capable of making fine plays in the outfield, all too often he was seen waving his arms and behaving like a bird while circling under a fly ball. Some say that Goose got his nickname because of his nose. It was likened to a beak. But others believed that he became the Goose because of the odd way he camped under fly balls.

In either case, it must have been an adventure to watch him play. Not always successful in his quest to become a better outfielder, especially early in his career, there had been a fly ball or two along the way that had hit him in the head. One bounced "as high as a hay stack," Smith wrote.

But the Tigers needed Goslin's bat, and he responded in 1934, his first year in Detroit, with a .305 batting average, a 30-game hitting streak, and 100 RBIs for an upstart team that came close to winning a World Series for the first time in the history of the franchise—only to lose in seven games to the St. Louis Cardinals.

It was a good season for him, but not Goslin's best, and had his time as a Tiger ended after one year, he never would have achieved the folk hero status that he did. Such a pedestal still wasn't guaranteed for Goslin when the Chicago Cubs began to call him "Goose Egg" for going hitless in the first two games of the 1935 World Series.

One at-bat, though, changed how he would be remembered. One glorious swing triggered a celebration that many considered the most joyous ever seen in Detroit.

This was the situation confronting the Tigers: needing just one more victory, they were at bat in the bottom of the ninth inning of Game 6 against the Cubs. The Tigers were within reach of winning it all, but they also had been within reach in Game 5 at Wrigley Field after taking three of the first four games.

Needing a hit to take the lead in Game 5 with two outs, a run already in, and runners on second and third in the top of the ninth, heroics eluded the Tigers when Flea Clifton's foul out to first ended the game. Goslin had contributed to the drama of Game 5 by getting the second of the Tigers' three consecutive singles that began the top of the ninth. And it was Goslin who was at third when they ran out of outs.

What the Tigers didn't accomplish in Game 5 they hoped to get done back at home in Game 6. But a one-run lead had turned into a 3–2 deficit by the end of the fifth inning. Trying to regain momentum and adding to the growing suspense, the Tigers tied the score on a double-single combination with two outs in the sixth.

Was there going to be a hero? Was there going to be a goat? Would the Cubs force a seventh game? With the pace quickening, it wouldn't be long before all questions were answered.

In the bottom of the ninth, the top of the Tigers' lineup was coming up against starter Larry French, with whom the Cubs had such trust that they let him hit with the tie-breaking run on third in the top of the inning. French's grounder back to the mound helped Tigers starter Tommy Bridges survive the threat, which had taken shape with Stan Hack's leadoff triple.

But suddenly the mist of unanswered hope cleared at Navin Field, and the opportunity at hand could not have been clearer. Since coming into the American League in 1901, the Tigers had never been in a better position to win a World Series. One run in the bottom of the ninth was all they needed. The crowd at Navin Field began shrieking with every pitch. But Clifton failed again in the spotlight by striking out for the first out. French was still looking sharp. With two singles

Cochrane had been a tough out all day. By handcuffing Billy Herman at second base in the ninth with an elusive grounder, Cochrane made it three singles. He took second on Charlie Gehringer's ground ball to first.

With two outs, that brought up Goslin, who hadn't gotten the ball out of the infield against French. He had popped out twice and grounded out twice. So there was nothing to indicate that he could hit the ball squarely against the pitcher he'd be facing yet again. Then, with two outs, it happened. "About that time," read the account in the *Detroit Free Press*, "the florid, waddling figure of the Old Red Gander stepped out of the batter's ring and into the box."

Here came the money player Cochrane had envisioned, and here, too, came the long-awaited championship. On French's first pitch, Goslin lined a foul to right. On the second pitch, Goslin singled to right. Deep at second, Herman leaped for the ball, but he would have needed a stepladder to grab it. Cochrane scored easily, and enthusiastically, from second.

The ballpark went crazy. The city went crazy. And the celebration lasted long into the night. Five days later, fans were paying 35 cents to watch a World Series highlight film at the Fox Theater in downtown Detroit and to meet the man—"Public Hero No. 1"—who had won it. Goose Goslin, the "Old Red Gander," Schnozzle and all.

10

ALAN TRAMMELL

He was the Tigers' shortstop, their manager, their leadoff hitter, and at one time even their cleanup hitter. Over the years Alan Trammell batted everywhere in the lineup. Then again, what didn't he do for them? He was hired by the Tigers, fired by the Tigers, let go by them, and brought back by them. He won with the Tigers and lost with them. He finished first with them and last with them, but before all that, he found a second-base sidekick with them.

From their first hit to their last, and within the artistry of all the double plays they turned, Trammell and Lou Whitaker were a pairing their entire careers. "We were called up the same day, made our debut in the same game, and even got our first hit off the same pitcher," Trammell recalled of his and Whitaker's entry into Major League Baseball.

It actually goes deeper than that, Tram.

Your last hit was off the same pitcher as well—but a year apart. "Our last hits were?" Trammell said. "I never knew that—amazing. That's even more closure than I thought we had. Our first and last hits off the same pitcher...that just shows how joined our careers really were."

Trammell and Whitaker, the Tigers' shortstop-and-second-base combination for a generation, played in their first major league game on September 9, 1977 at Fenway Park in Boston with right-hander Reggie Cleveland on the mound for the Red Sox in the second game of a doubleheader. Whitaker batted second; Trammell batted ninth. After Ron Leflore opened the first inning by striking out, Whitaker singled in his first major league at-bat.

An out later, Lou stole second and took third on Cleveland's throwing error. The rookie second baseman already was making things happen. But Steve Kemp's pop-up ended the inning with Whitaker at third base. The Tigers were retired in order in the top of the second, so it wasn't until the third that Trammell batted for the first time. "I remember being nervous," he said.

But he, too, singled off Cleveland on a line drive up the middle that he vividly recalls. Instead of being stranded, though, Trammell scored from first on Whitaker's double. "I don't care if you are 19 years old or 45," Trammell said of his debut. "You know when the ball leaves your bat if it's a hit. I knew."

Whitaker would get three hits in his debut; Trammell got two. Their careers were off to a good start. Side by side, they would man second and short through the 1980s and halfway through the 1990s; their tenure included a World Series championship in 1984. "We were together longer than a lot of husbands and wives," Whitaker said.

By 1995, however, Lou knew that it was time to retire, though he never called it retirement. Even now he prefers to say, "My career ended, that's all."

His last hit was a productive one. On September 13 at Tiger Stadium, Whitaker hit a three-run walk-off home run in the ninth off Milwaukee Brewers pitcher Mike Fetters, giving the Tigers a 5–3 victory. It wasn't his last at-bat (he went 0-for-11 after that), but it was indeed his last major league hit.

A year later, after 20 seasons with the Tigers, it was Trammell's turn to be at the end of his career. He had contemplated retiring when Whitaker did at the end of 1995 but decided to come back for one more season. And that one more season was ending for him on September 29, 1996, following a dreadful year for the Tigers during which at one point they suffered through a 5–39 stretch. As with Whitaker, the Tigers were facing Milwaukee but were trailing in the 10th inning this time. Sure enough, Fetters was again in the game for the Brewers.

Ruben Sierra led off with a fly ball to shallow left, but Curtis Pride followed with a single. The parallels were becoming uncanny. With the Tigers trailing Milwaukee at Tiger Stadium, Fetters was on the mound to face Whitaker one year and then Trammell the next. As he did with his first hit 19 years before, Trammell singled up the middle for his last hit. "I had like a flashback," Trammell said. "It was unbelievable. Was it meant to be? I guess so."

Pride stopped at second base, then stole third. But instead of the Tigers winning with a dramatic walk-off, the game ended on Travis Fryman's double-play grounder to short. Trammell, though, was no longer on base. He had been lifted for a pinch-runner before Fryman batted. But as Trammell walked off the field for the last time as a player, his career ended with the applause it deserved.

And also with the emotion it deserved. Trammell got through his postgame speech in fine fashion but only after losing it in the clubhouse tunnel following the game's final out. Once he composed himself, Trammell was ready to face the crowd and make the announcement that his playing days were over. It had only been speculated that he would retire, so the Tigers' final game had not been billed as his swan song.

A crowd of just 13,038 was on hand at Tiger Stadium because the only certainty going into the game was that the Tigers' dreadful season would conclude. Whatever suspense existed about Trammell's plans, however, soon ended. "Today was my last day," he announced, "and as much as it hurts to say that, it comes somewhat as a relief... I don't think I was great in any one area but good in a lot of areas. One thing I'm proud of is that I did it for one club."

Future Tigers manager Brad Ausmus, a Tigers player at the time, was on hand for the ceremony. Growing up in Connecticut, he had listened on the radio to the Red Sox game the night that Trammell and Whitaker made their debuts at Fenway Park. "Then 19 years later, I get to be Tram's teammate," Ausmus said. "That was incredible. I'm happy I was here to see it. I felt like I was also around when he started."

It's rare, and always will be, whenever Trammell or Whitaker is mentioned without the other. They were parallel players. But what made them such a fluid pair of infielders was their selflessness. For instance, in the game in which Whitaker got his last hit, it was Lou who started the final double play that the two would ever turn. But it was also Lou who said later, "If I had a wish, it was that Alan would have started one, too."

Trammell lasted longer in the Hall of Fame voting process than Whitaker. Because he played one more season, he wasn't in Whitaker's freshman class with Kirk Gibson and Lance Parrish that was knocked off the ballot after just one year. Maybe because of the uproar, voters were gentler with Trammell, who received 15.7 percent in his first year of eligibility after Whitaker had gotten just 2.9.

But it wasn't until his ninth year that Trammell's total exceeded 20 percent. And any chance that Trammell would build the needed momentum to get enough of a sentimental boost later disappeared when he dropped to a five-year low of 20.8 percent in 2014, his 13th year on the ballot. By then it was clear he wasn't going to make it. In 2016 a last-ballot bump did kick in, but at 40.9 Trammell still finished far short of the required 75 percent.

Perhaps the underwhelming display of support can be attributed to their personalities. "We were never really comfortable in the spotlight," Trammell said. Winning the American League's Most Valuable Player Award in 1987 would have helped him, but in a close vote it went to George Bell of the Toronto Blue Jays.

And instead of getting a boost by becoming the Tigers' manager in 2003, it probably hurt Trammell that his teams were so bad. Instead of favorable attention as a manager, Trammell received a combination of sympathy and blame.

His peers, however, knew what kind of player he had been. In an ultimate display of respect after Trammell's last game, Brewers manager Phil Garner, who would later manage the Tigers, kept his team on the field after the final out to watch Trammell's ceremony. Asked why, Garner said it was so his team could watch "a consummate player" bow out. "Guys like that belong in a class of their own," he added. "It's called the Hall of Fame."

Trammell's career compares favorably with that of Barry Larkin, the Cincinnati Reds' fine shortstop who was voted into the Hall of Fame in his third year of eligibility. But perhaps Trammell's own honesty about his career on his retirement day echoed throughout the years.

However, by saying he'd been good in a lot of areas but not great in any, he shortchanged himself.

Trammell was great playing next to Whitaker as arguably the best double-play combination ever, and to this day, their legacies are inseparable. Some of their stats are as well.

Whitaker ended up with 2,369 hits to Trammell's 2,365. And the fact that their final hit was off the same pitcher a year apart is downright eerie. "That's storybook stuff," Trammell said.

They would have enjoyed winning another World Series or two, of course. But neither player had any regrets about his career. Or about the way their careers ended. "As good as it gets," Trammell said of Whitaker's final hit being a home run. And of his own final hit? "I went out the way I came in," he said. "I hit my last one solid."

For whatever else Denny McLain's flamboyant career will be known—its ups and downs, the good and bad, the acclaim and the shame—there was a time when all the eyes of baseball were focused entirely upon him. It all came down to McLain winning his 30th game in 1968.

His was a feat we might never see again, and if we don't, it will be correctly attributed to changing times. McLain started 41 games in 1968 as part of a four-man rotation. That doesn't happen anymore. With a higher mound and without an emphasis on bullpen roles, he averaged eight and one-third innings per outing during a 29-start stretch that year. That doesn't happen anymore either. Even such a talented representative of today's generation as Justin Verlander has never started more than 35 times in a regular season—and probably never will. For that reason alone, it's unlikely a major league pitcher will ever win 30 games again.

But long before it was thought that Denny was on the wondrous pace to win 31 games in 1968, he was on no pace at all. The Tigers won his first two starts, but he didn't. McLain pitched well in both games, but they were won with walk-off home runs after he'd left. Being winless after two starts, though, would be his only stutter step. By the end of May, he was 8–1. By the end of June, he was 14–2.

With a record of 20–3 by July 27, however, his countdown was just beginning.

So was his awareness of having an extraordinary season. In his book, *I Told You I Wasn't Perfect,* McLain recalled being told it was the earliest anyone had won 20 games since Rube Marquard for the New York Giants in 1912. But he also recalled saying, "1912, what? Rube, what?"

He was a brash, talented right-hander more interested in the present than his place in history. Born outside of Chicago, McLain had

Denny McLain throws during 1968, the year he won 31 games, the Cy Young Award, and MVP Award. (USA TODAY Sports Images)

been the odd man out of a 3-for-2 roster crunch with the White Sox in 1963. Twenty minutes after the Sox placed him on waivers that spring, the Tigers signed him. But to this day, McLain believes he might not have reached the major leagues at all had it not been for Al Lopez, the manager of the White Sox back then.

It wasn't because Lopez believed in him that Denny got his chance. It was because Lopez did not believe in him. "I remember it as if it were yesterday," McLain said. "We had played an exhibition series in Mexico City during spring training. I'd thrown some scoreless innings and was feeling pretty good when Lopez called me up to the front of the plane back to Florida. He told me, 'This is very serious because you have two guys ahead of you [Dave DeBusschere and Bruce Howard], and if I had to throw someone off the bus right now, it would be you because all you have is a fastball.' Here I was floating on air, and my manager is telling me I'm never going to be a major league pitcher. Take that and go sleep in the back of the plane."

The decision would come down to how McLain and Howard performed in an exhibition game Lopez arranged between the team's minor leaguers and, as McLain called them, "the scrubbinis" of the roster. "There we were," McLain said. "Bruce and I were pitching for our lives. I gave up a home run to Dave Nicholson and lost 1–0. So he kept Howard, had already decided to keep DeBusschere, and let me go."

Before the Tigers claimed McLain on waivers, he called his fiancée, Sharyn Boudreau, the daughter of Hall of Famer Lou Boudreau. "That was the best decision I ever made because when I told her, 'Listen, I'm coming home because I don't know that anyone is going to pick me up,' she said she didn't want to marry a quitter. [She told me:] 'So you can't quit—because if you do, I might not be here.'"

Nothing more needed to be said. "That was the moment I told myself, *looks like I'm going to play baseball*. It was a big, big moment in my life because if Sharyn hadn't said that to me, I really believe I would have gone home."

McLain signed with the Tigers and reported to their minor league complex, "which I wasn't impressed with because of all the cockroaches," he said.

When McLain asked fellow prospect Leo Marentette what "those bugs" were, Marentette told him, 'They're roaches, and they'll eat you alive if you don't cover yourself while you sleep.' "That scared the crap out of me," Denny said. "I don't think I slept for a week." With the Tigers, though, he was on a fast track to the majors. On September 21, 1963, he made his big league debut in a start against the team that had let him go, the White Sox, who were still managed by Lopez. The Tigers won 4–3 with a complete game and a home run from McLain, the only home run of his career. "It's amazing how things turn out," he said. "But in my next game against Washington, I got the crap kicked out of me."

By 1965 he'd become a consistent winner. In the three seasons leading up to 1968, he won 53 games. But he also had begun to feel discomfort in his arm, so it was with the constant help of cortisone that McLain would excel in 1968. "God, I wish I'd never done that," he said of the anti-inflammation shots he began to take. "From 1966 on, I had 134 shots. I would have lasted longer without them, maybe, but I never would have won 30 games."

To get to 30, he needed victories in 10 in his last 15 starts. But he was rolling. After his 20th victory, he won his next five starts. All five were complete games. His 0.80 ERA was his lowest of any five-win stretch that season, as was his .172 opponents batting average.

With 10 starts left, McLain was only five victories away from the magic number. But in a 10–2 loss to the White Sox—a game in which he lasted just five and two-thirds innings—he suffered a setback. The Tigers' medical staff described McLain's shoulder as "tired" after that game, though to Denny, that merely meant another cortisone shot.

He felt better at Yankee Stadium but lost 2–1—the only time he would lose two games in a row all season. With eight starts left, he needed to win five. But the pressure had just gone up. Complicating matters was an ugly undercurrent of resentment. As McLain pointed out in his book, it was after the loss at Yankee Stadium that a *Life* magazine profile quoted an anonymous teammate who said, "It's good he lost. He was already starting to act like he'd won 30."

Manager Mayo Smith was on edge as well. McLain won his next game, but when he found himself down 2–0 to the Baltimore Orioles after just two batters, Smith hurried to the mound. Mayo was a worrier, McLain said. He asked Denny how he felt. "Pretty good" was the reply, "but maybe I'm overthrowing."

Concerned about his pitcher's precious shoulder, Smith asked if McLain wanted to be pulled from the game. Denny's response was a profane variation of no. Smith then asked catcher Bill Freehan how McLain was throwing. "How would I know?" the eventual 11-time All-Star replied, "I haven't caught anything yet."

McLain not only went on to win the game but made the play of the game, turning "a screamer to my crotch" into a triple play. When he won his next start as well to stand at 28–5 on September 6, he was ahead of Dizzy Dean's 30-win pace in 1934. The problem with such comparisons is that Dean won four of his 30 games in relief. With seven saves he was a closer as well as a starter.

Denny pressed on, getting his 29th victory on September 10 in a 7–2 victory in Anaheim against the California Angels.

With four scheduled starts remaining, he liked his chances of winning 30. So did everyone else. Approaching his next game, McLain reveled in the media attention. "It was heaven," he recalled in his book. But 40 years later, he admitted that he was "embarrassed to look back and read the braggadocio."

On Saturday, September 14, McLain pitched at home against the Oakland A's with history on the line. The crowd for the game at Tiger Stadium was substantial (33,688) but not a sellout. Oakland led 4–3 in the middle of the ninth inning; Reggie Jackson had hit two home runs and had also thrown out Don Wert at the plate. "That asshole," McLain recalled with a laugh. "I hung an 0-2 curveball to him the first time, and he hits it to Canada. Next time, it's 0-2 again, and you bet I'm throwing him another curveball. He hits it even farther. I was pissed at him for years."

The Tigers were facing right-hander Diego Segui, a converted starter entering his fifth inning of relief. Al Kaline led off with a walk. An out later, Mickey Stanley singled Kaline to third. Despite the fact that earlier in the season McLain had called them "the worst fans anywhere," a forgiving crowd was clamoring for history to be made.

Then came the break of the game. After fielding Jim Northrup's grounder to first, Danny Cater made a wild throw to the plate. Kaline's run tied the score. He had to crawl home after ducking under Cater's throw, but he scored all the same.

Stanley ended up at third. That brought up Willie Horton. The count went to 2-2. Willie hit the next pitch solidly. Upon seeing that Horton's liner to left would drive in the winning run, McLain jumped up and hit his head on the dugout roof. Kaline helped him to the field, where the celebration began. Denny would win his next start and had a chance to win his final two starts as well, but the Tigers lost them both by 2–1 scores. It was a season for the ages all the same.

McLain won 24 games, plus his second consecutive Cy Young Award, the next year. But with a bad shoulder, he burned out. Including a suspension from baseball and his two stints in prison, his life took one wrong turn after another, the most tragic being the death of his daughter, Kristin, in an automobile accident. "Nothing comes close to losing my daughter," McLain said. "It's the worst thing that's ever happened to me. I feel the pain of it every day."

But the cocky kid who once lived almost entirely for himself now lives to keep his wife, Sharyn, comfortable while helping her cope with Parkinson's disease. "I do about 200 card shows a year so we can pay for her nurse," he said. "I'm out there meeting people nearly every weekend in minor league ballparks." He also lost more than 150 pounds to get himself in better shape to take care of her. "It's the least I can do for the wonderful woman who's believed in me for 52 years.

Of his time with the Tigers, McLain speaks fondly: "Those were the days, I tell you. We sure loved the game."

Lou Whitaker, were you a great player?

"Oh, absolutely," he said, "one of the best to ever put on a major league uniform."

Interviewing Whitaker was like the box of chocolates that Forrest Gump talked about. You never knew what you were going to get. Sometimes nothing. Other times, because of his honesty, more than you ever expected.

If the soft-spoken second baseman was upset with himself after a game, he wouldn't break his bat or throw his equipment. Nor would he take his frustration out on the media by being disagreeable. He'd just be quiet, withdrawing to thoughts perhaps of a play he should have and could have made but somehow didn't. He was that way with his teammates, too. "That's often the best kind of player to have," Whitaker's longtime manager, Sparky Anderson, once said. "They show up at the ballpark, do their job, and never say nothin' good or bad. No muss, no fuss. You eventually get to respect those players as much as any."

That said, Whitaker could also talk your ear off, so much so that you would wonder out loud when the session was over, "Who just interviewed whom?" If you asked him if he had a minute, he might still be chatting a half hour later.

Whitaker was always acutely aware of his own ability, though, as indicated by his reply about being a great player. There was a playful smile on his face when he said it, possibly indicating that he didn't really mean it. But Lou usually meant what he said. "We were major league players," he added. "We were supposed to feel that way about ourselves. But I was very confident. I knew I was a great player. That's not bragging. That's not being cocky. It's just how I felt about myself. It's like when I was younger, and my sister would ask me what I wanted to be. I'd tell her, 'I'm going to be a pro.' But I would think that to motivate myself and get better."

Some who watched Whitaker's career believe that the five-time All-Star was more than a good player but not quite among the elite. For those, though, who considered him great—and there were many who did—it was a major injustice that when Whitaker's name appeared on the Hall of Fame ballot for the first time in 2001, he not only came up short of the required votes to be elected, but also of the necessary 5 percent to stay on the ballot. It was a stunning one-and-done for Lou. He needed 26 of the 515 votes but received only 15 from members of the Baseball Writers Association of America.

Knocked off the ballot the same year were Kirk Gibson and Lance Parrish, whose removals also were surprising but not nearly as much as what happened to Whitaker, to whom favorable comparisons with Hall of Fame second basemen Joe Morgan, Roberto Alomar, and Ryne Sandberg can be made.

According to Bill James' *Historical Baseball Abstract*, in fact, Whitaker is the 13th best second baseman of all time. But in all honesty, if Whitaker had been allowed to play his preferred position, he would have been a third baseman instead. He didn't ask to be moved to second base, nor did he feel he should have to move after playing third base so well in 1976 that he was named the Most Valuable Player of the Florida State League. Actually, the Tigers' front office wanted to move Whitaker from third to second during the 1976 season, not after. But Jim Leyland, who was managing the team in Lakeland, Florida, at the time, felt it would be so disruptive that he advised general manager Jim Campbell to wait.

Campbell initially rejected the advice but changed his mind. As soon as Whitaker's season was over in Lakeland and Alan Trammell's was done at Double A Montgomery, the two were whisked off to the Florida Instructional League in St. Petersburg, where they began to work out as a second-and-short combination under the auspices of Montgomery manager Eddie Brinkman. But that was the point of the switch all along: to pair Whitaker with Trammell as a dynamic young combo. "I was not happy about the switch," Whitaker said. "I might even have shed a few tears. My whole life had been at third, and you're telling me you want to make a second baseman out of me?"

That's exactly what they were telling you, Lou.

Later in his career—in the spring of 1985, to be precise—Whitaker had a chance to move back to third when Anderson became enamored with Chris Pittaro as a rookie second baseman, but he turned it down. "This is better for all involved," Lou explained.

Instead of thinking it brash, Campbell admired Whitaker's self-confidence. When they met for the first time, Whitaker introduced himself by saying, "I'm Louis Whitaker. I'll be playing for you soon."

With the Tigers liking what they saw during the Florida workouts, it was only a matter of how long it would take the two to become major league starters. Not long at all, it turned out. After spending most of the 1977 season at Double A Montgomery—playing for Brinkman, a former Tigers shortstop who monitored their progress—the two infielders were September call-ups to the majors. Neither ever played a game at Triple A.

As with Trammell, Whitaker was just a scrawny kid. At 20 he was a year older than his sidekick when they made their major league debuts, but neither had the strength yet to drive the ball. "When I first saw them," Anderson said, "you could knock the bat out of Trammell's hands, and Whitaker was hitting pool shots over third."

In fact, it took Whitaker until May of his sixth season to accumulate as many career home runs as he would eventually hit in a single season (1989), when he set a personal high with 28.

Whitaker achieved another personal best with 85 RBIs in 1989, more than making up for missing the final month of the previous year when he injured his knee while doing the splits on the dance floor at an anniversary party. "I believe Lou was embarrassed by that," Anderson said at the time.

Before he learned to turn on a pitch, there also was no way Whitaker ever could have envisioned clearing the right-field roof at Tiger Stadium as he did on May 13, 1985, off Burt Hooton of the Texas Rangers. With Whitaker becoming the first leadoff hitter to accomplish the feat—and the first second baseman as well—the blast made a believer out of Vada Pinson, who was the Tigers' hitting coach at the time. "You watch Lou for a while and you begin to feel he can do whatever he wants to at the plate," Pinson said. "He's so quick.

He's a natural. They tell me that last year he didn't even take batting practice much of the time."

It's true. Whitaker didn't always take batting practice during the Tigers' championship season of 1984 because many of the hitters preferred a practice pitcher who threw too hard for his liking. "[Former major league catcher] Dan Whitmer did a great job for a lot of guys," Whitaker said. "Darrell Evans loved hitting off him, so did [Dave Bergman], who said he was worth his weight in gold. But at 900 miles an hour, he threw too hard for me. The ball went past me too fast. It was too much to get ready for a ballgame. So I stopped taking batting practice and didn't resume until September. I can't speak for anyone else, but I just didn't need it."

Whitaker knew what he had to do to prepare for a game—even if it looked as if he didn't work as hard as others. For instance, he didn't take a lot of infield work—just 15 ground balls before every game. "Fifteen, that's all, and I'm ready," he said. "I mean serious, game-type ground balls. I don't think I was cheating anyone. I'd been playing baseball all these years. I should know what I need."

In any case, when Whitaker and Trammell opened the 1978 season as the Tigers' starting second-and-short combination, little did they know it was the beginning of an era that would last 18 years. Lou and Tram. Or the other way around. It didn't matter how you said their names nor in what order. As a tandem they defined the Tigers for a generation. What surprised some was that neither player ever came close to leaving the Tigers for another team. Instead of seeking more money elsewhere, Whitaker and Trammell remained loyal even when they knew it was costing them.

Besides, both of them liked the togetherness of the franchise. For example, when the Tigers signed Whitaker to a five-year contract for $3.5 million after the 1982 season, assistant general manager Bill Lajoie had tears in his eyes because he'd always been so close to Whitaker. "He meant a lot to me," Whitaker said of the late Lajoie, "and I meant a lot to him. I remember when he came down to my hometown [of Martinsville, Virginia,] to sign me, he asked if I could play. "I told him I was born to play. He loved that answer."

But Lou and Lajoie also had the kind of relationship in which they could kid each other.

"No wonder he was the happiest man in the room when I signed that contract," Whitaker said. "I'm not surprised he had tears in his eyes. He had just locked up the best second baseman at a third of the cost."

Whitaker credits the late Gates Brown for developing him as a hitter. "He changed me from an inside-out singles hitter to being able to turn it loose," he said. "He turned me into someone who could drive the ball."

Without Brown's help, Whitaker would not have become such an offensive force. But with these words once spoken by "the Gator," there's still hope that Lou will receive the ultimate honor and be voted into the Hall of Fame. "One of these days," Brown said, "but I don't know when."

13

TIGER STADIUM CLOSES

The old ballpark was closing. Its rust and dust would soon be part of the past. So on a warm September evening in 1999, it was time to look both forward and back because of the emotion and history involved.

Baseball had been played at the corner of Michigan and Trumbull in Detroit since 1896.

With an initial capacity of 5,000, Bennett Park came first. By all accounts it was rickety. With the stadium lacking stands in some areas of the outfield, spectators had to stand behind ropes.

But it served its purpose. The Tigers played in the World Series at Bennett Park from 1907 to 1909 but lost all three.

On the same site, but with home plate reconfigured to where left field had been, Navin Field—named for Frank Navin, the team's principal owner—opened in 1912. As Bennett Park had been, the new park was gradually expanded. Two more World Series were played there, and the Tigers finally won their first championship in 1935.

Navin Field became Briggs Stadium after Walter O. Briggs Sr. took over full ownership of the club following Navin's death. World Series came along in 1940 and 1945 with the Tigers winning the latter against the Chicago Cubs. Briggs believed in day baseball, so lights for night games weren't installed until 1948.

In its final incarnation as Tiger Stadium, the Tigers would win the World Series in 1968 and 1984. But it wasn't just the team—sometimes good, sometimes not—that made the ballpark special. For many the personal attachment began with that first view of green grass, especially from the upper deck, which thrilled generations of fans. "To me, it always was like home," said Detroit native Willie Horton. "That grass was so soft, I could have slept on it."

Toward the end of Tiger Stadium's time, though, it more than showed its age. From the upper deck, the initial view was still grand.

But in the lower deck, you could never be sure what was dripping on you from above. There were leaks. There were creaks. Creature comforts had long since become an issue.

The Tigers weren't particularly good in 1999, one of many not-particularly-good seasons they endured in later years. Some, actually, were worse than that. Other than the glorious good-bye that would take place at the end, it was a lackluster season. The closing of Tiger Stadium seemed light years away in April and May, but when summer came, so did the realization that a last hurrah was approaching. Appropriately, Ernie Harwell would refer to Tiger Stadium as a friend in his final game tribute. "Open your eyes, look around, and take a mental picture," Harwell said so poignantly. "Moments like this will live on forever. Farewell, old friend, Tiger Stadium. We will remember."

The Tigers played the Kansas City Royals in the last game. First pitch was moved up to a mid-afternoon start so that the program of festivities, including the relocation of home plate to Comerica Park, wouldn't last until midnight. Todd Jones struck out Carlos Beltran for the final out at 7:07 PM. Everything about the game was viewed as history in the making because it was.

In the fourth inning of the previous day's 6–1 victory against the Royals, Gabe Kapler hit a home run. But it wouldn't have been fitting for the last home run at Tiger Stadium to be hit in the next-to-last game. The occasion deserved something more dramatic than that.

Maybe Luis Polonia's leadoff home run in the bottom of the first inning would be the one remembered. Polonia signed with the Tigers as a free agent before the 1999 season after playing the previous two years in Mexico. He wasn't known for hitting with power, but as of the first inning of the final game, Polonia's home run was a candidate to be the last of its kind at Tiger Stadium.

It wasn't a candidate for long, though. Mark Quinn of the Royals countered in the second inning with a home run off Tigers' starter Brian Moehler, one that enjoyed a longer shelf life as the next three innings went by without anyone else reaching the seats. With the game tied in the bottom of the sixth, however, Karim Garcia put the Tigers in front with a two-run blast to deep left-center off Jeff Suppan. Maybe Garcia's was the one meant for posterity. It was more than a garden-variety blast, but in all fairness, the last home run at Tiger Stadium deserved to be more majestic.

And it would be.

Earlier in the day, making a good-natured prediction in the spirit of the occasion—but a prediction all the same—Tigers Hall of Famer Al Kaline had told Robert Fick that Fick was going to hit a home run. It was somewhat of a stretch to think so because Fick, a 25-year-old in his second season as a Tiger, hadn't yet hit a home run at Tiger Stadium. He'd hit five on the road but none at home, and after Garcia connected, time began to run out for the prediction to come true.

As the Tigers' designated hitter that day, Fick had hit a long fly ball for a sacrifice fly in the second inning. He walked in the fourth and then made solid contact to end the sixth with a liner to right that was turned into a double play. At that point there were two reasons to believe Fick would not get another at-bat. The first was that he'd been the last batter in the sixth, and manager Larry Parrish wanted at some point to give another young player, Frank Catalanotto, a chance to hit, so he also could say that he had played in the last game at Tiger Stadium. The second was that Fick, himself, already thought he was done for the day. "I'd told Cat he was going to hit for me if my turn came around again, but [Parrish] hadn't told him," he said.

When only one Tiger reached base in the seventh, it looked like it would become a moot point anyway. The Tigers would have to load the bases in the eighth for the DH to bat again.

No sooner said than done. Dean Palmer led off the eighth with a double. Damion Easley singled Palmer to third, and Garcia, whose home run in the sixth had given the Tigers the lead, was walked intentionally to load the bases.

It would have been monumental if Kapler, the next batter, had hit a grand slam as the last home run at Tiger Stadium. But he hit a comebacker to the mound instead. Pitching in relief for the Royals, Jeff Montgomery threw it home to get Palmer for the first out. Decision time had arrived. Was it going to be Catalanotto batting next as a pinch-hitter for Fick with the bases loaded? No one seemed to know—in part because the play at home on Palmer had been close enough for Parrish to discuss the matter with plate umpire Rocky Roe. Lost in the confab was that Parrish still hadn't told Catalanotto to grab a bat. "I'd been a good teammate and had told Cat he was going to hit," Fick said, "but the word from Parrish never came. He just forgot. So there I was on the top step of the dugout. Kapler had swung at the first pitch. and [Parrish] still hadn't told Cat. Since I was still technically in the game, I grabbed my batting gloves and my bat and went up there."

Destiny at work.

With the Tigers leading 4–2, Fick hurried to the plate because the score was still close, and any hitter worth his salt wants to be up in that kind of situation. As far as the umpire was concerned, Fick was supposed to be the hitter anyway. Robert figured he had "one swing coming up before L.P. would make the switch." Talk about making the most of one swing. "Oh, yeah, I remember the pitch," Fick said. "Middle away, middle down, it was middle. A meaty pitch, but a lucky hit."

And there it went. From the get-go, it had the distance as well as impressive height. Would it hit the facade of the third deck in right, the roof—or might it even clear the roof?

Fick's rising blast hit the roof and came back down to the field, but it was a grand slam all the same. And that slam would forever rank as the last home run ever hit at Tiger Stadium. "I was real blessed to be a part of that, for sure," Fick said. "It was a cool thing. That whole last week the fans had been nuts. That's how big the game was to them."

As he rounded the bases, though, Fick didn't think of himself or of his place in Tigers history. He thought about his father, Charlie, who had died the year before. "I always played the game for him because of how much enjoyment it brought him to watch me play ball," Fick said. "I wasn't going to let him down. At that moment, I could feel his pride."

Tiger Stadium closed forever with that game—and with those enduring memories.

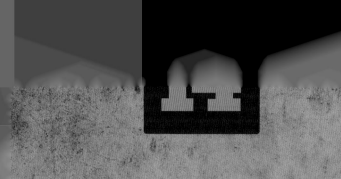

MIGUEL CABRERA

Miguel Cabrera needs no introduction. Not by most accounts, but by all, he is a great hitter, a lock for the Hall of Fame. "Everyone could see early on he was going to be good," Barry Bonds said. Added Tigers legend Al Kaline: "He's by far the best hitter I've ever seen in a Tigers uniform. There's no weakness in his swing. He does things I never did: hitting to the opposite field, for instance. He hits the ball to right field like left-handed hitters used to back in my day."

The acquisition of Cabrera was one of the great trades in Tigers history. It will also rank as one of the most lopsided because none of the six players that the Florida Marlins received in the deal made much of an impact for them. Going into the 2007 winter meetings, it seemed highly unlikely the Tigers would make a trade of such magnitude. But their track record of accomplishing the improbable was already impressive.

Starting in 2004, when he signed Pudge Rodriguez as a free agent, Mike Ilitch had become one of the most aggressive owners in the game. "Detroit had changed from being somewhere that big-name players didn't want to play, or just didn't think of playing, to being somewhere they did," Kaline said. "Mr. Ilitch changed that with the signing of Pudge and Magglio [Ordonez] in back-to-back years."

Adding Cabrera, however, would have to be done with a trade, not a signing. Ilitch's open mind certainly helped. "When [team president and general manager Dave Dombrowski] went to the winter meetings that year, it was Mr. Ilitch who said, 'Hey, can we get that guy, Cabrera?'" said Jim Leyland, who managed the Tigers from 2006 to 2013. "I'm only saying what Dave has said himself. I know he was thinking, *I don't think so*, but the owner told him to give it a try, and we walked out of the winter meetings with Miguel Cabrera. I mean, how can that happen? It was amazing to all of us."

More than being a good owner, that's being a difference-making owner. "The thing with Mr. Ilitch is that he knows the game, he played the game, and he's very perceptive about what's going on in baseball," Leyland said.

Cabrera didn't come to Detroit as a potential star. He already was one—with three consecutive .300-plus seasons for the Marlins, in each of which he also collected more than 100 RBIs. As a Tiger the Venezuelan native not only continued that journey but became the best hitter in baseball. In his first eight seasons with Detroit, Cabrera hit .326 while averaging 34 home runs and 115 RBIs. He was voted Most Valuable Player in the American League twice and ranked fifth or better in MVP voting another three times. He also won four batting titles. But it wasn't just because of his swing that he excelled. "He also has an IQ that's higher than most," Bonds said.

Cabrera stumbled a time or two with missteps in his personal life, but there've been no reported issues since 2011. He has since devoted much of his time to the Miguel Cabrera Foundation and to becoming an even better hitter than he was. His foundation, as described on its website, focuses on providing academic scholarships and revitalizing baseball fields in schools and neighborhoods. It also states that Cabrera's philosophy was "shaped" by the Triple Crown he won in 2012 for leading the A.L. in batting average, home runs, and RBIs.

In so doing he became the first player to win the Triple Crown since Carl Yastrzemski of the Boston Red Sox in 1967 and the first Tiger since Ty Cobb in 1909. What made the winning of it seem like an achievement that might never happen again was how much time had elapsed since it last happened—especially compared to how often it used to occur. Between 1901 and 1967, there'd never been a gap of more than 10 years without a Triple Crown being won. The feat had gone from being relatively common to unheard of. The fact that it had

ANOTHER RARE TRIPLE

There's something the Tigers have never done. They've never hit into an unassisted triple play. But they have pulled one off.

It happened on May 31, 1927 at Navin Field on a line drive to first baseman Johnny Neun, who caught the ball, tagged the Cleveland Indians' base runner who had been on first, and then ran to second base (instead of throwing the ball) to retire the runner there.

The runner at second, Glenn Myatt, seemed awestruck. After tagging him, Neun raced to the Tigers' dugout, where he broke into a happy dance resembling the hula.

It was the eighth unassisted triple play in the majors since 1900, but there have been only seven since. The feat didn't change Neun, nor would it, the *Detroit Free Press* reported. "Neun isn't apt to be besieged with theatrical offers that seem to be a weakness of folks made famous overnight," the story said. "Johnny is a home-loving man—and besides, traveling around the country, appearing behind the footlights would interfere with his bridge lessons."

been 45 years since the last one made Cabrera's Triple Crown even more celebrated.

It wasn't done without some nail biting, however, mostly by Leyland. Calling the fact he managed a Triple Crown winner "one of the great thrills of my career," Leyland wanted to be absolutely sure it didn't slip away. So he insisted on updates involving all scenarios involving the clinching of it on the final day of the 2012 season. Leyland positioned media relations director Brian Britten with his computer behind the Tigers' dugout in Kansas City. "When I told Jim before the game I was going upstairs to the press box, he told me I had to stay in case he had questions," Britten said. "So I was sitting at some beat-up old training table near the dugout with my charts, getting a lot of puzzled looks from the players."

But to Leyland, who checked with Britten between innings, it made perfect sense. "I didn't want to be remembered as the guy who pulled Miggy too soon," he said.

Miguel Cabrera readies to swing during 2012, when he won the Triple Crown by hitting .330, 44 home runs, and 139 RBIs. (USA TODAY Sports Images)

The bigger picture was that the Tigers had won the A.L. Central two nights before with a 6–3 victory against the Royals. It hadn't been an easy road for them. Not since 1972 had they won a postseason berth with fewer than 90 victories. But 88 would be enough in 2012. They swept the New York Yankees in the American League Championship Series but were held to only three runs in the last three games of the World Series and were anticlimactically swept by the San Francisco Giants.

The outcome of Cabrera's quest was far more suspenseful. Going into the final game, he was hitting .331 to Mike Trout's .324. But if Cabrera had gone 0-for-4 on the last day and Trout had gone 4-for-4, the Angels' outfielder would have nudged in front, .3287 to .3285. That's an example of what Leyland wanted to monitor.

Cabrera was 0-for-2 after his first two at-bats, while Trout was hit by a pitch his first time up for the Angels. After that, he grounded out to the pitcher. Trout would get hits in his last two at bats, but they wouldn't be enough. Finishing at .330 to Trout's .326, Miggy was home free on the batting average front.

Cabrera had no final-day worries about RBIs. He knocked in 139 runs in 2012. Josh Hamilton of the Texas Rangers was the runner-up with 128. Just one obstacle remained: home runs. Cabrera was at 44, but there were four other hitters in the A.L. with 41 or more. Britten had his work cut out for him, keeping it all straight and making sure Leyland knew the situation at all times. Homerless in his last eight games, Adam Dunn of the Chicago White Sox sat out the final day. He finished with 41 home runs. Edwin Encarnacion of the Toronto Blue Jays also didn't play, missing his third game in a row. He finished with 42. Hamilton, meanwhile, stalled at 43 home runs when he was one ahead of Cabrera. By the first pitch of the Tigers' final game, Hamilton had gone homerless again. Incredibly, he hit none in his last nine games.

That left former Tiger Curtis Granderson as the final challenger. But with only 41 home runs, he seemed to be too far behind to grab a share of Cabrera's crown by tying him. He'd have to hit three in his last game—improbable but not impossible. Granderson's bid grew stronger—but still seemed unlikely—when he belted a three-run shot his first time up against Boston. His chances dimmed when he struck out in his next two at-bats. But with the Yankees winning in a rout, Granderson came up again in the seventh and, sure enough, he led off with his second home run of the game, giving him 43. Suddenly he was within striking distance of Cabrera, his friend and former teammate who went homerless in his last game. To tie him, however, Granderson would have to bat again, which wasn't assured. But when the Yankees batted around in the seventh, it looked like he'd get that chance—until he didn't. Ahead 14–2 with two outs, the Yankees pinch-hit for Granderson, who didn't object. "I didn't think about it until CC [Sabathia] saw me sitting down and said, 'Man, you could have had one more,'" Granderson told *The Newark Star-Ledger*.

But the chase was over. Miguel had his Triple Crown. Cabrera was removed from the Tigers' game in the bottom of the fourth inning. Reacting with class, Royals fans gave him a standing ovation when his achievement was announced. "That ovation was unbelievable," Leyland said. "If it's not one of the 50 big moments in this team's history, something's wrong."

OZZIE VIRGIL BREAKS COLOR BARRIER

The Tigers were an all-white team until 1958. Some called them stubborn. Some said they were backward. Others would look back years later and say they were racist. Whatever they were, it remains an indelible stain on their history that they were the second-to-last major league team to integrate. In fact, it took them 11 years longer than the first team.

Baseball's color barrier was broken by Jackie Robinson of the Brooklyn Dodgers in April of 1947. Three months later, when he played his first game for the Cleveland Indians, Larry Doby became the first African American player in the American League. Two weeks after Doby, Hank Thompson debuted for the St. Louis Browns.

The process—not to mention the progress—stalled in 1948 but picked up again in 1949. For the Tigers, though, times didn't change. Doors didn't open. Season after season went by. The number of all-white teams in the majors diminished, but the Tigers were still one of two (the Boston Red Sox being the other) not to have a black player on their roster when the 1957 season ended.

Then along came Ozzie Virgil, who burst upon the Tigers' scene with a 5-for-5 performance in his first home game. On June 6, 1958, Virgil became the first non-white player ever to play for the Tigers. Born in the Dominican Republic to parents of Puerto Rican descent, Virgil considered himself more of a ballplayer than a trailblazer. He always thought the Tigers felt the same way. "I don't believe the Tigers called me up because I was black," he once said. "They called me up because I was a player." But John McHale Sr., the Tigers' general manager at the time, would admit later that "getting a black player was a priority of mine. We were a little slow getting into the 20th century."

Virgil's family moved from the Dominican Republic to the Bronx in 1947, the year he turned 15. New York had three major league teams, and all were good that year. One, in fact, was excellent.

The New York Yankees won 97 games and the World Series. The Brooklyn Dodgers won 84 games but lost the World Series. The New York Giants weren't as good as the other two teams, going 81–73, but with Johnny Mize hitting 51 home runs and Larry Jansen putting together a 21–5 record, there was plenty of talent on hand at the Polo Grounds in 1947.

For a young man such as Ozzie, entire days could be filled with baseball—living it, playing it, dreaming of it. Not only that, but the game was finally knocking down its barriers for players of color. Roster spots were opening even while some minds remained closed. For instance, as late as 1962, when Willie Horton reported for his first spring training in Lakeland, Florida, he carried his own bags from the bus station to the Tigers' complex because white cab drivers refused to drive him.

Horton eventually became the Tigers' first black star. But in 1958 it wasn't a matter of being a star; it was a matter of minority players hoping for any chance at all to play for the Tigers. The black community in Detroit wasn't happy with the pace of progress. They'd go to Briggs Stadium to watch visiting black players, but there weren't many. Four of the last five teams in the majors to integrate, after all, were A.L. clubs.

And while there was no disputing that the acquisition of Virgil by the Tigers was a step forward, the talent side of the January deal with the Giants was more about the acquisition of first baseman Gail Harris than Virgil, a third baseman for whom there was no immediate spot in the lineup. With Italian-born bonus baby Reno Bertoia getting the chance to start at third for the Tigers, Virgil began the year in the minors. He had spent the entire 1957 season with the Giants, hitting .235 in 96 games but wasn't yet a fit with the Tigers.

After Bertoia hit just .235 in their first 45 games, however, Ozzie got his chance. With his promotion on June 6, Virgil became "the Tigers' first Negro player," according to the *Detroit Free Press*. There was no accompanying fanfare. No banner headlines. Just a mention near the bottom of a jumped story, one that continues on another page.

Virgil, though, was back in the majors. So when the Tigers played that night at Griffith Stadium against the Washington Senators, a non-white player was in their lineup for the first time ever. "The only thing I didn't like was that the black people in Detroit didn't accept me," Virgil later said. "They wanted one of their own, a Larry Doby, someone they could identify with. I could understand that. I had Latin ancestry. They thought of me more as a Dominican player instead of a Negro. I heard that on the radio programs. If they called me black, fine. If they called me white, fine. If they called me Latino, fine. I didn't care what they called me. I just wanted to play."

And that's the chance the Tigers gave him. In Virgil's first game, he helped the Tigers beat the Senators 11–2, or, as Hal Middlesworth put it in his *Free Press* account, "Virgil, taking over at third base as the first Negro ever to wear a Tigers uniform, had a hand in the swatfest with a ground-rule double."

One hit led to another, then to several more. Virgil hit safely in his first eight games, all on the road. Among the hits was his first home run as a Tiger, which occurred in Boston. On the final stop of the three-city trip, Virgil doubled in a run and scored twice as the seventh-place Tigers upended the first-place Yankees 4–2 in the opener of a difficult four-game series at Yankee Stadium. And when the Tigers completed a sweep of the Yankees with doubleheader shutouts from Frank Lary and Jim Bunning, which meant they were heading home with seven wins in their last eight games, there were those who believed that the addition of Virgil had triggered the sudden reversal.

That was understandable because, to an impressive extent, it had. Two games below .500, the Tigers were suddenly feeling good about themselves but even better about their new third baseman. The fans felt good about him, too. Virgil's first home game as a Tiger was properly viewed as an historic event. A crowd of 29,794—huge for a Tuesday night—showed up at Briggs Stadium. (In comparison, only 6,603 attended the Tigers' next game.)

As he'd done during the just-completed trip, Virgil batted second. And what a memorable game he had. In his first at-bat, following a leadoff home run by Frank Bolling off the Senators'

Pedro Ramos, Virgil doubled down the third-base line. The crowd cheered. In his second at-bat, he led off the third inning with a single to deep short and scored—to more cheers—on Al Kaline's three-run home run. Batting a second time in the Tigers' seven-run third, Virgil singled to center. He already had three hits. The crowd loved it. Another win for the Tigers—their fifth in a row—was in the works. As Middlesworth would write about the eventual 9–2 victory, "Those wonderful, wonderful Tigers did it again."

In the fifth inning, Virgil reached first base on yet another infield single, and in the seventh, his fifth hit of the game was a blooper to left. Game stories described the crowd's reaction at that point as "thunderous." For Virgil, who admitted that he hadn't known what to expect when he got to Detroit, it was a golden moment. "I had never had a standing ovation before," he said.

But the glow was short-lived. Virgil was not destined to be a player of major impact for the Tigers. He began to slump. By August he wasn't playing at all. The Tigers, meanwhile, had a clearly identifiable flaw that prevented them from sustaining a surge. "We had a bad club," said Virgil years later.

There were no Ozzie comments, though, after his five-hit game. He was whisked away before reporters were allowed into the clubhouse because manager Bill Norman reportedly was miffed at the media, and "This was his way of getting even," wrote Joe Falls in the *Free Press*.

The Tigers and Virgil remained hot for another week. They climbed to a 32–31 record with a victory against the Baltimore Orioles on June 24, at which time Virgil was hitting .303.

But at that point the bubble burst. Hitting just .205 for the rest of the 1958 season, Virgil would spend all of 1959 in the minors before reappearing as a Tiger during the summer of 1960.

Ovations during Ozzie's second time around were more polite than thunderous. But at least they were polite.

As for the Tigers of 1958, after being one game over .500 on June 24, they spun their wheels the rest of the way, not even climbing to two over until September 17 before finishing with a 77–77 record. Slowly marching forward, they would sign Maury Wills in

October—their "second Negro infielder," he was labeled in print—but wouldn't keep the future seven-time All-Star shortstop. Doby would play 18 games for the Tigers in 1959. Though still early in the organization's age of enlightenment, it was too late in his career to matter. But the door, at long last, was open. And who had been the first player through it? Osvaldo Virgil, who served two years in the U.S. Marine Corps, played nine years in the majors, coached 19 years in the majors, and was also the first major league player from the Dominican Republic. That's called a magnificent career.

16

HARRY HEILMANN

An outstanding hitter and then a popular broadcaster, Harry Heilmann died thinking he was in the Hall of Fame, even though he wasn't. Heilmann was only 56 in 1951. But he knew his last breath was near.

He'd had a wonderful 15-year career with the Tigers despite never playing in a World Series. The teams on which he played simply weren't good enough. Only one of them finished as high as second place, and only three ended up within 10 games of first.

Heilmann's first year in the majors was 1914, five years after the Tigers lost the World Series to the Pittsburgh Pirates in seven games. His last year with Detroit was in 1929, five years before they lost to the St. Louis Cardinals in seven games again—so he was five years too late and five too early to make a series appearance.

But he did his part to help the Tigers compete, winning four batting titles in the 1920s. From 1921 to 1927, Heilmann's composite batting average was .380, topping out at .403 in 1923. Without a doubt, the man could hit. As one sportswriter of the era put it, Heilmann "specialized in line drives that threw off fire and smoke."

It was an era in which the Tigers transitioned from one great hitter to another, from Ty Cobb to Heilmann—after Cobb had averaged .379 from 1916 to 1922.

But near the end of Heilmann's life, it was time for his career to be honored. The process would feature one of the rare acts of kindness of Cobb's often unkind existence. As Heilmann lay dying of lung cancer, Cobb told him at his bedside that he had been elected to baseball's Hall of Fame. It hadn't happened—and wouldn't until the following year, months after Heilmann's death.

But Cobb told him otherwise.

By all accounts, of course, the news brought joy to the fading Heilmann, who had given up hope of eventually being elected.

Had today's Hall of Fame rules been in effect—with the stipulation that any candidate receiving less than 5 percent of the vote is removed from future ballots—Heilmann would have been removed three times. Despite being called "One of the five greatest right-handed hitters of all-time" by Ted Williams, Heilmann received less than 3 percent of the vote three times. In 1942 only four of 233 writers voted for Heilmann, who finished in a tie for 36th place.

An identical snub was happening to another Tigers great, Sam Crawford, who never received more than 4.2 percent of the vote. The Veterans Committee eventually elected Crawford in 1957, but Wahoo Sam would live to see the day. Sadly, Heilmann would not. Of solace, though, was that he thought he did.

It was out of character for Cobb to be kind to Heilmann. Then again, there are those who believe it was out of character for Cobb to be kind to anyone. They'd been longtime teammates, often vying for the same batting championship—a competition that created a distance between the two. But as his manager, and when it benefited him to do so, Cobb helped Heilmann become a better hitter by sharing batting tips with him. Even so, Cobb "wasn't really Dad's cup of tea," Heilmann's daughter-in-law, Marguerite, said.

In all likelihood, that was because their personalities were completely different.

Heilmann was considered a gentleman. Hall of Fame pitcher Ted Lyons of the Chicago White Sox called him "One of the most marvelous men I ever met in baseball." Such compliments didn't apply to Cobb, especially during his fierce playing career.

According to Heilmann, Cobb wouldn't even speak to him until they'd been in the same batting order for many years. But Cobb respected good hitters, though in the cases of both Heilmann and Crawford—another Tiger who Cobb helped get into the Hall of Fame— his feelings were concealed for years.

But it was his enduring respect for Heilmann that prompted Cobb to visit his old teammate "Slug" in his final hours. By then Heilmann's playing days had been over for 20 years but not his broadcasting career, which further endeared him to Tigers fans. And to future broadcasters as well. "I became a Tigers fan because of

Harry Heilmann," said Paul Carey, who was Ernie Harwell's broadcast partner for 19 years. Speaking shortly before his own death, Carey said Heilmann "had a pleasant, deep, mellow voice and was a good storyteller. I'll never forget some of his sayings, which were often tied to commercial sponsorships, such as 'He got on his Flying Red Horse [a plug for Mobil Oil] and caught that ball.' And for Bug-A-Boo insect spray, he would say 'Bug-A-Boo, another fly is dead.'"

Heilmann, though, never intended to be a broadcaster. When he played—for most of his career, at least—there was no such thing as radio play-by-play. But after his insurance company collapsed during the Depression, Heilmann had no livelihood. His baseball career had been a productive one, but most players of his era needed to work after they retired from the game. It was no different for Heilmann.

In 1934, when he was hired by radio station WXYZ in Detroit, he became the first former player to work in a broadcast booth. And there he stayed until he became too weak to continue during the 1951

THE THIRD OUTFIELDER

Bobby Veach was one of the most underrated Tigers of all time, a fine hitter about whom many will say, "never heard of him." That's because he played 100 years ago. A .311 hitter in a Tigers career that lasted from 1912 to 1923, Veach was part of an outfield that included Hall of Famers Ty Cobb and Sam Crawford. There've been few, if any, better threesomes.

But Veach was too easygoing for Cobb, who became his manager. So in 1921, to get the most out of him, Cobb instructed another future Hall of Famer, Harry Heilmann, to taunt Veach into becoming a more serious player, which worked.

Veach had his best season but at the cost of their friendship. Cobb told Heilmann he would take the blame at the end of the season for the taunting strategy, but he never did. Heilmann took the fall, and Veach never forgave him.

To this day, though, Veach—the son of a Kentucky coal miner—remains among the Tigers' top 10 in several offensive categories. He hit better than .305 in nine seasons and also led the American League in RBI three times. So he deserves better than "never heard of him."

season. But even then he stayed on the job until nearly a month before his death on July 9. At the All-Star Game in Detroit the day after Heilmann died, a moment of silence was observed at Briggs Stadium on his behalf as stars of both leagues lined the baselines.

It had been in the waning moments of Heilmann's life before the All-Star Game that Cobb told him he'd been elected to the Hall of Fame. His words became a silent pledge that he would work to make it happen, which he did. By calling baseball writers he knew, Cobb was true to his promise. In 1952—10 years after receiving just 1.7 percent—Heilmann was elected into baseball's Hall of Fame with 86.8 percent of the vote.

Had it been merely a matter of popularity among Tigers fans, of course, Heilmann would have been a Hall of Famer years earlier. And that's not just because of his four batting titles with the Tigers. Or because he was an amicable, outgoing outfielder who'd been an unassuming clerk in a San Francisco biscuit company when he was discovered. As author Fred Lieb described him, Heilmann was "handsome" and "pleasant-faced." Or because, despite becoming a .400 hitter, he never lost his humility after his first signing bonus, which consisted of nothing more than a spaghetti dinner. Or even because he was such a contrast to the angry Cobb.

No, it was because Heilmann became a hero off the field in Detroit before he became one on the field. In 1916, just his second season with the Tigers—and 10 full years after he had buried bodies from the earthquake that devastated his hometown of San Francisco—Heilmann saved the life of a drowning woman in the Detroit River.

In the process, he overcame the specter of his life's greatest tragedy. Harry's older brother, Walter, whose renowned curveball might have made him a major league pitcher, had drowned in 1908 while trying to swim to shore after his boat capsized. Walter was 17; Harry was 14. Both of them loved baseball. The loss of his big brother had to have been traumatic to Harry. The way Walter died, however, did not prevent Harry from reacting heroically when another drowning began to unfold right in front of him.

On July 25, 1916, Heilmann was nearby when a driver, who had his wife, daughter, and two houseguests in the car, lost control at the wheel on the banks of the Detroit River and plunged the vehicle into 18 feet of water. Maybe another person would have been frozen by the nightmare of his past. Heilmann, though, dove in and saved one of the houseguests, Lydia Johnson, who was the driver's sister-in-law.

"Mercy, I can feel the awful sensation yet," Johnson had said of the "sudden plunge" soon after the incident. "Some man rescued me, but I don't know who it was. The next thing I recollect, I was on the shore again."

The driver and second houseguest survived, but two passengers—the driver's wife and his three-year-old daughter—were not as fortunate. Trapped in the submerged automobile, they drowned. Yet from that point on—for what one newspaper called the "gallant rescue of a maiden"—there was a bond between the fans and Heilmann. The next day, the Tigers' modest outfielder received a standing ovation at Navin Field for his life-saving deed.

The unfortunate aspect of his career, of course, is that the Tigers never won an American League pennant, let alone a World Series, during his playing days. Even his four batting titles, all in odd-numbered years, didn't help. In 1921, when he won his first title, the Tigers finished in sixth place—27 games out of first. In 1923 the Tigers had to win 11 of their last 13 games just to finish as high as second place—16 games out. In 1925 they were out of the race by May 16 with an 8–22 start. And in 1927, when a push could have brought them closer to the vaunted New York Yankees, the Tigers dropped out of sight by starting a 3–19 plunge in late August.

Heilmann never did play on a winner, and, with arthritis developing in his wrists, his career was never quite the same after his last batting title. The Tigers eventually sold him to Cincinnati, where he ended his career in 1932. But it was in Detroit that Harry Heilmann played most of his splendid career and where he died in peace soon after Cobb whispered the premature truth to him that he finally had made the Hall of Fame.

17

HORTON'S THROW HOME

Without a close second, it is the most famous throw in Tigers history. A play of so many elements, and of such importance, that the re-living of it will never end. Chances are you're well aware what throw it was: Willie Horton's heave home to get Lou Brock at the plate in the fifth inning of Game 5 in the 1968 World Series. With that play as the catalyst, Horton changed the direction of the series.

Bit by bit from that point on, the momentum ebbed away from the St. Louis Cardinals, who had won three of the first four games. Despite Brock's one-out double, the Cardinals didn't add another run, and, creaking as if it were made of ancient oak, the pendulum inexorably swung toward the Tigers. It swung because Brock was thrown out at home by Horton, it swung because the Cardinals' lead remained at 3-2 instead of increasing, and it swung because the Tigers were able to stick with Mickey Lolich, their starting pitcher, who was having an outstanding series.

Despite falling behind by three runs in the first inning, Lolich was the only available pitcher Tigers manager Mayo Smith trusted at the time. "I can understand that," relief pitcher John Hiller said. "None of us in the bullpen had helped much."

The Tigers relied on Lolich so completely in fact when he was scheduled to hit in the bottom of the seventh with his team down by a run—and only eight outs away from being eliminated—Smith allowed him to bat. Mickey had actually hit a home run in Game 2, which the Tigers won 8-1 to tie the series at a victory apiece, but Lolich wasn't known to be a good hitter.

Allowing Mickey to bat in the seventh inning, with his team down by a run and facing elimination from the World Series, was an outright gamble. He had hit .114 during the regular season, and the home run he hit in Game 2 would be the only one he would ever hit. But there he was, ready to bat again "because Mayo was either a visionary or that dumb," Hiller said.

Possibly a bit of both. As it turned out, Lolich singled to start a three-run rally that put the Tigers in front to stay. But it never would have happened if the Tigers had fallen behind by more than one run in the fifth. And the reason they didn't was the famous play at the plate. If the speedy Brock had been safe, the Tigers would have been too far behind for Smith to extend his trust in Lolich. But with Horton's throw, good things began to happen for the Tigers.

Some called it a lucky out. Brock came so close to touching the plate while he was being tagged that it was an extreme test for umpire Doug Harvey to get the call right. More than just the call, though, had to go right for the Tigers. Every element of the play had to. The throw from Horton to catcher Bill Freehan was the product of teamwork, serving as a reminder even now that preparation sometimes pays off later rather than sooner.

The Tigers had talked to each other about being defensively aggressive with Brock on base. They knew his speed was a real weapon for the Cardinals. "He'd been causing us all kinds of problems," Freehan said.

But the Tigers also knew they couldn't let him run at will. He'd stolen 48 bases in the second half of the 1968 season, including 20 in September. Deservedly confident of his ability, Brock loved to challenge outfielders and catchers alike and easily won most of those challenges.

Mickey Stanley, who switched from center field to shortstop in a daring move by the Tigers for the 1968 World Series, had been especially helpful to Horton during Willie's quest to become a better outfielder. Stanley's advice enabled Horton to improve both his approach to anything hit to him in left field and his judgment about where to throw the ball. Without Stanley's help, it's possible that Horton would not have been as bold on the play involving Brock.

Willie was no gazelle in left field, but when he put himself in the correct position, he could make a strong throw. His arm was such that some clubs had originally envisioned him as a catcher. But suddenly, with a one-out double from Brock in the top of the fifth, the Tigers found themselves in a spot where there was no room for error. Everything needed to work in their favor when Julian Javier followed Brock's double with a sharp single to left.

Horton had to break well on the ball. He did.

He couldn't be turned in an awkward way when he got to it. He wasn't.

And the ball had to bounce just right to him, so there'd be no lost time transferring it from his glove to his hand. Sure enough, the bounce was true.

But as Brock neared third, after a crucial split-second hesitation to make sure the ball would make it to the outfield, it looked as if he'd score easily. There was a chance he would have to slide at the plate despite not being in the habit of sliding on throws home, but he had the advantage all the same.

Horton, meanwhile, depended on a nugget of information he had squirreled away for such a moment. An instinctive player, he always tried to make up for his lack of speed and agility by doing his homework. And it was about to pay off. "That particular play was two plays in one," Horton recalled. "But we definitely needed an out there. The feeling was that another score would have put the game out of reach. I knew where to position myself when Mickey was pitching. Usually, by the time he got to the fifth or sixth inning, you could make the field smaller. Plus I also knew how to position myself so that on most balls hit to me I could get to them quickly."

Horton, therefore, wasn't as deep in left as he might have been earlier in the game. And he got to Javier's hit in a hurry. What also helped was his knowledge of the scouting report on Brock. Going from first to third on a single, the Cardinals' speedster often would break his stride at second base. From second to home, he would do the same thing at third and tend to "drift in," according to Horton.

No matter the eventual outcome of the bang-bang play, it was Willie's awareness of the scouting report that enabled him to even entertain the thought of throwing out Brock. Thinking he could was the first step. But he still needed help to do so. Horton's throw to Freehan at the plate was accurate, a one-hopper chest high. Freehan didn't have to move for it.

Brock was already there, though, with time to slide safely under the throw despite how strong and accurate it was. But in a difference-making decision, he did not slide. He tried to score standing up. And Harvey ruled that his foot missed the plate, meaning Brock was out.

"It wouldn't have happened without teamwork," Horton said. "Coyote [third baseman Don Wert] put a good con on him, like he was going to cut it off, and Freehan wanted it coming through all the way. Yeah, I thought I was going to get him when I threw the ball. Lou still says he was safe, but when he does, I just reply, 'Then why did you go back to home to tag the base?' People don't remember that's what he did. He went back to the plate to touch it. When the call was made, all I could think of was to thank Stanley right away for all his help."

There is one other comment Horton makes whenever the Brock play comes up in World Series discussions, as it often does. To this day, it's one that underscores just how important the throw turned out to be. "Who got the rings for winning?" Horton asked. "We did, and that play there was the turning point."

Sparky Anderson usually accomplished what he set out to do. But when he didn't, he had a winsome way of making it sound as if he did such as the time he hit a home run off a future Hall of Famer. Well, almost hit one.

Sparky played one season in the major leagues, starting 152 games as the Philadelphia Phillies' second baseman in 1959. But he was not the National League's Rookie of the Year, which *The Sporting News* predicted he'd be. In fact, he would not play a second major league season after the first. As rare as it is to completely vanish, Anderson had one year in the majors as an everyday player but never had another big league at-bat. Instead, he played at Triple A Toronto during his last four seasons. Anderson hit .218 for the Phillies. He was capable defensively but clearly couldn't hit—especially not for power. With only nine doubles, his slugging average was .249.

Years later, though, when he managed the Tigers, Anderson said of his one season in the majors, "I took [Don] Drysdale deep."

"But Sparky," reporters replied, "the record shows you had no home runs as a major leaguer."

"That's true, I didn't. But I'm telling you I took Drysdale deep. It went foul, but it was deep."

That was Sparky Anderson for you. He could spin a memory with the best of them and leave you laughing. He could also fracture a comparison and leave you shaking your head. So impressed with Jose Canseco's strength, for instance, Anderson once said, "I'm not surprised he has so much power. The guy is built like a Greek goddess."

Prone to being too enthusiastic, Anderson had a way of anointing prospects as budding superstars, which they seldom turned out to be. Some ended up as solid players; others were never heard from again. For example, at the end of the 1989 season—his worst with the Tigers at 59–103—Anderson said, "At least I know I have two young starters I can depend on next year."

But those young starters, Brian Dubois and Kevin Ritz, combined for only five more wins as Tigers.

In search of success—or continued success as in 1985—Anderson sometimes tinkered too much with his team in spring training. After the Tigers won the World Series in 1984, he was going to move Lou Whitaker from second to third so he could play his favorite new prospect, Chris Pittaro, at second base. The experiment did not last long. Pittaro ended up with only 62 at-bats as a Tiger.

At times it was as if Sparky had two personalities. Then again, at times he did have two.

He was George Anderson, a quiet family man, in the offseason. But on the flip side was baseball's gregarious silver-haired skipper, one of the most outgoing individuals you'll ever meet. As Sparky—except for his refusal to manage replacement players in 1995—he was totally devoted to his job from the day he'd leave for spring training, starting with his annual trip by car from California to Florida. "Did you finally stop at the Grand Canyon this year?" he once was asked by writers who already knew the answer.

"Nope, never have, never will," he responded. "Don't travel, don't read."

Sparky wasn't a sightseer. He was a baseball manager and a darn good one—the first, in fact, ever to win a World Series in both leagues (with the Cincinnati Reds in the National League and Detroit in the American League). He won more games with the Tigers, but it was as a Cincinnati Red that he was inducted into baseball's Hall of Fame in 2000, saying he did so as a tribute to Bob Howsam, who gave him his first major league managing job.

Being fired by the Reds after the 1978 season remained an open wound for Anderson until he erased its pain by winning it all with the Tigers in 1984. He would manage them another 11 years but never to another World Series. But by the time the 1990 season arrived—after he had a weathered a personally turbulent 1989 season—there was another record in sight.

Manager Sparky Anderson, who won 1,331 games with the Tigers, watches play during the 1986 season. (AP Images)

It was an honor he cherished, of course, but not one he talked a lot about ahead of time—even after his 1,000th victory as Tigers manager on June 7, 1991. That's when the countdown began. For the rest of that season and most of the next, Anderson would be closing in on Hughie Jennings, the Hall of Famer who ranked first on the Tigers' all-time list of managers with 1,131 victories.

Jennings managed the Tigers from 1907 to 1920. In the 70 years since, no one had seriously challenged his record. Bucky Harris came the closest with 516 victories, which was compiled in two different stints. Harris, however, didn't manage the Tigers long enough to zero in on Jennings as Anderson was about to do.

With their tenures as Tigers separated by seven decades, Anderson managed in tamer times than Jennings, who thought nothing of making odd noises (such as shouting his famous "eeyah!") while coaching third base—as managers did back then. That's not all Jennings did. Partial to props, he once shook a rubber snake at an opposing pitcher, Rube Waddell. It was also said he tried to distract Waddell with a jack-in-the-box.

But despite representing different generations, Anderson and Jennings were similar in their timeless pursuit of success. Their tactics differed, but their goals were the same. And, to a large extent, so were their personalities. Both were tough individuals under friendly veneers who didn't tolerate having their authority challenged, though Jennings occasionally made an exception with Ty Cobb.

Anderson once reacted so violently to a report of his players calling a team meeting without his knowledge that he broke a telephone—and nearly his hand—while pounding his fist on his office desk. He also swore he would never again speak again to the writer whose byline was on the story—or to the newspaper for which he worked (in this case, the *Detroit Free Press*). Anderson huffed, puffed, and loudly fumed but relented the next day.

He also once yelled so loudly at Jack Morris after a game in Toronto that he didn't notice the media had been allowed into the clubhouse and were hearing his entire rant. What caused the explosion? It was that Morris, in Anderson's opinion, had showed him up by not immediately handing him the ball when he extended his hand for it at the mound. Sparky was easygoing most of the time. But if you crossed him, he could be fierce.

Another time he made it quite clear to me that he didn't like the use of a story in which fellow manager Billy Martin said, "I could make a living managing against that guy" (meaning Anderson).

But before I left his office, Anderson had declared a truce. "Tommy, my boy, you weren't the only one to run it. It was also in a Cleveland paper."

That, too, was Sparky—charming but every bit the boss.

As a shortstop, Jennings was a hard-nosed player who lasted longer and achieved much more in the majors than Anderson. For the Baltimore Orioles in 1896—when the Orioles were in the National League—Jennings hit .401. With the assistance of being hit by 51 pitches—a record that still stands—he also had a .472 on-base percentage that year. Applying today's analytics to Jennings' career, he led the N.L. in offensive WAR twice and in defensive WAR three times.

At first it wasn't of paramount personal importance for Jennings to be in complete control as a manager. He treated Cobb with a long leash, allowing him personal freedoms he didn't allow others. A trial lawyer before returning to baseball, Jennings recognized that the explosive Cobb wouldn't perform at his best if required to conform. As a result, Cobb flourished under Jennings. "There isn't anything I can teach you about baseball," Jennings is quoted in *The Detroit Tigers Encyclopedia* as saying to Cobb. "Do as you please. You have my support."

But Jennings wasn't a pushover. In his book *The Detroit Tigers*, Frederick Lieb wrote that Jennings' "enthusiasm and dynamic personality did wonders for the Tigers." Lieb called Hughie a "warm, friendly person" but a "live-wire manager who could be very firm." Lieb also wrote that a "determining glare" could come from Jennings' eyes. Decades later, the same could have been said of Anderson.

Both came from humble beginnings. Sparky was from South Dakota; Hughie was from the coal mines of Pennsylvania. Their paths finally converged, when Anderson tied Jennings by winning his 1,131st game as Tigers manager. Two days later, on September 27, 1992, he passed Jennings. "Thanks, players," was Anderson's message to his team on a banner in the Tigers' clubhouse after the game. "I couldn't have done it without you."

To which winning pitcher Walt Terrell, who had a 7–10 record, deadpanned, "He could have done it without me. Would have gotten there faster."

His players were overjoyed for Sparky, though, and were honored to be part of the moment. But he didn't stop there. By the time Sparky retired after the 1995 season, his Tigers teams had won 1,331 games. "When you think of all the years the game has been played, and all the managers there have been, it's really something," an emotional Anderson said upon passing Jennings. "How did I ever last this long? Tricked 'em, I guess. I know this. This record will last forever. Nobody else will ever be around long enough to break it." Once upon a time, Hughie Jennings probably thought the same thing.

19

PUDGE
USHERS IN A
WINNING ERA

The Tigers were a mess, an unmitigated mess. On the field, they'd been a laughingstock in 2003 with 119 losses. Only by somehow winning five of their last six games—after losing 16 of their previous 17—did they not set a major league record for losing. But they ended the season in a different universe all the same. Not only did they finish 47 games out of first place in the five-team American League Central, but they also were 25 games out of fourth.

Their season was one gruesome statistic after another. They had one pitcher who lost 21 games (Mike Maroth) and another who lost 19 (Jeremy Bonderman). Their No. 4 and 5 starters, Gary Knotts and Adam Bernero, went a combined 4–20. In contrast to the pitching, the Tigers' offense wasn't terrible. But it certainly wasn't good. To make matters worse, the future didn't look much brighter as they contemplated 2004.

They were also hurting at the gate. The bump in attendance provided by the opening of Comerica Park in 2000 had already disappeared—to the point that the Tigers were 13th out of 14 A.L. clubs after just four seasons in their new digs. They'd never been last in attendance since Mike Ilitch bought the team in 1992, but they'd been next-to-last five times. And never higher than seventh, even in the year Comerica Park opened.

Ilitch never said so, but it was high time for him to start getting a decent return on his investment. Any businessman worth his salt would have begun to think so. The dilemma was how to change direction. The Tigers had tried any number of plans, including short-term and long-term general managers and six different field managers from 1992 to 2003.

Plus their intended attraction, Juan Gonzalez, for whom the Tigers traded during the winter before Comerica Park opened, had flopped. Fortunately, Gonzalez didn't accept their generous offer to remain a Tiger and left as a free agent after one season. But the departure of Gonzalez left them back where they'd been: the wilderness as far as talent was concerned.

In 2001 the Tigers didn't have a hitter who drove in more than 75 runs. In 2002 they didn't have a pitcher who won more than eight games. Then it bottomed out in 2003. Without a record over .500 since 1993, the Tigers had virtually vanished from baseball's map.

Ilitch had two choices—one illogical, the other unlikely. He could begin to think about selling the team, which he wasn't about to do, given his commitment to Detroit. Or he could try to convince one star at a time that they could lead a resurgence. If he had to overpay them, so be it. The Tigers were desperate. But Ilitch chose wisely.

Catcher Ivan Rodriguez was coming off a World Series-winning season with the Florida Marlins. He was 33, and his batting average (.297) had dipped under .300 for the first time since 1994. Some concern existed about how much tread was left on his tires. No one was saying out loud that Pudge was washed up—or soon would be—but as proof of prevailing uncertainty, there'd been no bites on a long-term contract. Yet he was reluctant to settle for a single season. He was too proud, and considered himself still too talented, to sign for only one year. So he was still available when the Tigers began to wonder in January of 2004 if he'd consider signing with them.

What an unlikely match it appeared to be: a historic, but downtrodden franchise, wondering what it would take to become relevant again, was negotiating with a great player whose future nobody else trusted. Ilitch needed a star—or as Pudge acknowledged, "a very well-known player." And Rodriguez needed a contract. For the Tigers it was almost too good to be true, so to make sure it was really going to happen, Ilitch went to the hospital where Pudge was taking his physical before signing. "We talked. He even calmed me down before I had an MRI," Rodriguez said. "Still today, I call him, I text him. He's a very special man for me."

There'd been a hint of a back problem with Rodriguez going into the 2003 season with Florida, but nothing prevented him from having a productive season for the Marlins. His batting average had dropped, but in terms of RBIs and runs scored, it was his best season since 1999. Willing to take a chance, Ilitch gave Rodriguez a four-year, $40 million contract. Observers not only were surprised by the size of the agreement, but they also were flat-out stunned it was with the last-place Tigers. Rodriguez said it wasn't a cash grab. But even if it had been, both sides were happy with it. "I'll never forget [general manager] Dave Dombrowski telling me that if I came on board, we'd be in the World Series in two years," Pudge said. "When I signed some family and friends asked me if I was sure because of how many games Detroit lost the year before. But they didn't know about what Dombrowski told me. The Tigers were going to start putting together a good team around me."

The process already had begun, though not even the Tigers knew it at the time. When the Seattle Mariners' trade of Carlos Guillen to the Cleveland Indians for Omar Vizquel fell through, the Tigers ended up acquiring Guillen instead (for infielder Ramon Santiago and a minor leaguer). The trade took place a month before Rodriguez signed. With their newcomers the Tigers went from a 43–119 record in 2003 to being 72–90 in 2004—still not good but better. Adding Guillen was a shrewd move, one that paid many dividends, but the attention-grabbing signing of Rodriguez triggered the improvement. At the news conference at Comerica Park announcing the contract, manager Alan Trammell said, "this is how it starts. This is how we begin to get better."

On July 16, 2004, the Tigers won their 43rd game—as many as they won in all of 2003.

They were the happiest 43–46 team there could possibly be. Though far from being a contender, they were on the road to eventual recovery. And Pudge was the biggest reason why. His first-half start was nothing less than awesome. By the end of June, he was hitting .381 with 10 home runs and 56 RBIs. In June alone he hit .500 (43-for-86). To close out the month, he hit .600 in his last six games, five of which the suddenly relevant Tigers won. "I was locked in," he said. "But I didn't know about hitting .500 until after I did it. If I tell you this, you probably won't believe me, but never in my entire 21-year career did I think about hitting. I always thought about defense. I just stepped up to the plate and hit the ball. I didn't think about it. That's how focused I was on my defense."

Dombrowski came close to being correct with his prediction. It took the Tigers three seasons—not two—to get to the World Series after signing Pudge. Close enough. They added Magglio Ordonez as a free agent in 2005, then Kenny Rogers in 2006. The Tigers also hired Jim Leyland as their manager in 2006 as they continued to construct a contender piece by piece. "We knew we were a good team," Rodriguez said of the 2006 team that played the St. Louis Cardinals in the World Series. "The thing I liked the most was the great pitching staff we had. Healthy and solid all year long, it was the reason we got [to the World Series]. We had five quality pitchers who could go seven innings every time."

Four of them (Rogers, Bonderman, Justin Verlander, and Nate Robertson) started 30 games or more. "Then, when you can bring in Joel Zumaya in the eighth. and he's throwing 120 miles an hour," said Rodriguez, "it kind of makes my job easier."

The Tigers didn't win the World Series in 2006. Plagued by eight errors—all but three of them by their pitchers—they lost in five sloppy games to St. Louis. It was a crushing way for their season to end. But after 119 losses just three years before, getting to the series was an achievement in itself.

Following his fourth All-Star appearance in four years with Detroit, the Tigers picked up Pudge's option for 2008, but that's the year his All-Star streak ended, and by July, with the team struggling, it was apparent they weren't going to re-sign him. Annoyed he wasn't playing every game but not wanting to get traded, Rodriguez hit .358 during July of 2008, his second highest monthly batting average as a Tiger. That only enhanced his marketability. At the trade deadline, he was dealt to the New York Yankees for pitcher Kyle Farnsworth.

Although he played through the 2011 season, Pudge's best years were clearly over before his career was. "I didn't think I was going to get traded by the Tigers," he said. "I was surprised. Detroit was a lovely city to play in. I played five great years there. To be honest with you, I thought I was going to finish my career there. But it didn't happen."

About the importance of the signing, though, Trammell had been prophetic. Pudge was the first brick in rebuilding the franchise. As the star the Tigers needed, and found, he was how they began to get better.

20

HAL NEWHOUSER

The Tigers have had some astoundingly unique pitchers. Years before Mark Fidrych spoke to the baseball, Hal Newhouser would sometimes speak to his arm. Judging by the caliber of Newhouser's career, however, it worked.

From being a pitcher who rarely won to becoming one who rarely lost, Newhouser overcame several obstacles in his path to greatness. In 1943 the Detroit-born southpaw went 8–17 for the Tigers. In 1944 he went 29–9. One reason for his improvement was the welcome onset of maturity. Both insecure and ill-tempered in his early years, Newhouser was known as the hottest of hotheads, a player who once threw a case of Coca-Cola against the wall after a bad performance.

But he mellowed once he found success. The debate for years about Newhouser has been whether he started winning after learning to control his emotions—or whether it was the other way around. In whatever order it happened, though, it was essential that it did. But it is also true that Newhouser was a perfectionist and an eccentric. Not knowing others were eavesdropping one day in the Tigers' clubhouse at Comiskey Park in Chicago, Newhouser spoke to his left arm as if he were making up with a loved one after a dispute. "You have been good to me, baby," he was heard saying. In fact, it was written in the *Detroit Free Press* that Newhouser was once "purring" as he said to his arm, "It's about time I begin to appreciate you and start being good to you." While speaking softly, according to the account, Newhouser stroked his pitching arm "affectionately." Does that mean Newhouser was a Fidrych-like character? To a certain extent it does.

In any case, something clearly worked because after often being frustrated and showing it, Newhouser became a dominant pitcher. If anyone had dared to think that Newhouser would be the American League's Most Valuable Player in 1944, especially after what he went through in 1943, "That person," one from that era was quoted as saying, "would have been escorted to a resting spot, patted on the head, and advised to relax and take it easy."

Who saw it coming? In other words, virtually none. From 1940 through 1943, Newhouser was 34–51 for the Tigers. While there were indications he'd eventually become a better pitcher, there were more signs he was just plain wild. In two of those four seasons, he walked more batters than he struck out. And not until 1944 did he win more games than he lost.

Especially in 1941, when he was only 20, Newhouser was all over the map with his control. He blanked the St. Louis Browns with a complete-game victory that season, but 10 days later, he walked 10 New York Yankees, yet won again. In three other games in 1941, Newhouser walked nine. He was a brutally raw prospect—but an exciting one all the same because of his potential. Despite being an All-Star in 1942–43, he still wasn't close to being a winning pitcher.

Success during the war years often has been discounted. But to say Newhouser improved only because World War II depleted the major leagues of talent would be a disservice to him.

And he would prove that once the war ended. But it hadn't ended yet. After not looking like a future Hall of Famer in 1942–43, he definitely looked like one in 1944–45.

There were those, including Newhouser himself, who believed that catcher Paul Richards, who joined the Tigers in 1943, deserved much of the credit for Newhouser's development. In his Hall of Fame induction speech in 1992, he made that clear by saying, "I would not be here if it weren't for Paul Richards." Both as a catcher and eventually as a manager, Richards was an outstanding handler of pitchers—the wilder the stallion, the better.

In Newhouser's case Richards' psychological forte was his ability to keep a pitcher from getting down on himself, which Newhouser had a tendency to do. As a domino effect, his control would deteriorate when he was upset. The facts, though, underscore the entirety of his conversion. Holding onto stardom when he finally found it, Newhouser went 80–27 from 1944 to 1946 and was twice named the American League's Most Valuable Player. He also won 21 games in 1948 for the Tigers.

The story of Hal Newhouser, though, was not just one of wins and losses. His legacy was more about what he demanded of himself: the failure he simply would not accept, the mediocrity for which he would not settle. If it turned him into a grouch at times, so be it. "I'd try to get him to smile for publicity photos that would be taken before we pitched against each other," Cleveland Indians pitcher Bob Feller once said. "But he didn't smile too often when he was in uniform."

Newhouser vs. Feller was a marquee matchup whenever the Tigers and Indians met. What's more, it often lived up to its billing. "Hal took the game very seriously," Feller said. "In fact, I think it was more than a game to him. He was very proud of what he did and should have been. He was a great pitcher."

Newhouser was an intense but also very proper individual, earning the moniker "Prince Hal" because of the regal way he conducted himself. His wife, Beryl, once said she'd never even seen him with "his shirttail untucked." He knew how to growl and grumble, but Newhouser had such a soft side to him that in his Hall of Fame induction speech he would not have thought of thanking anyone before his 95-year-old mother, Emilie. It had been his mother who instilled in him his work ethic and discipline. What a poignant moment it must have been for both when Newhouser was inducted. In fact, the entire crowd in Cooperstown was so moved by his mother's presence that she received a lengthy ovation. "I'm so happy I'm still alive to see him honored this way," she said.

Months earlier, when he heard he'd been elected to the Hall of Fame, Newhouser's first call was to his mother. Hal asked if she was sitting down when she answered the phone. When she wondered why, he told her the good news, following which, he admitted, "We both wept."

After enjoying her son's career and the recognition he received to the fullest, she died at the age of 99 in 1996.

The nucleus of Newhouser's career encompassed the seven seasons (1944–50) during which his average won-lost record for the Tigers was 22–11. The only reason he wasn't an All-Star in all seven years was because there wasn't an All-Star Game in 1945, the last of the war years. All of his dreams eventually came true, though,

GEORGE "HOOKS" DAUSS

Jack Morris does not hold the record for most wins as a Tiger. Good guess, but he's fifth on the list. Even better guess, but Mickey Lolich doesn't hold it either. He's third. The pitcher with the most wins as a Tiger (223) is George "Hooks" Dauss, a right-hander known for his curveball who pitched for Detroit from 1912 to 1926 and won 20-plus games three times.

But he never pitched in a World Series. The closest Dauss ever got was in 1915, when he went 24-13 for a team that was 100-54, but the Boston Red Sox edged the Tigers for the American League pennant that year by two and a half games.

If 1915 wasn't a big enough year for Dauss on the field, it certainly was off of it.

Sometimes it was big—both on and off the field—on the same day. On May 29 Dauss got married in the morning in St. Louis and then beat the Browns 7-1 in the afternoon with a complete game.

A friendly, easy-going individual who even got along with Ty Cobb, Dauss never thought of himself as a star because, well, he never was one. In fact, in the book *Indiana-Born Major League Baseball Players*, Dauss is quoted as saying, "I wasn't a great pitcher and never pitched any remarkably good games."

He won 223 of those he did pitch, though—and that was remarkable enough.

including two victories in the 1945 World Series against the Chicago Cubs.

What was good for Newhouser was equally good for the Tigers. The club was patient while waiting for him to live up to the potential that manager Del Baker predicted in 1941 would eventually make Newhouser not just a great pitcher but "one of the most feared in the league."

Patience on the downside of one's career, however, seldom comes as easily. Time and again in his later years, Newhouser fell short of being as good as he once was. Despite winning 15 games in 1950, his downfall began in June of that season. He went 9-11 with a 5.11 ERA in his last 27 appearances and would never again be relied upon as a workhorse.

That's far from how it was in 1944, though, when Newhouser wasn't quite out of earshot while speaking to his left arm. "We had our differences last year and didn't get along so well," he was heard saying to it. "That was my fault. If I had known then what I know now, I never would have said a mean word to you. So now I'm apologizing."

When he finally noticed that his words were being overheard, he said he'd just had "a personal chat with my best friend." Then he went out and blanked the Chicago White Sox.

THE
35-5
START

When the Tigers began the 1984 season by winning 35 of their first 40 games, one compelling event after another took place. Jack Morris threw a no-hitter on a cold Saturday afternoon in Chicago against the White Sox. There was the walk-off win against Kansas City on an error by the Royals' usually dependable Frank White to stretch the Tigers' season-opening winning streak to nine games. And two more walk-off wins in a seven-game winning streak followed their first loss. "We did what we had to do," Lou Whitaker said. "We just did it all the time."

But off the field, there was one moment above all others—before their 40th game—that reminded the Tigers to stay focused and humble despite their lofty record. It happened in Anaheim, the night before they would depart for Seattle with their remarkable 35–5 record. The team bus arrived at the hotel, following a 4–2 triumph against the California Angels.

It had been a comfortable enough victory. The Tigers outhit the Angels 12–5, outwalked them 5–2, and could have blown the game open at any time. But to score only four runs was a warning sign that they weren't taking full advantage of their scoring chances. As he stepped down from the bus and began to walk through the lobby, manager Sparky Anderson, who was spending the night at the hotel instead of at home in Thousand Oaks, California, because the Tigers were to play an afternoon game the next day, was understandably pleased with the team's record. But he knew that maintaining such a pace wasn't realistic.

Being friendly with fans, as he always was, Anderson didn't turn away when a man approached him, wanting to shake his hand. But it wasn't a Tigers fan. It also wasn't an up-to-date fan. "Sparky Anderson, oh, my gosh," he said. "I'm from Dayton and was a huge fan of your Big Red Machine teams in Cincinnati."

Anderson thanked the Ohioan but kept walking. Even so, the conversation wasn't over. Sparky's new friend kept walking, too.

"Those were great teams," the Reds fan said.

"Yes, they were," Anderson replied.

"And I've always been a big admirer of yours," the man continued.

"Thank you very much," Anderson said again, signing an autograph while the two continued to converse.

Then came the comment that put the Tigers' sizzling start in perspective.

"By the way," the Dayton man said, "what are you doing now?"

Sparky froze in his tracks. If he'd been chewing gum, he would have swallowed it. Those nearby weren't sure they had heard the comment correctly. Not only had Anderson been managing the Tigers since 1979, not only had they been in contention a couple of times, specifically in 1981, a season interrupted by a work stoppage, but the Tigers were the toast of baseball at that very moment.

If nothing else, the question from the Dayton fan fully underscored just how much work remained to be done before the Tigers had accomplished anything worthwhile. The start was nice. It was great, in fact. But it was only a start—and nothing about it, especially after that jolt of reality—would be allowed to go to their heads.

In other words, the only ones not allowed to be impressed by their record-breaking 35–5 start were the Tigers themselves. No one knew that more acutely than Sparky. So he told the man from Dayton that he was managing the Detroit Tigers, then used the conversation as a reminder to his team of a saying he had on the wall back in his Detroit office: "Every 24 hours, the world turns over on someone who is sitting on top of it."

How timely. In Seattle the Tigers would suffer a three-game sweep in their next series, so sure enough, right on cue, the world was trying to turn over on the Tigers.

After going 35–5 to start the season, the Tigers would go 20–20 in their next 40 games and look a lot more beatable than they looked before. In fact, in the final 122 games of the season, the eventual third-place New York Yankees (70–52) had a better record than the Tigers

(69–53). And the eventual fourth-place Boston Red Sox had the same record as the Tigers.

But those teams hadn't had the same incredible springboard into the heart of the season.

When analyzing the 1984 Tigers, it's easy and appropriate, of course, to give individual credit where it's due, beginning with closer Willie Hernandez. But it's also essential to acknowledge the less heralded players. For his magnificent season, one in which he went 9–3 with a 1.92 ERA and 32 saves, Hernandez won both the American League's Most Valuable Player Award and Cy Young Award. Dan Quisenberry of the Kansas City Royals, who had 44 saves, finished second in the Cy Young voting and third for the MVP. First baseman Kent Hrbek of the Minnesota Twins was the MVP runner-up.

But Hernandez was not the Tigers' best relief pitcher during the 35–5 start. Aurelio Lopez was. Nicknamed "Senor Smoke," Lopez went 4–0 with six saves and a 1.47 ERA in the Tigers' first 40 games. Opposing hitters batted just .169 against him. Hernandez was 1–0 with seven saves and a 3.03 ERA in the first 40 games. Opposing hitters batted .223 against him.

Lopez, who tragically died in a car accident the day after his 44th birthday in 1992, would play second fiddle to Hernandez' achievements the rest of the season, but the impact he had on the start was profound.

On the hitting side, there is one Tiger who gets less credit than he deserves, and that's Cuban-born Barbaro Garbey, who was the Tigers' first baseman for much of the 40-game start.

Out of the chute, the Tigers had no fewer than seven significant contributors in their lineup: Whitaker, Alan Trammell, Kirk Gibson, Chet Lemon, Lance Parrish, Darrell Evans, and Garbey.

One can argue that Lemon and Trammell were the most impactful hitters. Lemon had the higher OPS in the first 40 games (.972 to Trammell's .953) and also led the Tigers with 32 RBIs.

Trammell hit .340 and topped the team with 36 runs scored. But the unsung Garbey, who was never better in his two years as a Tiger than he was early in 1984, led the team during the 35–5 start with a .355 batting average. His OPS was higher than those of Parrish,

Whitaker, or Evans, and though he played less than full time, his 20 RBIs in the first 40 games equaled Gibson's total and were more than Whitaker had. Garbey hit .261 the rest of the year and wouldn't remain a Tiger beyond 1985, but his contributions should not be overlooked.

As for their starting pitching, Morris contributed much more than a no-hitter. He went 9-1 during the 35-5 start. But teammate Dan Petry was 7-1, and Milt Wilcox was 6-0. In their 30 combined starts, the Tigers were 28-2. The real surprise was that none of them won 20 games that year. But Morris, who had the best shot at winning 20, went 10-10 with a 4.59 ERA the rest of the way to finish with a 19-11 record. With a chance to win his 20th in his final start of the season, Morris came away without a decision in a 2-1 loss to the Yankees.

What hurt him and possibly his future—because one more 20-win season would have helped his Hall of Fame resume—was that he was 17-8 on August 25 with seven starts remaining but went 0-3 in his next four. To finish with 20 victories, Morris had to win his last three starts but won only two. He shrugged off the disappointment by focusing on the challenge still facing the Tigers. "Remember," Morris said after his last start, "the regular season doesn't mean doodly."

But it had meant that the Tigers had played well enough to get into the postseason, where they would win the World Series in five games over the San Diego Padres. It had meant they had a chance of winning wire-to-wire and would do so. But without 35-5 and a timely boost from that man from Dayton, it would have been far more difficult. Maybe too difficult.

WILLIE
HORTON

Willie Horton stepped off the bus in 1962. The journey to Florida had not yet been memorable, but he was a black man going to work in the Deep South for the first time. It would soon become a watershed moment in his life. At the station in Lakeland, Florida, the city where the Detroit Tigers still train, Horton gathered his belongings and summoned a taxi to take him to the Tigertown complex. There were no problems until the driver noticed the color of his skin. "I can't take you," he told Horton.

"What do you mean you can't take me?" Willie replied. "What am I going to do with all my luggage?"

It didn't matter to the driver if Horton had two suitcases or 10. He repeated what he already had told him: "I can't take you."

And with that, the driver either drove away or waited until there were white people who wanted to get in his cab. Willie doesn't remember nor—in the emotion of the moment—did he care what the driver did next. He had just faced blatant discrimination. "At first I thought someone was playing a joke on me," Horton said. "You know, a rookie joke."

But it wasn't a joke. So he angrily picked up his bags and, instead of putting himself in the position of being turned down again, he started walking. One mile, two miles, maybe more. "I walked all the way to Tigertown," he said. "But during that walk, I started thinking about how people should treat one another, and it was then that Lakeland became part of who I am. I still think of that walk and how important those miles became for me."

Later that same spring, Horton and Mickey Stanley, another prospect who would become his good friend and longtime Tigers teammate, decided to go watch the big leaguers play at Henley Field, the old ballpark the Tigers used before Joker Marchant Stadium was built. "When we got there, a man told me I could only watch from a corner of the grandstand," Horton said. "Then I saw the water fountains that said 'black' and 'white' like one of them was poison." They didn't stay. Instead of watching the game from separate sections, Horton and Stanley walked back to the minor league complex. "We still talk a lot, Mickey and me," Horton said. "He's a good man, a good human being."

Horton and future teammate Gates Brown also became good friends, but Gates used to kid Willie about how he differed from other African American players. "They can get rid of us, but they can't get rid of you," Brown would say. "You're the franchise player."

It wasn't the first time Horton had heard the term, but he wasn't sure what it meant. "When I heard myself referred to as a franchise player, I thought they were saying I had some sort of sickness," he said. "So I'd reply, 'Don't call me that; I'm a ballplayer.'"

Horton's respect for "ballplayers" still runs so deeply that he easily tears up while talking about them. That's how much his profession meant to him and how much being a Tiger meant to him after starring for Detroit's Northwestern High School. He said Tiger Stadium "was like home to me. Even before I played there, as kids we'd sneak in behind the concession trucks and hide in the dumpsters until the coast was clear." Horton sobbed when he was announced to the crowd after the final game at Tiger Stadium in 1999. "I would tell the kids in the clubhouse never to let my Tigers uniform touch the ground," he said. "That's how much I respected it."

A special assistant with the Tigers since 2002, Horton is a local legend, but the 262 home runs he hit for them are only a small percentage of the reason why. His accomplishments on the field also don't fully explain why he's revered, why his uniform No. 23 has been retired, why there is a statue of him in center field among those of the team's Hall of Famers—and why every October 18—his birthday—is

now known in Michigan as Willie Horton Day, as decreed in 2004 by the governor at the time, Jennifer Granholm.

If Al Kaline was the heart of the Tigers, Horton was their soul, a man as deeply committed to caring as he was to winning. Equal opportunity has always been one of the subjects he's cared about. When Willie walked out on the Tigers for four days in 1969, many thought it was because he was in a slump. But he later told author Bill Dow that an underlying cause was the racial imbalance of the team. "I got it off my chest and carried the torch as best I could," he told Dow. "It paid off because we started to get more black players after that."

To be sure, Horton was a productive hitter and had some outstanding moments as an outfielder, among them his throw home in the fifth inning of Game 5 of the 1968 World Series against the St. Louis Cardinals. It was the play that changed the course of that series. Horton's throw, which prevented Lou Brock from scoring, is one of the great defensive moments in Tigers history. But to Willie it was an important product of teamwork—right down to Stanley jumping for a batted ball at short that he had no chance of catching. "Whenever an infielder jumps for a ball, it freezes the runner for a moment," Brock said. That's all the Tigers needed—a split second—to keep Brock from scoring.

Playing for the Tigers meant everything to Horton—except for a momentary lapse in his devotion in 1971 when he told manager Billy Martin he was going to retire. It wasn't similar to his first walkout. Bumps and bruises caused this one. "I'm tired of bleeding," Horton said of frequently being hurt. But he was often in Martin's doghouse that year and had for the first time clashed with the media as well.

Horton's intention to retire didn't last long. After that he became fond enough of the fiery Martin to believe that the Tigers would have won more than one World Series if they'd been managed by someone like Martin rather than Mayo Smith. "I wish Mayo had been harder on us the year after we won," Horton said. "We got off to a good start, then relaxed. With a Billy Martin-type, we would have won. I still get mad thinking we didn't win more with the team we had."

Respected by teammates and opponents alike, Horton was feared as well, such as when future Tigers pitcher Frank Tanana—in his second full season with the California Angels in 1975—threw a pitch too far inside for Willie's liking. "You're too young to be messing with me," Horton growled at Tanana during the scrum that followed.

Fortunately, for one of those involved, no punches were thrown. "I would have gotten killed," Tanana said years later. "I know that because Willie poked me several times in the chest with his finger, and even that hurt for a long time."

Horton's concept of togetherness in team sports was based on what one of his boyhood mentors taught him. "He's one of the people without whose help I would not have been a major league player," Horton said of Ron Thompson, a longtime Detroit high school coach who became so well known for the guidance he gave young athletes that he was elected to the Michigan Sports Hall of Fame. "We were kids from the projects on a team called the Ravens. Coach Thompson would make us get in a circle when we were eight or nine years old. Then he told us to throw our baseballs and gloves on the ground and hug each other. He said we couldn't learn to play team sports until we learned to care for each other."

To this day it would be difficult to find an athlete better known for caring about his teammates than Horton. It would also be difficult to find an athlete to whom Detroit means more. For several generations Horton has been a community leader. The late George Cantor, who covered the Tigers as a beat writer for the *Detroit Free Press* and as a columnist for *The Detroit News*, once said there had been no link between the Tigers and the black community until Horton reached the majors.

But it's not just been during the good times that Horton and the city he loves have supported each other. With racial unrest developing into deadly riots in 1967, Horton went to the troubled streets asking for peace to prevail. "I was still wearing my uniform when I got there," he said. "I put my clothes in a bag and pretty soon there I was, talking to people on 12th Street from the top of a truck."

His pleas, however, went unheeded. Those in the streets cared about his safety but not about the wisdom of his words. Even for a Detroiter as popular as Horton, the situation was too far gone to prevent it from getting out of control. But he had tried all the same. "The way I was raised, there was no color," Horton said. "It was about doing right in life for all people. I went there to bring peace. I didn't look at black or white. I just looked at people."

Horton was one of 21 children raised by his parents. While he was playing winter ball in Puerto Rico before his first full season in the majors in 1965, his mother and father were killed in a car accident on a Michigan highway. It was New Year's Eve.

From his mother he had learned how to treat people the way he would want to be treated. From his father he learned fairness but sometimes in difficult ways. When Horton damaged the first car he purchased as a professional ballplayer, his father sold it out from under him. "You have work to do," Horton said his father told him. "You won't need a car until you are 21." To avoid his father's fairness again, Horton kept his next car at a friend's house.

Horton would play for five teams other than the Tigers in his career. It was for the Seattle Mariners, but against the Tigers in 1979, when he would hit his 300th home run. Actually, he basically hit his 300th twice. The first time, it struck a speaker 110 feet above left field at the Kingdome and fell to the artificial turf as a single. But the next night, the speaker didn't interfere.

After the game, Horton's true feelings about no longer being a Tiger—and about the trade that sent him to the Texas Rangers in 1977—spilled over. "I dedicate that home run to Ralph Houk, who got rid of me, and to Jim Campbell for letting him," he said of the Tigers' manager and general manager at the time of the deal. "I worked hard for that man Houk, but he stabbed me in the back."

Feeling unappreciated, Horton lashed out. He'd always been a proud Tiger. He wanted Detroit fans to remember that. With steadfast affection to this day, they do.

PLAYER/MANAGER
MICKEY COCHRANE

othing happened during Mickey Cochrane's tenure as a player/manager for the Tigers.

Nothing at all. *Except...*

The Tigers lost a World Series in his first year. They won a World Series in his second year. He got seriously sick in his third year. He was nearly killed in his fourth. And in his fifth year, after all that Cochrane was fired, ending the most eventful half-decade in Tigers history.

It was in 1934, Cochrane's first season as player/manager, that the Tigers lost the World Series in seven games to the St. Louis Cardinals. The high point in getting to the series was the club's improvement from the year before—and from a long stretch of years before. They hadn't been in a World Series since 1909.

The low point of that first year occurred when fans at Navin Field pelted Cardinals outfielder Joe Medwick with garbage during a series-ending 11–0 loss. Medwick had slid hard into Marvin Owen at third base, kicking him twice after getting stepped on. Tempers flared; benches emptied. When Medwick offered to shake hands, Owen refused. But to make matters worse, when order was restored on the field, trouble escalated in the stands.

Angry about the fracas at third but also upset that the Tigers had fallen apart with two losses at home after needing just one victory to win their first World Series, the fans in left field got unruly when Medwick went to his position in the bottom of the sixth. Begging them to calm down, Cochrane had no effect as the situation got worse. "Every face in the crowd, women and men, was distorted with rage," wrote columnist Paul Gallico. "It was a terrifying sight. All fists were clenched."

Throwing fruit and glass bottles while chanting "Take him out," the crowd prevented Medwick from taking his position the three times he tried. Saying he had seen him "kick at Owen" and that the action "warranted punishment," commissioner Kenesaw Mountain Landis ordered Medwick off the field so that the series could be played to its conclusion. The ejection satisfied the fans, many of whom soon began to leave with the score so lopsided.

Cochrane, understandably, preferred the ending of his second season. In 1935 the Tigers won the World Series in six games over the Chicago Cubs. Emerging from the Depression and rebounding from the previous year's disappointment, Detroit was delirious over its first baseball championship. But one year of joy did not lead to another. Instead it led to health issues for Cochrane, a life-threatening injury, and an eventual dismissal.

In 1936 he collapsed in the dugout during a game. Some called it a nervous breakdown. The Tigers called it an illness (hyperthyroidism). In 1937 a pitch broke three bones in Cochrane's skull, nearly killing him. He survived, but the injury ended his playing career.

And in 1938, when he didn't adjust well to being a bench manager after being a player/manager and when his team didn't respond well, he was fired.

Lasting only five years, the Cochrane era was a whirlwind, starting with his first day on the job in December 1933. The team's improvement began at the same time. When the Tigers traded with the Philadelphia Athletics for Cochrane to manage and catch after they'd been under .500 for six straight seasons, it was their first step toward reinventing themselves as a contending team. Or as Grantland Rice wrote when assessing the Tigers' future, Cochrane "should make a high-class manager for Detroit. He has the personality that should lift any club from the rut."

The Tigers, however, weren't just any club in any rut. From the standpoint that they hadn't been a contender for years, they were hardly a manager's dream when Cochrane took over. In fact, they had not finished within 25 games of first place since 1926. And only four times since their last World Series appearance in 1909 had the Tigers finished within 10 games of first.

Well respected in his own right as a manager, Bucky Harris was so disappointed in how they played en route to a fifth-place finish in 1933 that he resigned before the season ended.

"I'm not going to sit around and blame the breaks," Harris said upon departing. "I'm resigning in order to give them the opportunity to get another man to run the club. Perhaps he can do better."

In addition to their 75–79 record, the Tigers' other bottom line also was bad—even worse—in fact. Attendance at Navin Field had tanked. No one was going to their games anymore. In 1933 attendance dropped to an embarrassing 320,972, the worst it had been since 1918, a war-shortened season.

In terms of talent, however, the Tigers were beginning to put together a nucleus with genuine promise, including some future Hall of Famers. Entering his second full season in 1934, Hank Greenberg would become one of the game's premier sluggers. Already an excellent hitter, Charlie Gehringer was about to get even better, hitting higher than .350 not just for the first time in his career, but also for the first of three times in four years. On the pitching side, both Tommy Bridges and Schoolboy Rowe went into the 1934 season regarded as future 20-game winners. As it turned out, Rowe would win 24 games that year, and Bridges would win 22.

So there was talent to build upon when the 1933 season ended with a six-game winning streak following an eight-game losing streak. Clearly missing, however, was consistency—plus a manager to help them achieve it. The Tigers thought Gordon Stanley Cochrane, known as "Mickey" in public but "Mike" to those close to him, could be the answer. That's why they targeted him two months before they hired him.

Despite denials from both teams, a deal was in the works between the Tigers and Philadelphia A's almost as soon as the 1933 season ended. Connie Mack, the owner of the A's, needed cash. The Tigers, in turn, needed Cochrane, a future Hall of Famer. After first being reported in October, the deal got done in mid-December. Mack received backup catcher Johnny Pasek and $100,000 in the deal, just shy of the $125,000 he'd been seeking. Even so, the trade helped him stay in business. "Now we have the funds to rebuild," Mack said of his team's overhaul. But the A's continued to be a doormat.

As for the Tigers, paying such a hefty price was a sign that they meant business, and Cochrane's impact was immediate. As he stepped

THE TIGERS' BEST CATCHER

The more you study Bill Freehan's case, the more you grasp how good he was. For several years he was the best catcher in the American League. There are those who believe that Mickey Cochrane would have been the Tigers' best catcher ever had he played longer for them. That may be true. The same can be said about Pudge Rodriguez.

And if Lance Parrish had opted to play his entire career with the Tigers instead of leaving for the Philadelphia Phillies as a free agent, he might be remembered as the Tigers' all-time best catcher.

But he didn't. And he isn't.

Freehan occupies that spot for the 11 times he was an All-Star, for the five Gold Gloves he won, and for finishing second in the voting for the American League's Most Valuable Player in 1968, the year the Tigers won the World Series. More than just being an All-Star, though, Freehan was the A.L.'s starting catcher for seven consecutive years (1966–72). "He knew the game better than anyone I ever played with or for," Denny McLain said.

Perhaps Freehan's greatest catching feat, however, was when—in a matter of seconds—he caught Tim McCarver's pop-up to end the 1968 World Series and was then able to catch and carry Mickey Lolich, who jumped into his arms after the final out. "He's not a small man," Freehan said, "but it was a great feeling."

off the train upon his arrival in Detroit, the new manager asked if the deal for Goose Goslin had been made yet. It would be agreed to within the week with outfielder Johnny Stone going from the Tigers to the Washington Senators in return, but it was immediately evident that Cochrane had been thinking about how to improve the Tigers. "Maybe Stone will be a better player than Goslin three or four years from now," said Cochrane, "but we're not running next year's race three or four years from now. I want somebody out there who can deliver next summer."

Goslin delivered. He finished third in the league in total bases (278) for the 1934 Tigers, but would permanently etch his name into their book of heroes with a World Series-winning single the following year.

By the time the 1934 season began, Cochrane had made a hugely favorable impression with his optimism. Before the Tigers ever took the field, they felt like a rejuvenated team. "We are set for the big drive," Cochrane said. "I am sure we will have a first-division club."

Upbeat and energetic, Cochrane was all about hustle. In a speech during his first month as manager, he said effort was a matter of "aspiration, inspiration, and perspiration." The fans loved it. What's more, they loved him in sickness and in health, both of which he experienced.

Healthy in his first two years as a Tiger, Cochrane hit .320 and .319, respectively. In 1935 he realized the greatest joy of his career when he scored the winning run of the World Series on Goslin's ninth-inning single in Game 6 against the Cubs. It was Cochrane's last full season as a player.

Sickness not only afflicted him, but also severely curtailed his 1936 season. Held to just six at-bats after June 4, he played in only 44 games all year. Of his collapse in the dugout, Cochrane said, "I was suddenly seized by a dizzy feeling. My heart started beating at a rapid rate. I thought I was going to die." He said he didn't feel right the rest of the year. "First, everything goes black," Mickey told the *Detroit Free Press* of his symptoms. "Your heart pounds so hard, you think it's going to tear loose from your body. You can't see, you can't breathe. It scares you to death."

By the next season, Cochrane was back in the Tigers' lineup but for less than two months. Just as Cochrane was finding his stroke in 1937 with a 10-for-17 stretch, he was struck in the head on May 25 by a pitch from New York's Bump Hadley, making the home run Cochrane hit off Hadley in his previous plate appearance the last official at-bat of his career.

The incident happened with two outs in the top of the fifth of a tie game at Yankee Stadium. Hadley was a durable but unspectacular right-hander who won 161 games in a 16-year career that ended in 1941. He hit eight batters in 1932 and, though it was the only time he led the A.L. in that category, he was never known for good control. Twice he led the league in walks. Cochrane had been hit by Hadley once before, but this time, as the great Grantland Rice put it, "a swerving in-shoot" struck him in the right temple.

The three fractures in his skull were so severe that the incident led to renewed interest in the use of protective helmets. Incredibly, however, the rule requiring helmets to be worn was not fully enforced in both major leagues until 1970. Sensing that a career-changing moment had just taken place, Rice called Cochrane "the greatest catcher of all time, a deadly hitter, and a smart, hustling leader who knew how to keep a team fighting to the finish. He was the major spark plug of baseball."

Despite reports of Cochrane being near death, doctors in a week were encouraged by his improving condition, calling it "uneventfully rapid." By the end of the month, it was reported in the *New York World-Telegram* that Cochrane was "done for all time as a player." It was not known, however, if he would continue as the Tigers' manager. Cochrane did indeed come back, but when the Tigers stumbled in 1938, he was fired on August 6.

It was written more than once that Cochrane was different as a bench manager than he'd been as a player/manager. Sitting and watching did not agree with him. No easy outlet existed when he became agitated. His relationships with players suffered. The marvelous match between Mickey and the Tigers no longer existed.

The Cochrane era in Detroit was over. But its legacy remains constant to this day.

"We needed someone to take charge and show us how to win," Greenberg said. "That's what Mickey did. He was an inspirational leader."

SAM CRAWFORD

The weather was chilly, but wishes were warm that August day in 1917 when Tigers fans said a fond farewell to Sam Crawford at Navin Field. Wahoo Sam had been their favorite. He'd given the Tigers 15 wonderful years during a career that eventually landed him in baseball's Hall of Fame, where emotion overcame him on his induction day in 1957. "I had a speech ready," the 77-year-old Crawford said with tears in his eyes when he began to speak, "but I don't think I can go through with it."

So he didn't. He just sat back down. Perhaps there were just too many memories for him to continue.

Hailing from the tiny town of Wahoo, Nebraska, Crawford had played beside the great, but often difficult, Ty Cobb in the Tigers' outfield. He'd been in three World Series with the Tigers, though they were series they didn't win, and had carved a niche for himself because nobody has ever hit more triples in the major leagues than his 309.

But his days as a Tiger were coming to an end. It was time to honor him. According to the account in the *Detroit Free Press* on August 25, 1917, "Fans are determined to give the Wahoo slugger a reception he will remember all his life. Apparently, everybody in town that ever went to a ballgame wants to be present on this occasion. It will be the friendliest crowd that ever gathered to pay tribute to a fine athlete and a fine fellow."

Crawford wasn't retiring. He would play four more years for the Los Angeles Angels of the Pacific Coast League, beginning with the 1918 season. But at 37, his career as a Tiger was over. There were speeches that praised him during the pregame ceremony. There were cheers, and, of course, there were gifts. The Tigers gave Crawford $1,200 in cash (roughly $25,000 now)—their net profit from the gate receipts that day. Fans presented him with a diamond ring. He was also given a watch.

And despite going hitless in his last full game as a Tiger, Crawford was cheered throughout the afternoon. Good-bye Wahoo Sam, they were saying. Thanks for everything you've done. And thanks for everything good that you were. At the height of his career, the *Free Press* wrote that "If there be anybody in Detroit who thinks that ballplayers, as a class, are a roistering, ill-mannered crew, Sam Crawford is the best argument in the world that they are wrong."

Had it not been for a squabble between the National and American Leagues, however, Crawford might have played his entire career for Cincinnati instead of most of it for Detroit. Basically, it came down to this: to prevent the Tigers from moving after the 1902 season to Pittsburgh, where the National League already had a profitable team that didn't want American League competition, Crawford was transferred from Cincinnati to Detroit after he'd accepted advance money from both teams in a bidding war.

If it had been up to him, though, Sam would have stayed with Cincinnati. "I firmly intended to be with the Reds again this year," Crawford told the Cincinnati media. "I've been with Cincinnati ever since '99. All my friends are there.

After signing with Detroit, I regretted it for I knew I should be homesick. As the matter now stands, however, it would seem I shall be forced to stick to the Detroit contract. But I'm sorry to have quit Cincinnati."

With that in mind, Detroit sportswriter Joe S. Jackson wrote, "It looks as if we shall have to arrange for a torchlight parade and brass band reception for Sam Crawford when he reports to demonstrate to the outfielder that the city isn't such a bad place, after all."

Fortunately for the Tigers, after his initial hesitation, he liked it. In fact, Crawford and his new city took to each other almost immediately. But there was sadness to overcome first. The day after Crawford's admission of regret about signing with Detroit, coverage of the Tigers veered to explanations of why their newly appointed player/manager, Win Mercer, had taken his own life by inhaling gas fumes in a San Francisco hotel room. A letter was found in Mercer's room that began with "A word to my boy friends; beware of women and games of chance. With tears in my eyes, I say good-bye forever."

Mercer had gone 15–18 with a 3.04 ERA as a starting pitcher in 1902, his only year with the Tigers. He'd been such a matinee idol at one point that when the handsome Mercer was ejected from a Ladies Day game while playing with the Washington Senators, a group of angry women attacked the umpire who booted him.

Instead of Mercer being his first manager with the Tigers, though, Crawford played for Ed Barrow, for whom Detroit served as an early stop before he joined the New York Yankees.

As an executive and eventual president of the Yankees during their initial glory years, Barrow would enjoy far more success in New York than he did in his one and a half years of managing the Tigers.

By July of 1904, he was gone from Detroit. Crawford, though, wasn't. Known as one of baseball's great sluggers of the Deadball Era, Wahoo Sam immediately endeared himself to Tigers fans by leading the American League in 1903 with 25 triples and hitting .335, second to Napoleon Lajoie's league-leading .344 batting average. Applying today's sabermetrics to Crawford's first year as a Tiger, he finished third in the A.L. in offensive WAR. In other words, whether judged by traditional numbers or by today's criteria, Crawford excelled.

Crawford also never stopped being a likable individual on and off the field. Even now you can watch him on YouTube talking to the late Lawrence Ritter in an interview that contributed to Ritter's book, *The Glory of Their Times*. Crawford remembered the simplest of his simple beginnings by telling Ritter that a highlight of growing up in Wahoo during the 1880s was to watch the town's only lightbulb turn on each night. "It was a big deal," Crawford told Ritter.

But it was also a big deal to Crawford not to live beyond his means. When reporters interviewed him after he'd been elected to the Hall of Fame, they found him living a quiet life in Pear Blossom, California, tending to his fruit trees and tinkering with his 1935 Ford, whose 162,000 miles didn't prevent Sam from referring to it as "my baby Lincoln."

But it was the Ritter book that put Crawford back on the map as a personality. The two started conversing after Ritter, by happenstance, met Crawford while they were washing clothes at the same laundromat. The Hall of Fame outfielder quoted philosopher George

Santayana and wanted to discuss the works of Honore de Balzac as well. Finding him fascinating, Ritter said that Crawford "turned out to be one of my closest friends."

Once thought to have a sluggish disposition, there was even enough showmanship in Crawford for him to gain royal approval. On a world tour with major league players in 1914 on the eve of World War I in Europe, Sam brought joy to King George V of Great Britain by hitting a home run during an exhibition game in London. "I started out with the intention of making the king get rid of a certain bored look, which seemed to hover over his face," Crawford told the *Detroit Free Press*. "I figured a home run would be the only feature that could sufficiently excite the interest of the ruler. I waited for my chance to drive the ball as far as possible, and the opportunity came after I had almost given up hope. The ball came over the plate just right, and I slammed it."

As Crawford crossed home plate, he looked up at the usually dour British monarch, who was enthusiastically clapping his hands. "For the rest of the game, he displayed real interest," Crawford said. Just like that, the man from Wahoo had won himself another fan—a king, no less. What a thrill that had to be, even bigger—perhaps—than watching a lightbulb.

25

NORTHRUP'S WORLD SERIES TRIPLE

Some say he never achieved stardom, and when the usual criteria are applied, that appears to be correct. Jim Northrup never made an All-Star team, never hit 30 home runs, never drove in 100 runs, and never came close to winning a batting title. "As good as Jimmy was, it ate him alive not to have more of what it took to be a great player," teammate Denny McLain remembered. "But he got so much out of himself."

And in 1968 the intense Tigers outfielder contributed as much to a championship season as any celebrated star could ever hope to. Even if Northrup hadn't hit the triple of all triples in the World Series that year, it would have been a season of significant achievement for him. It was the year in which he hit five grand slams, including three in one week, two in one game, and one in the World Series.

What's more, the two he hit in the same game were in consecutive at-bats. It was also the year in which Northrup became a stats leader for the Tigers with a team-leading 90 RBIs and the year in which he replaced Al Kaline in right field after a pitch broke Kaline's left wrist. Northrup played so well, in fact, that he simply could not be displaced when it came time for manager Mayo Smith to make a crucial decision about his World Series lineup.

Against the St. Louis Cardinals, Smith moved Northrup to center, returned Kaline to right, and opted to bump his regular center fielder, Mickey Stanley, to shortstop as a replacement for light-hitting Ray Oyler. The decision was one of the biggest gambles in World Series history.

And "one of the most ridiculous I ever heard of in my life," Kaline said. "I loved Mayo, but to move your center fielder to play shortstop in a World Series?"

It worked, though. The Tigers beat the Cardinals in seven games in large part because those involved in the switch played well. And because Northrup came through in the 1968 series with the most remembered hit, a pivotal triple in the seventh inning of Game 7 that eluded Curt Flood in center. If Northrup never got the credit he deserved for being a solid ballplayer, neither did the biggest hit of his career receive enough acclaim for being a great offensive moment.

Instead, most of the attention focused on Flood's reaction in center and whether he would have caught the ball had he not slipped on the grass. It's a theory that riled Northrup until the day he died in 2011.

To say the triple might have been catchable diminishes the power with which Northrup hit it, making the play more a matter of blame than of credit. Even now it seems clear on video that to catch the ball would have required a jump the caliber of which not even the frequently flawless Flood was capable. Dissenters argued that if Flood had not taken a step in, had he immediately broken back and then laterally on a ball hit far over his head, had he not momentarily lost it in the tricky background at Busch Stadium, and had he not compounded all his mistakes by slipping as he turned, maybe he would have caught it. But with everything going wrong, it became a perfect storm of blunders for Flood, who broke badly and stumbled. "We'll never know what would have happened," Kaline said, "because when he took that first step, the ball shot past him."

One of the reasons Flood played it badly, though, was that Northrup hit it so hard, making a quick and correct reaction essential. But Flood wasn't alone in always thinking he could have made the play. "I thought he'd catch it," Cardinals manager Red Schoendienst would later say of his initial reaction.

So the argument rages on. It is such an iconic moment in Tigers history that discussing it never gets old—even after all these years. There were other reasons it became such a gamechanger. Norm Cash and Willie Horton had chipped away at Bob Gibson's dominance in the seventh inning with two-out singles that turned Northrup's plate appearance into a scoring chance. Gibson had an outstanding World Series. He hadn't been unhittable in his first two starts but dominated the Tigers to the extent that they knew he'd be formidable to face in a third start as well.

If opportunities occurred, they could not afford to be wasted. Fortunately, Mickey Lolich was equally tough on the Cardinals, which was why Game 7 was still scoreless in the seventh.

Even when the biggest scoring chance of the game arrived for the Tigers, it did so haltingly.

Cash's full-count single to right off Gibson with two out didn't qualify by itself as a scoring chance. There was even a difference of opinion about how hard he had hit the ball. Broadcaster Harry Carey on television called it a "line smash." Ernie Harwell on radio called it a "bloop" single.

For Horton, who was hitless with five strikeouts in nine previous at-bats off Gibson, to bounce a first-pitch single through the hole at shortstop after Cash's hit, well, that was something entirely different. Horton's hit maybe, just maybe meant that Gibson was tiring. But even if he wasn't, the thought he might be gave the Tigers more hope than they justifiably could have entertained earlier.

Now Northrup was batting. Taking a pitch wouldn't knock in Cash from second, but being aggressive might. Therefore, Northrup's plan was to swing at the first strike. If I put in play, it might find a hole. As he stepped into the batter's box, Northrup noticed that Flood was shading him slightly to right, thinking he might pull a pitch as Northrup had done against Gibson with a long home run to right-center in Game 4.

The Breckinridge, Michigan, native, though, crossed him up. He not only swung at Gibson's first pitch, but he also scorched it to the left side of center field—away from Flood. In an instant it changed the game. "I don't want to make any alibis; I misjudged it," Flood said. "It was my fault. I started in on it, didn't pick it up out of the background until I knew it was over my head. Then I slipped."

In short, Flood made a total mess of it. In his defense it would have taken everything that went wrong to go right for him to have a shot at catching the ball. "The guys on the [Tigers'] bench all said he would not have caught it even if he hadn't stumbled," Northrup said.

For good measure, Freehan followed the triple with a full-count double off Gibson, giving the Tigers a three-run lead that was safe in Lolich's hands. When Northrup died more than 40 years later, McLain said he never "bought the argument" that Flood would have caught the ball. Not one to mince words, McLain said that Flood "blew it."

He was right, but it's understandable why Northrup always bristled about it not being considered a clean triple. In his opinion he had hit the ball too sharply and too far for Flood to make the catch. Eventually, Northrup took to task anyone hinting otherwise. Bleacher Report's Greg Eno wrote, "I might as well have poured gasoline on a raging fire" for mentioning Flood's role in the triple 30 years after it happened. "Look at the film," Northrup barked at him. "Look at the film."

That's why it is still one of baseball's great disputes. Flood was a seven-time Gold Glove winner. Those who believe he could have caught the ball can't be dissuaded. But that didn't alter the reality the Cardinals were left to accept. "When I saw [Flood] look for the ball, I knew I was in trouble," said Gibson, who never pitched in another World Series but had a Hall of Fame career all the same.

Playing in Detroit until 1974, Northrup also would never take part in another World Series. When the Tigers disassembled their 1968 World Series team, he was traded to the Montreal Expos. Cash was released the same day that Northrup was traded. Ready to retire, Kaline played his final season in 1974 as well. The champion Tigers may have gotten old, but the glory of what they accomplished has never faded.

26

JUSTIN
VERLANDER

Brandon Inge, as his longtime teammate, is well aware of Justin Verlander's vast talent. "How can you not be aware of it when you see someone throw 100 miles an hour as late in a game as he could?" Inge said. "That's when you know a pitcher is special." Inge believes that Verlander has been blessed with two essential ingredients of greatness. "The first is God-given ability, which you can't control," he said. "The second is his work ethic, which you can."

If you were to make a Mount Rushmore of Tigers pitchers, a case can be made for any of seven starters. But only one of the seven is still active during the 2017 season, and that, of course, is Verlander. So if he isn't yet on the Tigers' Mount Rushmore, he is the only one with a chance to still earn a spot. The Super Seven are Verlander, Hal Newhouser, Mickey Lolich, Jack Morris, George Mullin, Tommy Bridges, and Hooks Dauss, the pitchers with the best credentials.

Mark Fidrych had a great season, and Denny McLain had more than one, but their career stats don't compare with the seven already mentioned. And while there also are relief pitchers who had fine careers as Tigers, they don't quite qualify to have their likenesses carved into a cliff.

Dauss won the most games as a Tiger (223). He never pitched in a World Series, but that wasn't entirely his fault, especially in the three seasons he won more than 20 games. At .584, Bridges had the second best winning percentage of the seven and he, too, won more than 20

Justin Verlander, who won the 2011 Cy Young and MVP Awards, throws in Game 3 of the ALDS of that same season. (USA TODAY Sports Images)

games three times (in consecutive years, no less). He also won four World Series games for the Tigers, including two in 1935, when they won the series for the first time.

Mullin was second to Dauss in victories with 209, but with the help of pitching in the deadball era, he had the lowest ERA of the seven at 2.76. He won 20 or more games five times as a Tiger, and his best record was 29–8 in 1909, a World Series season. Lolich is the left-hander with the most wins in Tigers history with 207. For winning three games in the 1968 World Series, he not only was named its MVP but also earned a spot as a favorite in the hearts of Tigers fans.

Morris is on the list for the 198 games he won, as well as for his two victories in the 1984 World Series. Few pitchers owned an entire decade as much as Morris owned the 1980s, when he led the majors with 162 victories. And Newhouser, of course, is a Hall of Famer who won 200 games as a Tiger and put together an amazing 80–27 record in 1944–46. He went 29–9 in 1944, winning his 29th game in his last start of the season. Had he not lost a game in relief on an unearned run nine days earlier, though, he would have won 30 games that season.

If the choices were to come from only those six, it would be a stellar Mount Rushmore.

However, before he's through as a starting pitcher, Verlander will complicate matters even more than he already has. He won't have the lowest ERA in franchise history, but he could challenge Dauss for the most wins, Lolich for the most strikeouts, and he'd have to fall apart from this point on to not have the best winning percentage of the seven.

With all due credit to such honorable mentions as Wild Bill Donovan, Dizzy Trout, Schoolboy Rowe, Frank Lary, Jim Bunning, and Virgil Trucks—not to mention the impact that Todd Jones and John Hiller had as relief pitchers—the list of Rushmore candidates doesn't suffer when limited to seven. My vote goes to Verlander, Newhouser, Lolich, and Morris.

What's been undeniably true about Verlander's career so far is that neither his will to win nor his preparation ever wavers. So while

A SHORT-LIVED FLAMETHROWER

What happened to Joel Zumaya was a shame. He had all the talent in the world, all the velocity, and by the time he was 25, he had thrown his last pitch because of injuries. "For me it ended fast," he said, "I think about it every day. I relive it a lot. I wish I was still out there."

Zumaya isn't listed here because of what he was but because of what he could have been.

"One of the best," Justin Verlander said. "That's what he could have been."

With a fastball of 100-plus—sometimes considerably plus, like that 105-miler he once threw—Zumaya had all the makings of being a dominant relief pitcher for many more years than the one truly great season he had in 2006. That's when he burst upon the scene with a 1.94 ERA in 62 games for the Tigers. "There was so much talent there," Jim Leyland said. "He threw some pitches no human being could have hit."

Now he's a commercial fisherman near San Diego, seeking and sometimes finding Bluefin tuna but enjoying the challenge. In fact, he calls it just as exciting as pitching. "I would say the butterflies and adrenaline are about the same," he said.

Sometimes tempted to see how hard he can throw, Zumaya tested his arm during the Tigers' 2016 Fantasy Camp. "A lot of people said it looked firm," he said of his velocity. "I could still throw 90 to 93 if I wanted to. But that's not good enough. People would say, 'What's wrong with him?' if I went out there with that." When 100 to 103 used to be your trademark, that's probably true.

Verlander might have thrown his last triple-digit fastball—though don't bet against it—he's comfortable and confident with less.

As was a mentor before him. "One of the most important influences on his career was Kenny Rogers," said Inge, referring to the successful southpaw who also learned to make the most of less. "Justin might not have listened to anyone else, but he listened to Rogers. I think Kenny gave him the mentality to pitch in the majors a long time."

En route to pitching a long time, 2011 will go down as a spectactular year for Verlander. He not only went 24–5 but also won the A.L.'s Cy Young and Most Valuable Player Awards. He won pitching's Triple Crown that year, finishing first in wins, strikeouts, and ERA. Against the Blue Jays in Toronto, he also threw his second career no-hitter. "They were way different," Verlander said. "In the first one, I didn't even have a slider, just a fastball, curveball, and change. In the second one, my curveball was horrible, but I had a slider."

What also was different was Justin's immediate reaction to them. After the final out of the first one, which came against the Milwaukee Brewers in Comerica Park in 2007, Verlander—while the ball was still in the air to right field—started jumping up and down on the mound. It was difficult to do so with catcher Pudge Rodriguez hugging him around his neck, but the reaction was one of unmitigated joy. Verlander said he had "pure adrenaline" running through his veins.

His reaction to his second no-hitter, reflecting the "calming feeling" he said he felt, was a methodical mix of joy and business. He was four years and 62 victories older. Plus he was emulating his hero. "I idolized Nolan Ryan, who pitched a bunch of no-hitters," Verlander said. "He eventually reacted to them like it was his job."

It was thought a third no-hitter might soon follow for Verlander, but even when it looked like he had no-hit stuff—and it often did— the years began to fly by without another. "There were games when the only hits off him were flukes," Inge said. "I remember days [in 2011] when I thought if the other hitters are honest about it, they'll admit there was no pitch they could have driven."

That was the year in which it looked like Verlander was capable of throwing a no-hitter in any given game. Nine times he allowed fewer than four hits. But it was when he battled through tough times without complaint or self-pity in 2014–15 that his maturity began to be, and deserved to be, noticed—much to the prideful delight of his parents, Kathy and Richard.

To see their son handle good times and bad equally well was rewarding, and while they've enjoyed all of Justin's accomplishments in their own well-grounded way, they have never lost sight of how it all began. In an interview for MomsTeam.com, Justin's father,

Richard, said, "I really wish parents could flip a switch that would take them to a time when their children are grown up and gone, so they could realize how great those early years were—and how special the days spent as a family are running back and forth to sporting events, cheering and traveling together, and loving one another. The future will come soon enough. Don't get so caught up in tomorrow that you lose sight of today. As the father of a MLB superstar, I can tell you that my fondest memories of all are of the summer days with me and my boys on the Little League diamond."

Success comes in many forms. Within families it can be measured by the depth of what they've shared and still hold dear. In that case Justin Verlander—son, brother, and star—whether you end up on Mount Rushmore or not, you've known success from the start.

27

TANANA'S GEM TO WIN DIVISION

They just kept fighting, clawing, and not giving in. Although falling short of reaching the World Series, the Tigers were immensely proud of their 1987 season and deservedly so. Steadily gaining confidence after a sluggish start, they pulled themselves up from the depths one spot at a time. In the seven-team American League East, the Tigers were in sixth place after 34 games, fifth after 50, fourth after 59, third after 109, and second after 159 games.

On the final day of the season, they completed the journey by winning the division on a 1–0 masterpiece by Frank Tanana against the Toronto Blue Jays. It was one of the great triumphs in Tigers' history, a game in which they scored early and held on as Tanana skillfully guided them around all hazards.

Larry Herndon provided just enough offense by hitting a fence-scraping home run to left field in the second inning off Jimmy Key, after which Tanana was a crafty left-hander at his best, blanking the Jays on six hits. It was the signature game of Tanana's career, a clutch performance. But the Blue Jays should have scored. By Tanana's own admission, it should have been 1–1 after nine innings, not 1–0. "I balked," Tanana said. "With a runner on third, I've always thought I balked, and they didn't catch it."

And because it wasn't caught back in 1987, Tanana remains reluctant to specify what he did wrong. "Let's just say, it was something only a pitcher could feel," he said.

When did it occur? Well, only two Toronto runners reached third in the game. The first time was in the fourth inning when Manny Lee tripled after Cecil Fielder was thrown out on what will forever appear in the box score as a steal attempt—the first of Fielder's career. But "It was a botched hit-and-run, not a steal," Tanana said. "Cecil took off from first, which was supposed to be a complete surprise. And believe me, it was. Not a badly designed play. But Lee didn't swing at the pitch."

Despite being relatively svelte at the time compared to his productive years in Detroit, Fielder didn't beat the throw, so he was called out, even though replays suggest that Lou Whitaker never tagged him. If today's replay rules had been in place, the Blue Jays may have won a challenge of the call. "But in those days, you were out if the throw beat you," Tanana said.

With Fielder no longer on base, Lee's triple didn't manufacture a run, just a threat.

Did Tanana balk at this point? His right elbow appeared to twitch before he threw a pitch to Garth Iorg with Lee at third. But it was too minor a move for the umpires to rule that Tanana had started and stopped his delivery. No balk was committed, and Iorg eventually flied out to center.

The second time the Jays had a runner on third was when Lloyd Moseby stole second in the eighth and advanced on a fly ball to Scott Lusader in right. With two outs Tanana did some awkward toe-tapping with the pitching rubber on his delivery to Jesse Barfield. "My footwork wasn't smooth," Tanana admitted.

But the blunder wasn't blatant. Maybe it hadn't been noticed. In any case, Tanana weathered the balk scare in the eighth by getting Barfield to hit a comebacker to the mound, though not a routine one, on the first pitch. Equal to the challenge of protecting a one-run lead with a pennant on the line, Tanana retired the side in order in the ninth.

In winning the division, the Tigers did not follow a familiar path. Far from coming close to their 35–5 start of three years earlier, the 1987 Tigers stumbled out of the gate. When their record sank to 11–19, they had lost 15 of their last 20 games. At nine and a half games out, they were closer to last than they were to first. "I still think we have a good team, but something is missing," manager Sparky Anderson said at the time. "We have to do something."

Efforts to make a trade, though, went nowhere. Looking to acquire a right-handed hitter, the Tigers made pitcher Dan Petry available. They were hoping to pry third baseman Brook Jacoby loose from last-place Cleveland, but the Indians turned them down. The Tigers would have to get better with what they had. That took a while. Kirk Gibson missed the first 24 games because of torn muscles in his ribcage. Upon returning, he didn't start contributing on a regular basis for another two weeks.

Although catcher Matt Nokes would have a fine rookie season with 32 home runs, the Tigers initially felt the loss of Lance Parrish, who had signed with the Philadelphia Phillies as a free agent, the first defector from the core of the Detroit team that had won the 1984 World Series. Plus the Tigers just weren't scoring. They were tied for 11th place in runs scored among A.L. teams through 30 games. But suddenly reversing course, they led the league in scoring in the last 132 games.

At one early point, though, it got so frustrating that third baseman Darnell Coles took a ball thrown to him between innings and heaved it over the roof at Tiger Stadium—no easy feat. Coles was removed from the game for losing control of his emotions, but his teammates empathized with him. "I've felt a few times like doing that," Alan Trammell said. "But I don't have that kind of arm. I didn't want to embarrass myself."

It was a miserable five weeks. But to Anderson, the first milestone of the season always had been the 40-game mark, not the 30-game mark, and by winning eight of their next 10, the Tigers began to turn around their season. What had been urgently needed when the Tigers were 11–19 was an anger-purging, air-clearing blowout. They got it with a 15–2 victory against the California Angels, a game in which they had 14 runs by the fifth inning. Would it be an isolated splurge or the start of something? Until then, "When we had a good game," Trammell said, "it hadn't meant much. We still couldn't get going."

This time, though, it meant something. The Tigers started winning. They won 13 of their next 15 and then 17 of 25. By the end of July, they were only three games out of first place. Just like that, they'd become contenders. Both Tanana and Jack Morris got hot at the same time. Beginning in mid-May, Morris went 12–4 and Tanana

11–5 in their next 18 starts. When Walt Terrell started to win steadily in mid-July and newly acquired Doyle Alexander began working his magic in August, the Tigers were poised for an exciting finish. "I don't go for that destiny stuff," Tanana said, "but I knew we had a good team and were playing good baseball."

HERNDON HELPS TANANA...BUT DOESN'T WANT TO TALK ABOUT IT

Larry Herndon was known for being a good ballplayer, a great teammate, and for not commenting. It was Herndon, for instance, who hit the game-deciding home run in Game 1 of the 1984 World Series and then asked for his street clothes to be brought into the trainer's room, so he wouldn't have to talk about it.

And it is Herndon you see on footage of the final out of that World Series because he's the outfielder who caught the ball. Among Herndon's other career highlights was the home run he hit in the final game of the regular season in 1987, giving Frank Tanana enough support to clinch the division with a 1–0 victory.

He also blasted an absolutely monstrous home run off the facing of the second deck in center field at Tiger Stadium on Opening Day 1987. "The granddaddy of them all," Tigers coach Dick Tracewski called it. "You'll never see another one like that in a lifetime."

In four consecutive at-bats in 1982, Herndon hit four home runs. They spanned two games with an off day in between—unlike Charlie Maxwell's doubleheader achievement in 1959—but they left some who witnessed the feat permanently impressed. "One of the highlights of my entire time as a Tiger," Alan Trammell said.

It's also important to remember the extent Herndon would go to defend his teammates. When the Tigers and Minnesota Twins got into a vicious brawl in 1982, nobody waded into the middle of it more fearlessly than Herndon. "He was protecting his teammates by throwing haymakers," Trammell said. "Oh, my God, the punches Hondo threw in that fight."

When the brawl was over, Herndon didn't comment, of course, but he always refused so politely and was such a pleasant individual that the media got along with him. They just seldom had the chance to quote him.

On September 26, though, the outlook wasn't all that bright. The Tigers trailed the Jays by three and a half games with eight games remaining. But they won a key game the next day in Toronto on Kirk Gibson's RBI single in the 13th inning after Gibson already had tied the game with a dramatic home run in the ninth off Tom Henke. Sensing something special was possible, Gibson said the Tigers "might be setting the biggest bear trap of all time."

They were.

After they split a four-game series with the Baltimore Orioles while the Jays were losing three straight to the Milwaukee Brewers, a season-ending series against the Blue Jays at Tiger Stadium would eventually decide it all. With relief help from Mike Henneman, Alexander won the opener 4–3. Now the two teams were tied for the division lead with two games remaining.

On Trammell's bases-loaded, 12th-inning single through the legs of Lee at short, the Tigers gained sole possession of first place.

But the Jays still could have forced a one-game playoff had they won the Sunday game with Tanana starting for the Tigers. So it was up to the former flamethrower to see that they didn't. Tanana's first advantage was that he had already beaten Toronto twice that season and left another game after seven innings with a 2–0 lead. In those three starts, he allowed only two runs in 23⅔ innings. "Every time he pitches against us," Barfield said, "he's Cy Young."

Said Tanana of the Jays, "They had trouble with off-speed stuff, and I gave them a lot of it, so that my 85 [mph] would look like 95." With shadows lengthening, and Key on the mound for the Jays, "It was tailor-made to be 1–0," Tanana said.

Tanana called his performance in the fascinating game "my crowning achievement," but there were some who couldn't bear to watch. Sparky for one. Then again, was always more comfortable with power pitchers than those with finesse. In fact, he had once gone up to Tanana with a one-word question after he'd thrown a shutout: "How?"

"What do you mean 'how?'" Tanana replied.

"How do you get anyone out with that crap?" Anderson said.

As the pennant-clinching masterpiece came closer to its conclusion, Anderson kept looking down at the notepad he was holding. "From the seventh inning on," Tanana said, "he didn't watch a single pitch because he knew who was on the mound."

But when it was all over, Sparky planted a big kiss on his winning pitcher's cheek. "He knew the artistry it took," Tanana said.

Sure he did. Even without watching he knew.

JACK MORRIS

J ack Morris didn't win the most games as a Tiger, nor did he have the most strikeouts. He didn't talk to the ball, nor did he ever come close to having a 31-win season. But he won a World Series with the Tigers. What's more, he won the most games of any major league pitcher in the 1980s and was such an irrepressible bulldog that he still might end up in the Hall of Fame. It depends on if the Era Committee (what used to be the Veterans Committee) votes him in. But if it does…

"Anyone who knows me knows how emotional I can be," Morris said. "I don't know if I could get through a speech."

Despite his success, Morris' career wasn't a walk in the park. It was more of a squawk in the park. Jack was often vocal. He could be snarly with hitters and media alike. He also could be difficult with umpires. Since his playing days ended, though, he's been known to apologize for being such a grouch. "I've tried to make it right any way I can, but it was part of who I was," he said.

Morris admits he had some maturing to do as a pitcher and a lot of growing up to do as a person. And although both missions were eventually accomplished, his reputation as a hothead still haunts him. "It never completely goes away," he said.

Driven to excel, Morris wasn't easy on himself. But the more ways he could help his team win a game, the better. "Jack isn't hardheaded," pitching coach Roger Craig said of him. "He just believes he can do anything."

Along those lines, oddly enough, Morris grew to enjoy

pinch-running, which manager Sparky Anderson frequently called on him to do. In 1983, en route to winning 20 games, Morris pinch-ran seven times. But what manager today would allow his ace to risk injury by pinch-running? "Ultimately," Morris said, "a memo came down from the front office, saying 'no more. You're going to get this guy hurt.' I was upset about that. Pinch-running made me feel a part of it when I wasn't pitching. One time, though, I was picked off second base. Carlton Fisk got me."

Morris pinch-ran 19 times in his career. He would have enjoyed interleague play as well because it would have allowed him to hit, but he was out of baseball before interleague baseball was implemented in 1997. "It wasn't until about halfway through my career that I realized, 'know what? I'm a pitcher now,'" said Morris, who would take grounders at shortstop before every game he didn't start. "It was my way of staying loose. Some pitchers long toss, but for me throwing across the diamond was good enough."

"Initially," Alan Trammell said, "Jack thought he was a better shortstop than I was. That was just his mentality."

For a while everything seemed to be more fun than pitching. "I didn't have fun pitching until, in my mind, I started becoming a good pitcher," Morris said. And he didn't do that until he perfected his split-fingered fastball in 1983.

There were three distinct segments to Morris' career: 1) the years he pitched for the Tigers (1977–82) without a splitter, 2) the years he pitched for the Tigers (1983–90) after adding a splitter, and 3) the success he enjoyed in 1991–92 with the Minnesota Twins and Toronto Blue Jays.

Morris' arrival in the majors in 1977 unfortunately coincided with Mark Fidrych's early exit from the big leagues. The beginning of one outstanding career marked the beginning of the end for another. They never had a full season together in the majors. At the time of Morris' promotion from the minors, there were concerns about the right arm of "the Bird." No one knew then, but Fidrych wouldn't ever come close to being what he had been in 1976. "I think about it all the time—what it would have been like to be in the same rotation with a healthy Bird," Morris said. "It was unbelievable how good he was."

After dropping into and out of the Tigers' starting rotation his first two seasons, Morris was their undeniable ace for the next 12 years, beginning with a start on May 13, 1979. He had been the last pitcher cut in spring training that year, but after heeding the words of his Triple A manager, Jim Leyland, to stop pouting—and with his Mother's Day victory for the Tigers in his first ever start as a springboard—he was back in the big leagues to stay. "Happy Mother's Day, Mom," an elated Morris yelled in the Tigers' clubhouse after the victory. "This is probably the happiest moment of my life."

Except for a rehab start at Lakeland in 1989, Morris never pitched in the minors again. His next 394 appearances for the Tigers were starts. On the Tigers' all-time list, he ranks second behind Mickey Lolich (459–408) in career starts.

Morris pitched well in his first four years of starting, averaging 16 wins, but felt he needed another pitch. He said he wanted to add a "strike three" pitch because his slider "had started to flatten out." That's when he began to experiment with the splitter. Beginning in 1983 he increased his strikeouts by 40 percent. It did little to lower his ERA, but the split-fingered fastball—he called it his forkball—gave Morris a two-strike confidence that might have ebbed had he not added it. He went from averaging 4.5 strikeouts per nine innings in his first four years as a Tiger to 6.3 in his last eight. "Because it was thrown with the same delivery as a fastball," Morris said, "hitters had to look for one or the other and hope. If they guessed wrong, they were out. "

Teammate Milt Wilcox introduced Morris to the pitch when he realized his own fingers were too short for him to throw it effectively. After making some adjustments and observing that the pitch could be "ridiculously nasty," Morris mastered it. Not only that, he was the only pitcher in the American League throwing it. "In 1983 and 1984, before other pitchers picked it up," Morris said, "it was almost as if I was throwing an illegal pitch, like I was cheating."

Morris won 20 games for the first time in 1983 and seemed headed for even more the next year. In fact, none of his seasons began more auspiciously than 1984. He was 5–0 by the end of April and 10–1 by the end of May, leading to thoughts that he could possibly win 30.

Jack Morris, the major leaguer with the most wins in the 1980s, pitches against the New York Yankees during 1988. (AP Images)

"[The media] kept saying I was ahead of Denny McLain's pace," he said, "so at that point, I had no reason to think I couldn't do it."

The highlight of Morris' sizzling start was a no-hitter—the only one of his career—against the Chicago White Sox at Comiskey Park in April. Sure enough, the final pitch of the game was a splitter that Ron Kittle missed by a mile. "Two miles," Morris said.

The game was a graphic example of how confident Morris had become. To a fan in the stands who heckled him by constantly mentioning he hadn't yet allowed a hit, Morris replied, "You might want to stop drinking and pay attention, sir. History is going to be made today."

When Craig feared that Jack had jinxed himself, Morris said to him, "relax, Rog, I'm going to get it." After the game, plate umpire Durwood Merrill told Bill McGraw of the *Detroit Free Press* that Morris' masterpiece hadn't been "a Picasso, but might have been a Rockwell."

What took place later that season, however, was far from a work of art. Morris threw such a tantrum in July about ball-and-strike calls that Craig said, "As we all saw, he still has some growing up to do." Even taciturn teammate Lance Parrish said, "We've all spoken to Jack about his temper, but everybody's talked out. He has to do it on his own."

Eventually he did, but only after he stopped talking to the media for nearly two months. He said one of the reasons for his silence was that "Tom Gage annoys me to death. He knows nothing about the game. He should be covering shuffleboard. I decided it was enough."

When asked by the *Free Press* to comment, I said, "I don't think it matters to Jack how I feel. He's found his scapegoat."

Morris would later say his silence was designed to remove distractions, but it backfired. "By shutting up I got even more attention. Looking back, it was one of the dumbest things I ever did," he said. "It took me awhile to grow up, no question about it."

The worst of times for Morris in 1984 were the three months from mid-June to mid-September. He went 6–9 with a 5.60 ERA and was hit by opposing batters at a .293 clip. "He's not hurt," Sparky kept insisting. "He's just in a slump."

From that prolonged slump Morris rebounded with three strong starts that enabled him to finish with a 19–11 record. Morris won all three of his postseason starts, including two (Game 1 and 4) in the 1984 World Series.

But he would get far more postseason attention for his performance as a Twins pitcher for his 1–0 victory during Game 7 of the 1991 World Series against the Atlanta Braves. "I've heard that being in the zone means total focus," Morris said. "You can almost predetermine everything that happens before it happens because your will drives your focus. I never once thought the Braves were going to score. I had more positive inner energy in that game than I'd ever had—or ever again would have. And at the end of that game, I knew there was no way I could ever top it. I've said many times I wish every human being at some point in their lives experiences the same total joy I felt that day."

The discussion of whether Morris ever will be a Hall of Famer has lasted longer than he pitched. Not enough members of the Baseball Writers Association of America voted for Morris during his 15-year window of eligibility for him to be elected. He needed 75 percent of the vote. But the most he received—notably in his second-to-last year on the ballot—was 67.7 percent. Instead of a sentimental boost putting him over the top, his support inexplicably dropped to 61.5 percent.

Yet he might still make it via the Eras Committee because of what he accomplished in his career. Morris earned 233 of his 254 victories from 1979 to 1992. Of the 17 major league pitchers who've won the most games in a 14-year span since 1947, his total ranks 12th. But he is the only one of the 17 not in the Hall of Fame. So until he makes it, his journey to Cooperstown will remain an ordeal. His career wasn't an ordeal, though, well, maybe at times.

BOBO NEWSOM'S EMOTIONAL WORLD SERIES

They called him Bobo. But, more often than not, others knew him as ol' Bobo," a down-home nickname for a down-home kind of guy. Come to think of it, Bobo Newsom had as many names as his personality had quirks.

His family called him Buck. Reporters who covered his colorful career sometimes referred to him in print as "Large Louie" because Louis was his real first name. And because he clearly wasn't small. Nor was he quiet. Or mild-mannered. Bobo Newsom was big, brash, confident, loud, and lovable. He would talk your ear off—whether he met you on a train or in a hotel. Then he would pitch his heart out. "I just can't shut up," he readily admitted.

There was no one quite like him. Bobo's time as a Tiger was relatively short, yet so packed with personality, gladness, and sadness that Newsom will forever rank as one of the team's great characters. He was a comet streaking across a three-season sky, shining brightly before dimming. And for one glorious season in particular, he was one of the Tigers' great pitchers.

Bobo was well traveled by the time he became a Tiger before the 1939 season. He was in his 11th year as a major leaguer yet less than halfway through a career that began in 1929 and would end in 1953. Bobo was a big league hobo. He would have five different stints with the Washington Senators, three with the St. Louis Browns, two each with the Brooklyn Dodgers and Philadelphia Athletics, and one with five other teams, including the Tigers.

He would win more games for the Senators than he would for the Tigers during a career that saw him win 20 games or more three times but also lose 20 or more three times. And although one of those 20-loss seasons occurred with Detroit in 1941, he had his best winning percentage as a Tiger, compiling a 50–35 record. Considering such extremes, it should come as little wonder that Bobo ended up as one of only two 200-game winners in the majors who would also lose 200. His career record for the nine teams with which he played was 211–222.

But when he was good, he was very good, even outstanding, and for the 1940 season—one in which the Tigers would reach the World Series against the Cincinnati Reds—Newsom was at his all-time best with a 21–5 record. It was the signature season of his career, showcasing his talent, his showmanship, and his personality. But it was a personal loss at the end of the season—and his response to it—that would indelibly endear him to Tigers fans.

Upon hearing that his father had died of a heart attack in Cincinnati the night after Bobo won the Tigers' World Series opener at Crosley Field, he not only remained with the team for the rest of the Series, but also would blank the Reds in his father's honor in Game 5. And it was Newsom who would try to win Game 7 as well—on one day's rest. "I won Game 5 for my daddy," he said. "But I want to win Game 7 for ol' Bobo."

More than that, Newsom wanted to win it for all the Tigers because after pitching much of his career for teams with no chance of winning a World Series, he had found a home with one that could. Newsom admired Detroit manager Del Baker and also spoke highly of the team spirit with which Baker led the 1940 Tigers.

Then again, Bobo was willing to speak, highly or not, about almost anyone or anything.

There was the day, for instance, when Newsom told reporters that he was ready to take on Detroit's own Joe Louis, the heavyweight champion of the world. "Fellows, I've got an idea that I could lick Joe Louis," he told the *Detroit Free Press*. "Somebody has to bring the fight business back in order, and I think ol' Bobo is the boy to do it."

When asked how many times he had lost a fight, Newsom recalled only one—the time an elderly female fan hit him for striking out Babe Ruth. "Ol' Bobo isn't going to counterpunch a nice old lady," he said.

Newsom, who was a right-hander, was not above taunting other teams, which explains the time when, knowing the New York Yankees were having trouble against left-handers, he decided to play a game of catch while throwing left-handed within easy view of the Yankees' dugout at Briggs Stadium. On a subject no player today would dare tackle, Newsom also shared his honest assessments of other teams to reporters. Of the other contenders in the 1940 pennant chase, for example, he predicted in mid-June that the Cleveland Indians were "not good enough." He also said they were "hampered by a bad tradition: they always fold about the time of the All-Star Game." Of the Boston Red Sox, who were leading the American League at the time of his comments, Newsom told a *Free Press* reporter that the Sox did not have enough pitching.

That was Bobo for you. In his own words, he just couldn't shut up.

He was hell-bent, however, on not only pitching the Tigers to the World Series, but also on winning it once they got there. Newsom had never been to a World Series, and for more reasons than one, as summer wound down in 1940, he wanted the personal drought to end. Time, you see, was running short for a loved one at home. Back in South Carolina, Bobo's father wasn't doing well. Asked what his thoughts were about his father's poor health, Bobo said, "it sure would be nice to have him see ol' Buck pitch in a World Series game."

With each start Newsom became more intent on getting to the series. Not even a broken thumb in the second half of the season—an injury doctors said would take four weeks to heal—kept Newsom out for long. Hurt on July 17 but returning on July 28, he defied medical advice to return to the mound. Newsom would lose his first game back but soon reeled off four victories without a loss to head into September with 17–2 record.

The Tigers had teams nipping at their heels until the very end of the season but clinched the 1940 American League pennant with a gem of a game from unheralded Floyd Giebell against Cleveland's Bob Feller on September 27. Finishing the season on an 18–7 roll, they would begin the World Series in Cincinnati on Wednesday, October 2, with Newsom getting the call in the opener.

Despite ailing since June and knowing how arduous the trip from Hartsville, South Carolina, might be, his father, Henry, wasn't going to miss it. The *Free Press* would later report that when friends told Bobo they had wished him a safe return as he left home, Henry replied, "I'm not coming back."

Ol' Bobo treated his dad to a masterpiece. He beat the Reds 7–2 in the World Series opener. After the Tigers scored five runs in the second, it was never close. There's no record of what Henry thought of the game, or how it felt to see his son pitch, but one can only imagine it was with immense pride that he returned to his hotel room after the final out.

And died.

Henry Newsom had a heart attack at the hotel, then another in the hospital to which he was taken. He did not survive the combination of the two. Bobo couldn't hide his emotions, nor did he try to. Upon being told of his father's death, he was seen sobbing. "Tears streaming down his cheeks unchecked," according to eyewitness reports.

Stunned and saddened, Bobo vowed to remain with the team, saying his father would have wanted it that way. Before his father's body was taken back home, there was a small ceremony.

But now—gosh darn it, or whatever Bobo would have said—there was a World Series to win. The Reds took two of the next three games after the opener, but with a three-hit shutout that Newsom dedicated to his father in Game 5, the Tigers pulled to within a victory of winning the World Series.

There were no travel days, however, between venues back then. From Newsom's Game 5 gem on a Sunday, the Tigers went straight to Cincinnati, where their bats fell silent in a 4–0 loss to right-hander Bucky Walters on Monday. The series came down to Game 7 the next day, and without a rested starter available that they trusted, the Tigers once more turned to a willing, but weary Newsom.

Bobo was emotionally spent. But, amazingly, he more than matched the Reds' Paul Derringer to take a 1–0 lead into the bottom of the seventh. By then, Newsom had thrown 16 consecutive shutout innings—the last inning of Game 1, nine in Game 5, and six more in the seventh game.

But his streak ended in the seventh inning of the seventh game when Tigers shortstop Dick Bartell miscalculated Frank McCormick's location on the bases as the Reds' runner, who had hesitated, tried to score from second on a double off the right-field screen by journeyman Jimmy Ripple. Instead of throwing home in an effort to get the lumbering McCormick—who would have been "a dead pigeon," according to Charlie Gehringer—Bartell held the relay as the Reds tied the game. Ripple was sacrificed to third. Then he scored on a sacrifice fly. That's how the Reds won the game 2–1, as the Tigers were unable to muster anything more than an unearned run in the third inning.

Bobo's noble effort was over. So was his greatest season. He would go 12–20 in 1941 and was sold to the Senators just before the 1942 season—never quite to be the same again.

We're all in agreement, no doubt, that no one was nicer than Ernie Harwell. No one was kinder than Ernie. No one in baseball was more popular than Ernie, the Tigers' longtime broadcaster who was well into his career when he came to Detroit in 1960. No one ever heard Ernie swear. No one ever saw him get mad. No one had ever irritated him so much that he lost his temper—until Leo Durocher did the impossible by goading Ernie Harwell into a fight.

Harwell was broadcasting New York Giants games in the early 1950s when Durocher was their manager. Teams weren't flying from city to city yet; they were still taking the train.

It was an era that has been richly romanticized, mostly by those who did not experience it. To those who did, it could be equally enchanting and disappointing.

For instance, the late Joe Falls, who eventually wrote for three Detroit dailies in his Hall of Fame career, could not have been more enthralled with train travel after sitting up late one night to hear Tigers broadcaster Mel Ott tell baseball stories on a trip in 1956. "They were so interesting I couldn't wait to get back on the train the next time to hear him tell more of them," Falls remembered. "With my work done, I went right to the club car where everyone had gathered again. And what happened? Mel told the same stories he had told before. I couldn't excuse myself because I was the person sitting the closest to him, so I was stuck there."

Falls had run afoul of repetition.

What happened to Harwell was that he ran afoul of Durocher being Durocher. "We were coming back from Chicago, and I was sitting in a compartment with Russ Hodges," Harwell recalled in Curt Smith's overview of baseball broadcasting, *Voices of the Game.*

Hodges was famous for his "The Giants win the pennant! The Giants win the pennant!" call of Bobby Thomson's dramatic home run in 1951. Harwell had worked the TV side of the same game. But as the two were relaxing and reading on the journey back to New York from Chicago, Durocher "came in and slapped the newspaper, which hit my face," Harwell said. "That was Leo. He'd do those things just to see how far he'd get with you."

But this particular time, Durocher messed with the wrong Marine. It's true. Ernie had been in the United States Marine Corps from 1942 to 1946. He could take care of himself. Still, it must have surprised Durocher when Harwell reacted the way he did. "I jumped up and put him in a hammer lock until Russ broke us apart," Ernie said.

Years later, Harwell couldn't recall any other time he had lost his temper. Even once, however, was more than most of his friends would have guessed. Then again, everyone was Ernie Harwell's friend, even if they had never met him. You didn't have to know him personally to take him on vacation with you—to Charlevoix, Petoskey, or any number of summer venues where you could get the Tigers' games on the radio.

And you also didn't have to know Ernie for him to be close by while you were mowing the lawn on a sunny Saturday in June. His was the first voice you heard on that treasured transistor radio you were given for your 11th birthday. His was the last voice you heard before drifting off to sleep when the Tigers were on the West Coast. And, of course, his was the only voice that told you a man from Kalamazoo had just caught a foul ball—Ernie seldom knew where the fan really was from, of course, but it became one of his most endearing traits as a broadcaster to pretend that he did.

There probably wasn't a town in Michigan that didn't eventually have a resident snag a foul ball—and when it happened on the road, such as in Seattle, Washington, someone from Pullman or Puyallup caught the ball. But if listeners wanted to believe that Harwell knew where the fortunate fans were from, so much the better. They loved it because they loved him. And deservedly so.

With his comforting, soft Georgia drawl and neighborly smile, Harwell was endlessly gracious. But he was also endlessly enamored with the game that became his life's work.

In what he called his prose poem entitled "A Game for All America," which he wrote in 1954 and delivered as part of a speech at his Hall of Fame ceremony in 1981, Harwell's lyric love of the game and his sheer humanity glowed throughout as a constant theme. "In baseball democracy shines its clearest," he wrote. "Here, the only race that matters is the race to the bag. The creed is the rulebook. Color is something to distinguish one team's uniform from another. Baseball is a ballet without music. Drama without words...just a game, as simple as a ball and a bat. Yet as complex as the American spirit it symbolizes."

Ernie was a caring man who often would rely on his faith in everyday situations. Getting a ride to the ballpark in Anaheim from a beat writer, Harwell quickly said a prayer when told the writer's young

Beloved Tigers announcer Ernie Harwell pauses during a break in the action of a 1993 game against the New York Yankees. (AP Images)

son was having ear surgery that day. But he timed it for when the car was stopped at a red light so the writer could bow his head, too. That was Ernie.

As capable as he must have been to broadcast other sports, which he did until the 1960s, it's difficult to imagine Harwell's style being applied to football. He was a man associated with his phrases, after all. In football there was no equivalent to a batter taking a called third strike. It couldn't be easily said of a linebacker, for instance, that "he stood there like the house by the side of the road." And while it could be said of a receiver racing down the sideline for a touchdown that he was "lonnng gone," Harwell didn't start using that phrase as his home-run call until later in his career.

He belonged to baseball, not to other sports, so his last football assignment was a Michigan State game in 1963. After being the voice of the Baltimore Orioles following their long existence as the St. Louis Browns, Harwell also belonged to Detroit. And to Michigan. "People meet Ernie and they are happy," Smith wrote in *Voices of the Game.* "He probably could be elected mayor of Detroit, if not governor of the state. He has that hold on people. Kids, mothers, grandfathers, cops, firemen, teachers, bankers, and insurance men spend their summers with Ernie Harwell...a cherished friend."

There were times when it appeared that the Tigers didn't value Harwell's integrity as much as he did. But his good sense always prevailed. For instance, he didn't like being asked in 1968 by Tigers general manager Jim Campbell to withhold a vital out-of-town score from his broadcast in order to build the tension at Tiger Stadium, but he followed orders all the same.

When Don Wert singled in Al Kaline, Harwell announced, "and the Tigers have won their first pennant since 1945," which was true. But they'd already clinched it with a loss by the second-place Baltimore Orioles.

In *Voices of the Game,* Harwell said that "The stadium was packed, and Jim felt that if we posted the score on our scoreboard, the fans were sure to pour out of the stands, and we'd have to forfeit. So he held back the score and asked me to do the same. I didn't totally agree with him. It was a kind of censorship. But I could see his point."

With only one significant setback along the way—when he was told that the 1991 season would be his last with the Tigers, only to have new owner Mike Ilitch bring him back in 1993—Harwell continued to broadcast Tigers games until his retirement in 2002. It was an emotional moment for all when he signed off. But it wasn't farewell. "Rather than saying good-bye," Ernie said, "allow me to say thank you for letting me be part of your family. Thank you for taking me with you to that cottage up north, to the beach, the picnic, your workplace, and your backyard. Thank you for sneaking your transistor under the pillow as you grew up loving the Tigers. Now, I might have been a small part of your life, but you have been a very large part of mine, and it's been my privilege and honor to share with you the greatest game of all."

The great Ernie Harwell died on May 4, 2010. He was 92. To pay their respects as he lay in repose next to his statue at Comerica Park, fans by the hundreds were lined up when the gates opened at 7:00 AM. They wanted to say a last good-bye to the nicest man in baseball.

31

101 WINS IN 1961

The cruelest seasons in Tigers history have been those during which they won 100 or more games—only to go home empty-handed. No postseason, no playoffs. And it's happened twice.

In 1915 they won 100 games but finished in second place, two and a half games behind the Boston Red Sox. The Tigers had an outstanding team that year. Ty Cobb hit .369, stole 96 bases, and scored 144 runs, and Sam Crawford and underrated Bobby Veach knocked in 112 runs each. On the pitching side, George "Hooks" Dauss won 24 games, and Harry Coveleski won 22. Unsung to this day, no pitcher has won more career games as a Tiger than Dauss' 223. But the Red Sox—with Babe Ruth having his first good season (with an 18–8 record as a pitcher)—were better. The Sox went to the World Series and won in five games over the Philadelphia Phillies.

So much for 1915. For that matter, so much for the next 19 years.

The Tigers wouldn't finish in first place again until 1934, the year they lost the World Series in seven games to the St. Louis Cardinals.

Sometimes they've been good but not good enough. Other times they knew well in advance they weren't going anywhere but home when the regular season ended. What made 1961 so entirely different, however, is that no one foresaw the Tigers challenging the New York Yankees for first place. And certainly no one foresaw the Tigers winning 101 games after only 71 victories the year before. But suddenly they were good. They were also immensely entertaining to watch so much so that on September 1 they had a chance to win the American League pennant.

Make no mistake, the Tigers were underdogs the entire way in 1961—and when they fell out of first place on July 25—they wouldn't see it again. The mighty Yankees had Mickey Mantle. They also had Roger Maris. Impressively, the M&M boys combined to hit 115 home runs that year. (Maris had 61; Mantle had 54.) And to lead their rotation, the Yankees had left-hander Whitey Ford, who finished with a 25–4 record that featured a 14–0 streak. But despite all of that, the Yankees weren't pulling away from the Tigers in August.

The Tigers would begin to fade, falling to three games back, even four a couple of times. Then they'd bounce back. They were as tough as their best pitcher, Frank Lary. Not one to give an inch, Lary went 5–1 with a 1.17 ERA in August.

With a 22–9 record, August was superb for the Tigers. Their hitting was relentless but had been for a while. From June 1 to September 1 and on his way to winning a batting crown, Norm Cash hit .382 with 22 home runs and 70 RBIs. Making an impact following a tepid first season as a Tiger after being acquired for Harvey Kuenn, Rocky Colavito caught fire in the same three months as Cash. From June to September, Colavito hit .304 with 27 home runs and 88 RBIs. Not to be outdone, future Hall of Famer Al Kaline hit a helpful .306 during the same time frame. It was an exciting summer of baseball in Detroit. Attendance for the year jumped 37 percent from 1960.

And when September finally rolled around, there were the Yankees and Tigers in first and second place, respectively, one and half games apart with no other team close. The third-place Baltimore Orioles were 10½ games back. To make matters even more dramatic, a Labor Day weekend showdown pitted the two contenders against each other in a three-game series at Yankee Stadium. Mathematically, the season wasn't on the line for either team, but for the upstart Tigers, who were getting a rare dose of national attention, it was a chance to gain ground or maybe even take over first place with a sweep. "Why the Tigers Can Win It" read the headline in the *Detroit Free Press*.

But they had their hearts broken in the first game—then again in the third. The pitching matchup in the opener was between left-handers Don Mossi for the Tigers and Ford for the Yankees. Both were enjoying outstanding seasons. Ford took a 22–3 record into the game. Mossi was at 14–3 but was the hotter of the two pitchers at the time. Mossi had been 4–1 with a 2.04 ERA in August. Ford was 3–1 but with an abnormally high 4.26 ERA.

Baseball sizzled with anticipation. The two teams were hot. The weather was hot. But hotter still was the pennant race. Center stage was nothing new for the Yankees, of course. Since the Tigers' last trip to the World Series in 1945, the Yankees had been there 11 times, winning eight. It was no surprise, therefore, when the Tigers quickly looked like the team trying too hard.

In the opener two of their runners were picked off first, and Kaline, who rarely was guilty of any mistakes, made the overaggressive blunder of trying to stretch a single into a double in the eighth when the runner in front of him, Billy Bruton, had already reached third.

The showdown between the starters ended when Ford left the game in the fifth inning because of a pulled hip muscle. But with the game still scoreless, Ford's replacement, Bud Daley, proved just as stingy. Meanwhile, Mossi retired 21 of the first 22 hitters he faced. Mantle was no factor throughout the game, striking out three times. Maris didn't do any damage either.

Neither team did anything offensively—until the bottom of the ninth. That's when the difference in how the game is played now— with assigned bullpen roles and stats-based strategy and how it was played in 1961 with its lack of precise information—decided the outcome. With two outs in the ninth and the bases empty after a frustrated Mantle struck out for the third time, the Tigers and Yankees seemingly were headed for extra innings. Mossi had been masterful. So, when Elston Howard singled with two outs, Tigers manager Bob Scheffing did not remove his starter from the game.

Managers today might go to their bullpen in such a situation, but other than closer Terry Fox, the Tigers' bullpen wasn't entirely dependable. Neither Phil Regan nor Hank Aguirre had been extensively used since July. So, Scheffing let Mossi pitch to Yogi Berra, who singled Howard to third. Now there was trouble—and a decision to make with the formidable Bill Skowron at the plate. Today's comprehensive scouting reports would have come in handy.

But it was 1961 with rudimentary available information.

Skowron was coming off his best August since taking over as the Yankees' full-time first baseman in 1956. And when their careers were done, Skowron had more hits off Mossi (31) than any other pitcher. The Tigers' sudden predicament called for a pitching change. It screamed for one actually. But Scheffing stayed with his starter, a tiring left-hander facing a right-handed hitter with the game on the line.

Predictably, the Tigers paid the price. Skowron singled in Howard on a 1–1 pitch for the winning run. "One lousy curve," Mossi said after the game. "I had everything going the way I wanted, then I get to two outs in the bottom of the ninth and throw a terrible pitch." Said Scheffing, "It hurts. We had chances, but blew them. We should have wrapped it up a couple of times."

To gain a game on the Yankees after dropping the opener, the Tigers needed to win the next two games of the series. But after a two-run home run from Colavito in the first inning of the second game, their bats cooled in the Yankee Stadium heat. Scheffing's strategy backfired again. With the Tigers trailing 3–2 in the eighth inning, he stuck with Lary, his starter, for two more hitters after a one-out single by Yankees pitcher Luis Arroyo. Both of the hitters singled.

Scheffing had no choice but to take Lary out of the game at that point, but Aguirre quickly showed why his manager had hesitated in calling for him in the opener by allowing a two-run home run to Maris, the first batter he faced. The home run was Maris' second of the game and his 53rd of the season.

Losing the first two games was not what the Tigers had envisioned—nor obviously had hoped for. But neither was what happened next. In danger of falling behind by four and a half games on Sunday if they were swept, the Tigers did precisely that. But they did so in bubble-bursting fashion. After Jake Wood's two-run single in the top of the ninth inning of the series finale, the Tigers led 5–4 only to have Gerry Staley give up a leadoff home run to Mantle, followed by Howard's three-run shot off Ron Kline. For the Yankees it was a momentous turn of events. New York manager Ralph Houk called it, "the most exciting series of my lifetime."

For the Tigers, it was shattering. "None of us expected to get the complete broom," said a stunned Scheffing. As for the headlines that had been so optimistic, there was a complete reversal. "The party's over" announced the *Free Press*. But instead of the best, the worst had happened to the Tigers. They lost all three games and would not come close to recovering. In another week with their hopes gone after losing five more in a row in Baltimore and Boston, including a second consecutive 1–0 loss for Mossi, they were 11½ games out of first. The Tigers would win 12 of their last 15, but by then it was too late. When the season ended, they quietly went home with 101 wins as their only consolation.

32

JIM LEYLAND

Jim Leyland has always had a marvelous ability to look forward and back at the same time. It wasn't just the hallmark of his managing career. It is who he is as a person, an admirer of the past and of the future simultaneously. It's why those who think they know him often don't. It's why those who think he's a throwback miss the mark. And it's why those who believe they accurately describe his personality by calling him old school underestimate him. He's far more complex than that.

Leyland began and ended his career in uniform in the Detroit organization. From Perrysburg, Ohio, he signed out of high school as a catcher. He ended his managing career with the Tigers at the conclusion of the 2013 season. In eight years, he guided them to two World Series, winning neither but getting them there all the same. Also in those eight years, Leyland's teams reached the postseason four times. That number becomes five if a 163rd game in 2009 against the Minnesota Twins to decide the division winner is included.

When he came on board, the Tigers were non-contenders but beginning to put some pieces together. When he stepped down, many more of the needed elements were firmly in place.

He knew both joy and sadness as their manager. He barked at the media a little bit but only a little bit. He barked at his players about as often. It's all part of who Leyland is. He's gruff; he's gracious. He's abrupt; he charms. He's old; he's new.

And, yes, while not a throwback overall, he does have some of those characteristics. As he once said about his computer when he had not yet learned how to use it, "I don't Google, I don't Goggle." Another time in Chicago, while sitting in the visiting manager's office, he told a writer he didn't think his cell phone was working. "Give me a call to see if it rings, okay?" he said. The writer called him. His phone rang and quickly went to voicemail, but it rang. Jim was satisfied that it was working. By the time the writer had reached his seat in the press box, maybe 10 minutes later, he'd received a return call. "This is Jim Leyland. Who's this?"

Those eight seasons of covering Leyland's major league teams were special—just as it had been interesting to know him as a minor league manager hoping to get a break with the parent club. He wanted to be a coach with the Tigers, feeling he had paid his dues with 10 seasons of managing in Clinton, Iowa; Lakeland, Florida; Montgomery, Alabama; and Evansville, Indiana. He had a prime-time baseball mind, but there was no room for him on Sparky Anderson's coaching staff. Leyland understood that. As much as he wanted it to be otherwise, he understood and would later explain that "Sparky wanted his own guys."

It's a painful part of the job that a manager can't hire everyone he would like to as a coach. Leyland found himself in the same position with Lance Parrish when he became manager of the Tigers; there were only so many spots. It's not criticism to say Leyland has a fierce way about him. His eyes surveyed the scene with uncommon intensity, absorbing as much as they possibly could. He also studied the game fiercely, jotting down notes on a pad of paper, asking questions of experienced observers he respected.

With his Frankie Avalon references—"show me a manager who looks like Frankie Avalon at the end of the season, and I'll show you one who didn't work as hard as he needed to work"—it's not hard to envision Leyland as a teenager. A good son, brother, and athlete, he stayed out of trouble but definitely had a stylizin' side to him. His first car was a Studebaker Lark. He loved that Lark. But after he purchased it, he'd cruise the neighborhood on hot summer days with the windows up, so that people would think he had air-conditioning. One can almost envision Leyland being "the Fonz" before there was such a character.

Sports and family were his guiding lights in life. On his high school football team, he was the quarterback. In his senior class, he was voted most popular. And while there were Cleveland Indians fans in the house who wished the Tribe had been interested in him, it was with the Tigers that Leyland signed as a wiry catcher out of high school.

It was still the dead of winter when he left for spring training in 1964. Leyland had never been much of anywhere, but there he was boarding the bus that would take him to Florida—and to the rest of his life. "It was a little tough saying good-bye to my parents," he said. "I got homesick."

Just 19, he was a wide-eyed kid who had no idea what lay ahead. But he had four things on his side: he was smart, a quick learner, open-minded—and he wasn't shy. What he couldn't do, as he eventually found out, was hit. But his long career was just beginning all the same. "I signed with the Tigers," he said, "for absolutely nothing, no bonus, just $400 a month to come down for a shot to play professional baseball. I'll never forget it. I rode a double-decker Greyhound bus. Remember those? And I had a seat that was up high. When we finally pulled into Lakeland, you could see from where I sat the Tigers working out at Henley Field. All I could say was, 'Oh, my God.'"

It was actually coming true for him. Jimmy Leyland was a Detroit Tigers prospect for about a day before reality set in. "There were three beds in my room at the barracks," he said. "The two guys who were already in the room were catchers like me—except they were both All-Americans. At that point, I said to myself, 'I'm in trouble.'"

Leyland "had no idea what kind of player I was compared to anyone else who'd be there. I just knew I was getting an opportunity. I didn't know if I'd be around a month, a year, two years, or get sent home. It was just a new experience in life for me." It was the first of many he's had in baseball. "It's been a long, long career," Leyland said.

He lasted seven seasons in the minors, hitting .224 but never rising above the Double A level. Through as a player in 1970, he turned to managing in 1972. In the minors he managed many of the Tigers who would eventually become World Series champions in 1984. But by then he was in another organization. With no big league job being offered by the Tigers, he became a coach on Tony La Russa's staff with the Chicago White Sox in 1982.

At 37, Leyland was finally in the majors for the first time and would remain the White Sox third-base coach for four years before managing the Pittsburgh Pirates for the next 11. The pinnacle of his

managing career would come with a World Series championship with the Florida Marlins in 1997.

But do you measure success by how your teams perform, or by what you meant to the individuals you guided? In the case of what Leyland meant to Mark "the Bird" Fidrych, the memory of one poignant moment will never fade. Fidrych was attempting a comeback in 1980 that really wasn't one. His glory season for the Tigers had been in 1976, but amid his many setbacks, both he and the Tigers kept hoping he would somehow become an electrifying pitcher again. Sadly, it never happened. As manager at Triple A Evansville, Leyland had been assigned the task of helping Fidrych get back to the majors for one last try. "By then," Leyland said, "we had become very close. But obviously he was never quite the same."

In September of 1980, in what would become Fidrych's last home-game victory, "Lo and behold," said Leyland, "he pitched a complete game against the White Sox." It was an 11–2 victory in the first game of a doubleheader. In his last hurrah, Fidrych allowed no earned runs and only seven hits. Leyland attended the game with his parents. "Mark stayed at my house and had met them," he said. "My mom cooked him eggs and bacon for breakfast. He loved that."

So at the end of the game against the White Sox, when it would have been fully understandable for Fidrych to be thinking only of himself, he gave the game ball to Leyland's mother. "My mom didn't know what to do. She nearly passed out," said Leyland. "It was a great gesture by the Bird, one I'll never forget because even then I think he pitched in pain."

Built upon respect, the salute from Fidrych to Leyland and his family was for what they had done on his behalf in the grand but futile effort to make him great again. So therein lies the answer to how a manager's success is measured—sometimes with a one-of-a-kind moment.

33

WHAT A DEBUT!

The day was April 25, 1901, and in many ways, a whole new world was evolving.

On the streets, cars were replacing horses. There were so many cars that something new—a license plate—was about to be required. The cost of a first-class stamp was two cents. William McKinley, the president of the United States, would be assassinated in Buffalo in September. It was becoming a bustling, noisier world—nowhere more so than in Detroit, where the Tigers were preparing to play their first ever American League game.

Originally scheduled for the previous day, rain had postponed the opener. But skies on this Thursday afternoon were clear. Baseball would be played, and history would be made. Then again, history couldn't help but to be made. After all, the game had a new and hopefully enduring framework. The Tigers were in the recently named American League, which had declared itself a major league after four smaller franchises in the Western League were replaced with teams from Baltimore, Boston, Philadelphia, and Washington. Unimpressed, one National Leaguer felt that the American League was just "a highfalutin name for the old Western."

Already existing teams, along with Detroit, were in Chicago, Cleveland, and Milwaukee. The Baltimore franchise would last only two years before being replaced by the Highlanders of New York, who eventually became the Yankees. Known earlier as the "Wolverines," Detroit's baseball team from 1881 to 1888 had been in the National League, which is still regarded as the "senior circuit" because it is 25 years older than its younger sibling.

But on this bright afternoon, the past and the future didn't matter as much as the present. It was time to play ball. The Tigers' ballpark was called Bennett Park—named for Charlie Bennett of the

Detroit Wolverines. In a train accident several years earlier, Bennett had lost his left foot and right leg.

The popular catcher survived the mishap, though, and would throw out every ceremonial Opening Day pitch, no matter what league Detroit was in, from 1896 to 1927.

The ballpark was built at the corner of Michigan and Trumbull, the location where Navin Field, Briggs Stadium, and Tiger Stadium would follow. But the playing field was positioned differently. Home plate at Bennett Park was where right field would later be situated on the same site. That was not the only difference.

Made of wood, Bennett Park never held more than 14,000 fans. Its size was substantial for the day, however. With Detroit not yet known as the Motor City—it was the stove manufacturing capital instead—its population was around 300,000. Even though the city was excited about its first game in a new league, Ty Cobb wasn't a Tiger yet, and neither was Sam Crawford. Cobb's first season would be 1905; Crawford's was 1903. So there was really no telling how good the Tigers were going to be—or how bad.

As it turned out, they would be competitive, finishing third with a 74–61 record.

Rookie right-hander Roscoe Miller was the Tigers' best pitcher in 1901. He ended up with a 23–13 record, which he never came close to equaling before his death from unknown causes at age 36 in 1913.

Shortstop Kid Elberfeld would lead the team with a .308 batting average. Elberfeld was a fiery, physical player known for spats with other players and for arguing with umpires—when he wasn't throwing mud in their mouths, which he once did. With the Highlanders four years later, Elberfeld was the player whose hard knees (when applied to the back of one's neck) began to convince then-rookie Ty Cobb not to slide headfirst anymore. After that Cobb came in "spikes first," Elberfeld recalled, "so I had to protect myself."

They were colorful players in colorful times, and, fittingly, there's never been a game with a wilder conclusion than the 1901 Tigers' home opener against the Milwaukee Brewers. Despite the excitement of the day with its pregame parade downtown and with the Tigers

TIGERS OWNERS

They've only had 10 of them.

James D. Burns (1901)—The first owner of the team as an American League franchise, he owned a brickworks and later was sheriff of Detroit. He bought the team for $12,000 and sold it a year later for $20,000.

Samuel F. Angus (1902-03)—His businesses were railways and life insurance. Described as a portly and prosperous gentleman, he started the concept of spring training for the Tigers and signed Sam Crawford.

William H. Yawkey (1904–07)—The son of the richest man in Michigan, he took little interest in the operation of the team, so he left that to Frank Navin. He bequeathed most of his estate to his nephew, Tom, who bought the Boston Red Sox.

Frank Navin (1908–35)—He was the bookkeeper for Angus and worked his way up from there. The month after the Tigers won their first World Series in 1935, and after saying "if we can with it, I could die completely happy," he did exactly that while riding his horse.

Walter O. Briggs Sr. (1936–52)—His business was Briggs Manufacturing, which produced automobile bodies and plumbing fixtures. His teams won one World Series and also lost one while he was owner. He also expanded Navin Field and changed its name to Briggs Stadium.

Walter O. (Spike) Briggs Jr. (1952–56)—He loved owning the team but was forced to sell it by family estate administrators. He stayed on as general manager and executive vice president, but his affiliation with team ended in 1957.

Fred Knorr (1956–60)—A radio executive, he headed the syndicate that bought the team from the Briggs family for $5.5 million. He integrated the team in 1958. He died of burns sustained from a fall into hot bath water.

John E. Fetzer (1961–83)—The broadcast executive built his first radio station when he was 22. He was highly respected in baseball circles but not a hands-on owner. His Tigers won the World Series in 1968.

Tom Monaghan (1983-92)—He founded Domino's Pizza and was owner of the team when it won the World Series in 1984. He sold the Tigers in 1992 and Domino's in 1998 in an effort to divest himself of material luxuries and devote his wealth to Roman Catholic causes.

Mike Ilitch (1992-present)—The founder of Little Caesar's Pizza was a former Tigers minor leaguer. Comerica Park was built during his ownership. He is known for his knowledge of the game and generous player payrolls.

playing a beatable team that would end up 48-89 for the year, the game did not start well for the home team. By the ninth inning, much of the capacity crowd had left. The weather was good—"Just enough breeze to make the air pure and invigorating," according to a local weather report, but the brand of baseball was not.

At least it wasn't good for the home team, spoiling the first eight innings for "the noisy patrons," as they were called. Spectators were both numerous and rambunctious.

An overflow crowd had warranted a ground-rule stipulating that any ball hit into the ring of fans around the outfield would be scored a double.

According to Dennis Pajot's outstanding account for seamheads. com, "Oom Paul, the Tigers' mascot dog, was brought out and placed on home plate," and the band struck up the tune, "There Will Be a Hot Time in the Old Town Tonight." With the music and ceremonies, the day was off to a festive start. And the game followed suit when two Milwaukee base runners were thrown out at the plate in the top of the first—one on a grounder to third, the other on an attempted double steal.

With the help of four Tigers errors in the second inning, though—including two by Elberfeld—the Brewers took a 2-0 lead. They stretched it 7-0 in the third, and by the seventh, it was a 10-3 game. At the end of eight innings, the Brewers led 13-4. Disgruntled fans who had left the ballpark, however, missed what still ranks as the greatest ninth-inning comeback ever.

With Pete Dowling—a gentle but tormented soul whose brief career would end that same season with a 12–25 record and who died four years later when he was struck by a train—on the mound in relief for the Brewers, the Tigers suddenly erupted. One hit followed another. So did the runs. As the crowd became more of a factor around the perimeter of the outfield, the Brewers called for time so encroaching fans could be pushed back.

But when play resumed, the Tigers went right back to hitting—and to scoring.

Milwaukee's lead was quickly cut to seven runs, then to four. This was crazy. This was wild. The Tigers were getting closer and closer. The fans who hadn't left were now totally into the comeback. Men began to throw their hats in the air. By the time Detroit's Frank "Pop" Dillon came to the plate for the second time in the ninth inning—and with three ground-rule doubles in the game already to his credit—the Tigers were behind by only one run with two outs.

It's not known why Dillon was called "Pop," but it was not for the thump in his bat. Dillon hit only one home run as a major leaguer and, beset by appendicitis, he would hit just .208 in 1902. He had one good season in the majors, and 1901 would be it with a .288 batting average. But as Pop stepped up to the plate with a chance to win the game—when just minutes earlier the Tigers had trailed by nine runs—he was about to establish a major league record (which he still shares) with his fourth double.

A few moments later, one can only think that the Milwaukee team could not believe what was happening. Dillon had hit the ball hard and far again. His fly ball disappeared into the ring of fans around the outfield, the same fans who would soon be joyously hoisting him onto their shoulders.

Incredibly, the Tigers had rallied for 10 runs on 10 hits and a walk. Turning resilience into an early habit, they would win their first five games, exploding onto the A.L. scene by coming from behind two more times in the ninth and once in the eighth during the streak. In fact, they would be in first place for the first month of the season before their shortcomings—particularly their defense—caught up with them.

DETROIT TIGERS

No matter how well you hit or pitch as a team, it's difficult to overcome the hole you dig for yourself when you make 410 errors. Granted, the game of baseball was scored differently back in 1901. Many more individual errors were called, the fields were bumpy, and gloves were primitive. *But 410 errors?*

Kid Gleason, the Tigers' second baseman, made 64, Doc Casey, their third baseman, made 58, and now we can understand why Kid Elberfeld was so often in a sour mood. As the Tigers' shortstop in 1901, he was charged with 76 errors. But American League baseball—often for better, sometimes for worse—had come to Detroit to stay.

HILLER'S HEALTH

John Hiller's comeback remains unrivaled. He had his best years—not after struggling or being injured—but after nearly dying. Hiller was 27 years old on the day that would change his life. He was a major league pitcher who routinely woke up on a cold winter morning during the offseason. Nothing was amiss. There was no warning.

Then the pain began. Deep in his chest, down his arm.

It couldn't happen to a man that young, but it did on January 11, 1971. Hiller, a left-hander who'd been with the Tigers for four years, was having a heart attack. "At first, I thought I was having some kind of trouble with my lungs," he said. "I had just returned from a snowmobile trip into the wilderness and was having my usual breakfast of a cigarette and coffee when it hit me."

Not just once, but again and again. "I felt it three times before I went to the hospital," Hiller said. Suddenly it wasn't only his career that was in jeopardy; it was his life. Complications ensued. In one medical procedure, doctors removed seven feet of his intestines. Hiller got weaker. In the weeks ahead, his weight dropped from 210 to 145. Surely his career was over.

Understandably, his family was distraught. "When my mother saw me after I got out of the hospital, she cried," he said. "I'd look at myself and wonder if I was going to live, let alone ever pitch again."

But he survived. Hiller's future was in shambles, though. He missed the entire 1971 season, of course. Nobody recovers from a major medical crisis that quickly. A year later, however, as the 1972 season approached, Hiller needed a job—any job. "I think the Tigers felt sorry for me," he said. "I was broke, had moved in with my in-laws in Duluth...I had nothing."

But finding work did not provide an immediate path to a normal life. "The Tigers hired me for $7,500 that spring to be the pitching coach of their Single A team in Lakeland," Hiller said. "But I sent every check home," which meant he left himself virtually penniless while on the job.

At first, he slept on the floor of the minor league clubhouse and scrounged for leftovers.

"We got $5 per day for our trips," Hiller said. "I'd cut that in half to make it last two days. If I was lucky, I'd have 75 cents on a Friday night to buy myself a beer."

But sleeping on the floor literally made his skin crawl. "When the lights were turned off at night, that's when the roaches came out," he said. "Hundreds of them, climbing on my mattress, climbing on me...I couldn't sleep, knowing the roaches were crawling around me."

Getting enough to eat was just as much of a challenge. "When the clubhouse guy was about to throw out the old bologna or ham," said Hiller, "I'd save it. I saved the cheese, too. I'd keep it all so long, I eventually had to cut the green mold off it. God, that was awful. For breakfast I found a local restaurant that would give me a lot of oatmeal for $1. The perk was that when no one was looking, I'd grab extra crackers so I could make a sandwich with the old meat when I got back to the clubhouse."

Back from death's doorstep, this was no way to live. Hiller could not go on that way. After begging the Tigers for a room in the dorm, he finally moved out of the clubhouse. But Hiller knew time was running out. His minor league job was designed to be temporary.

"One day in Vero Beach," he said, "I saw [Tigers general manager Jim Campbell] out near some outfield seats. It was unusual for him to be in Florida for our games after the big club left, but I knew why he was. I went straight up to him and said, 'If you're here to release me, forget it.' And I walked away. He later told me that's exactly why he was there."

What Hiller really wanted was to start pitching again, but getting medical clearance proved to be a major obstacle. One cardiologist after another told him he was done. Eventually, there was only one hope left. "Dr. Clarence Livingood was the team doctor," Hiller said. "The man was a saint. He refused to give up on me, but the cardiologist who was going to see me, the doctor that Clarence sent me to, was also President Johnson's doctor. That got complicated. Because of the president's problems, the doctor had to cancel appointments with me twice. I understood that, naturally, but it was a difficult time. I'd always thought of myself as a fighter...still, when it happened a second time, I had to go home to Duluth to see my family."

Hiller had survived his heart attack. He also had overcome the indignity of sleeping with roaches and eating moldy food. But down to his last doctor, with his future hanging in the balance, was he ever going to get a break?

Eventually, he did. Hiller's third appointment wasn't canceled, so off to Atlanta he went with the hope of salvaging his career. This time the diagnosis was different than any previous finding. "After all sorts of tests, the doctor said he could have me pitching again in a matter of weeks," Hiller said. "Without that and Dr. Livingood's faith in me, I really don't know how my life would have turned out."

Getting his medical clearance was tough enough, but what manager would be bold enough to take a chance on him? Before his heart attack, Hiller hadn't exactly established himself as indispensable. "I hadn't been much of a pitcher," he said," just a left-handed spot starter who wasn't in very good shape."

But now Hiller was in the best physical condition of his playing career. What's more, he had learned to throw a pitch that changed his career. "Before adding a change-up," he said, "I had an all right fastball and a little curve but nothing else." There was no way, though, to judge Hiller's potential effectiveness like they do in today's game. "Remember," he said, "it was 1972. There were no rehab assignments back then, and I hadn't faced a batter in a year and a half.

"But [Tigers manager] Billy Martin kept asking for me. I don't really know why because I wasn't that great of a pitcher before, but Billy was in my corner. He kept saying, 'Get me Hiller.'"

What Billy wanted, Billy usually got. Even so, it was no minor miracle that on July 8, 1972, Hiller returned to a major league mound in a game against the Chicago White Sox.

"I pitched three innings," Hiller said. "Dick Allen hit a home run off me, a ball he nearly hit completely out of Comiskey Park. But I didn't walk anyone my last two innings, and that really impressed Billy."

Not only that, but Martin loudly let it be known that he was impressed. "To this day," Hiller said, "I can hear him saying to the other pitchers in the dugout, 'this [f---ing] guy comes back from the dead and throws strikes right away. How come you guys can't throw strikes like that?'"

Incredibly, Hiller was back. He didn't walk anyone in his next eight appearances and put together a 2.03 ERA with a 1–2 record in 24 appearances for the Tigers the rest of that season.

He also worked three and a third scoreless innings in the 1972 American League Championship Series against the Oakland A's that the Tigers lost in five games.

Poised to become a major contributor in 1973, Hiller advanced directly to stardom. He saved 38 games for the Tigers, 11 more than Sparky Lyle saved for the New York Yankees as the A.L.'s runner-up in saves. Hiller's 65 appearances also led the league. With every hurdle cleared, he was among the best relief pitchers in baseball—if not the best. "I just wanted to get back to baseball," he said of his ordeal. "But I can't say I envisioned anything I eventually accomplished."

Those accomplishments included recording a 1.44 ERA in 1973 and winning 17 games in 1974—two of the most amazing seasons ever for a Tigers relief pitcher. His biggest victory, though, is the same now that it was then. John Hiller's story was a profile in perseverance if ever there was one.

THE KUENN/COLAVITO TRADE

Within 48 hours of their first game in 1960, the Tigers stunned the baseball world by trading a steak for a hamburger. But they got the last laugh because the burger was better. The Tigers dealt Harvey Kuenn to the Cleveland Indians for Rocky Colavito on April 17, 1960, the first and only time a batting champion has ever been traded for a home run champion.

Opening Day was just two days away. So, understandably, the deal jolted both players and both teams. For that matter, it rocked both cities—a blockbuster trade if ever there was one. Cleveland's general manager Frank Lane was stunned that Indians fans hated it. In parting with Colavito for Kuenn, Lane explained he had acquired a steak for a hamburger. Tigers president Bill DeWitt countered by saying he liked hamburger. And with that, the Tigers completed one of the most memorable deals of their existence—Kuenn for Colavito, a hitter for a slugger.

It was bold. It was big. It's been fun to talk about ever since, though not so much for Indians fans because one club clearly got the better of it, and that club was the Tigers.

As suddenly agreed upon as the trade—with its huge headlines—seemed to be, the two teams had discussed it for weeks. One tried harder to discuss it than the other, though, because the Indians really wanted Kuenn. But their first offer for him—a package of players that would not have come close to impacting the Tigers the way that Colavito did—was rejected. The Indians' interest, though, didn't vanish.

Make no mistake, Kuenn, the American League's Rookie of the Year as a shortstop in 1953, a batting champ with a .353 average in 1959, and a hitter still in his prime after compiling a .314 average in eight seasons for Detroit, had been a quality player for the Tigers. They had listened to the Indians' overtures for him—but only sort of. Even so, the rumors wouldn't go away. In February, Tigers general manager Rick Ferrell discounted the chance of a trade, saying, "That's mostly Frank Lane talking because he's not been able to get Rocky to sign a contract yet."

But in March, the buzz got so hot that the two teams, in a highly unusual move, called a press conference to announce that the deal was dead—when it really wasn't. Simultaneously to being told the fire was out, it was learned that the two teams had discussed it for three hours.

"I asked Frank to come over here [to Lakeland, Florida] because I think Kuenn possibly has the idea that a deal is in the wind," DeWitt told reporters. "While Mr. Lane has a high regard for Kuenn, he also has a very high regard for Colavito. There is no deal at this time. This press conference is to let Harvey know that if he signs, it will be with Detroit."

At the time, Kuenn was balking at the contract being offered to him by the Tigers. But within 24 hours of hearing that talks were off, he signed for $45,000. Although secretly concerned his legs were getting heavy, the Tigers valued Kuenn to the extent that he was going to earn $3,000 more in 1960 than Al Kaline, who, in turn, was about to make more than any Tiger since Hal Newhouser in 1951.

Even then, the rumors would not go away for two reasons: the Tigers needed power and were intrigued with the idea of acquiring Colavito's home run bat and they were dealing with a general manager who wasn't called "Trader Lane" for nothing. Lane already had made a deal with the Tigers that spring, sending little known first baseman/outfielder (and future batting champ) Norm Cash to Detroit for infielder Steve Demeter.

But the Kuenn/Colavito talks were higher profile. If the trade could be worked out, it was going to be huge. "Anything can happen because baseball is a day-to-day, almost pitch-by-pitch business," said Lane, refusing to let the flame go out. "I'm very strong for Kuenn, but there is just no meeting of the minds at this time."

The deal that wouldn't die was made six weeks later. Those words were spoken on March 6. Spring training had just begun, and the Tigers' season wouldn't start until April 19. There was plenty of time for the two front offices to mull it over despite their denials.

Contrary to the way Lane characterized it, a steak had been traded for a steak. Both Colavito and Kuenn were impact players, but the swap turned out lopsidedly in Detroit's favor.

Colavito hit 139 home runs in four years for the Tigers. Kuenn hit .308 for the Indians in 1960 but was traded to the San Francisco Giants after the season for outfielder Willie Kirkland and pitcher Johnny Antonelli. Those Indians fans old enough to remember it still rue the day that the Kuenn/Colavito deal was made. Attendance tanked in Cleveland that season.

Bad became worse after that for the Indians, who wouldn't top more than a million fans at the gate again until 1974. Trashing the player he'd just traded, Lane explained his end by telling *The Sporting News*, "he'll hit you a home run about every 14th time at-bat. But he'll kill you with plenty of nothing on the other 13. Home runs are over-emphasized."

Lane said he traded 40 home runs for 40 doubles, but he had also added 50 singles for 50 strikeouts. Kuenn was told of the deal while smoking a cigar in front of his locker. He reacted by stoically saying, "these things happen in baseball." Colavito was told while he played in an exhibition game in Memphis as the Indians made their way home from spring training. He was on first base when manager Joe Gordon came out to remove him from the game, saying, "Rocky, you've just been traded."

Colavito reacted with shock. So did his batting average. In what he called the worst game of his life, he went 0-for-6 on Opening Day for the Tigers against his former teammates, striking out four times and hitting into a double play. As fate would have it, the Tigers and Indians opened the season against each other in Cleveland. With two hits in his debut, Kuenn fared better than Colavito, but neither performance had any bearing on the outcome—a 4–2 Tigers victory in 15 innings.

Kuenn got off to a slow start with the Indians. After 11 games, the first four of which the Indians lost—much to the increasing chagrin of a grumbling fanbase—he was hitting .216.

Catching fire after that, he hit .432 in his next 11 games, but attendance was already suffering. For a day game on April 30 against Kansas City, the Indians drew 3,666.

Colavito, meanwhile, bounced back from his Opening Day debacle by hitting home runs in each of his next three games as the Tigers ran their season-opening winning streak to five.

But his productivity at that point took a nap. In his next 26 games, Colavito hit .138 with just one home run, so by early June the deal was looking like a dud for both teams.

It didn't stay that way, though. As the weather warmed, so did Colavito. In the months of June and July, he hit .308 with 17 home runs and 44 RBIs.

But the final verdict about the trade took shape more in 1961 than in 1960. With career highs of 45 home runs and 140 RBIs, Colavito helped the Tigers win 101 games in 1961, while Antonelli—the two-time 20-game winner the Indians acquired from the Giants for Kuenn after the 1960 season—didn't win a game for Cleveland. With a 0–4 record, Antonelli was sold to the Milwaukee Braves in July. Kirkland, the outfielder the Indians received in the Giants' deal, averaged 21 home runs and 71 RBIs in three seasons for Cleveland while hitting .232. Despite the fact that Kirkland led the team with 27 home runs and 95 RBIs in 1961, Indians fans still pined for their darling Rocky.

Kuenn-for-Colavito wasn't a perfect trade for either team. It made the Tigers better but didn't win them a pennant. And when it came time for the Tigers to part with Colavito, which they did in a deal with Kansas City after the 1963 season, they were happy—but also relieved—it was happening. Colavito had become a headache to Tigers management, which he felt didn't fully appreciate him. He told Joe Falls of the *Detroit Free Press* that he was "glad to get away from Detroit…from the front office."

The headlines that bade farewell to Colavito were a lot smaller than those that had said hello. But that's understandable because no matter who'd been the steak that April day in 1960, there had never been a bigger trade.

WILLIE HERNANDEZ

With spring training of 1984 winding down, the Tigers had been on trade alert for a week. But instead of couching their expectations about the likelihood of a deal, they were saying one was likely by Opening Day. "I hope there is a trade," said manager Sparky Anderson. "I would bet there will be." The Tigers were looking for a left-handed pitcher and a left-handed hitter. But they had just told free-agent outfielder Oscar Gamble "no thank you." Something else was stirring, something significant.

On March 24, they announced what it was. In a trade with the Philadelphia Phillies, the Tigers had landed what they needed—Willie Hernandez and Dave Bergman. In return, they parted with catcher John Wockenfuss and Glenn Wilson, a young outfielder with potential.

As with any trade, the Tigers didn't know how it would turn out. Some deals had burned them. But they were immediately confident about this one, even though they initially had tried to pry outfielder Greg Gross loose from the Phillies. When they couldn't land Gross, Bergman became their target. The problem with turning their attention to Bergman was that he was a member of the San Francisco Giants—not the Phillies—at the start of the day on which the trade was made. A deal between those two teams had to be engineered before a swap involving Detroit could be finalized. Using whatever leverage they had, the Tigers were insistent. "Bill Lajoie made the Phillies go get Bergman," Anderson said in praise of the Tigers' general manager.

Fortunately for the Tigers, the Giants agreed to send Bergman to the Phillies for outfielder Alejandro Sanchez, a perennial prospect who ended up as a Tiger in 1985. Sanchez's predictable downfall was his over-aggressiveness, among other shortcomings. In 215 career plate appearances in the majors, he walked only once. But the Giants liked Sanchez's raw talent enough to part with Bergman, and the Phillies, in turn, quickly gave the Tigers what they wanted for Wockenfuss and Wilson.

Catcher Lance Parrish hugs Willie Hernandez after the 1984 Cy Young and MVP closes out Game 5, the final game of the 1984 World Series. (AP Images)

The early verdict was that the Tigers gave up too much. In fact, with 1,140 *Detroit Free Press* readers calling in to express their opinion, 52 percent didn't like the deal. "They gave up the next Mickey Stanley," one caller said. "Trading Wilson will haunt Sparky," another said. Among those who liked it, one said, "the Tigers got a good reliever in Hernandez. That beats two utilitymen any day."

With an odd batting stance, Wockenfuss had been popular with the fans. But in 10 seasons with the Tigers, he'd had more than 200 at-bats only three times. Plus he'd gotten noisy with his feelings of being underpaid and had recently said he would welcome a trade. Tired of his grousing, the Tigers welcomed it as well.

A Delaware resident, Wockenfuss had hoped to be traded to the Phillies, so he'd actually be home when the team was home. He was thrilled to get his way, but after one typically useful season with the Phillies, his playing career ended in 1985. Wilson, meanwhile, had indeed looked like the next Mickey Stanley when he came up to the majors in 1982. Not only did he play a superb center field as a rookie, but he also hit .292.

By 1984, however, when an experiment to move him to third base ended early in spring training, Wilson neither knew what position, nor how often he would play. In the weeks before the trade, he drifted into and out of the Tigers' plans while fans complained of Sparky's "shabby" treatment of him. Chances are Anderson already knew that Wilson would be playing for another team by the end of March. Upon being told of the deal, Wilson said he was "bitter about some things, but am tickled to death." Asked what he was bitter about, he replied that his mother had always told him, "Don't say nothing bad, if you don't have nothing nice to say."

Wilson would be an All-Star in 1985, his second year with the Phillies, but never again achieved that status in a major league career that lasted 10 years. It was mostly because of Wilson's perceived potential that the deal wasn't immediately popular with the majority of Tigers fans. But before long, nothing mattered more than the Tigers' spectacular start.

The start was so compelling, in fact, that it wasn't even an issue that Hernandez had a 4.86 ERA with only two saves by the end of April and still hadn't taken over as the full-time closer. Or that Bergman was hitting .200. The Tigers were 18–2—en route to 35–5.

They had proceeded directly to first place and seemed intent on staying there—with or without significant contributions from their new acquisitions. As it turned out, the season unfolded with their help, not

THE ROLLER COASTER

With 235 of them, Todd Jones is the Tigers' all-time leader in saves. He was with the Tigers twice—the first time in 1997–2001, the second in 2006–2008. Upon his Detroit return, he felt he was a more complete pitcher. "The difference was that when I came back, I was finally able to command multiple pitches," he said.

But there was a downside to Jones, one he acknowledged as the years went by. He fit Ernie Harwell's nickname for him. He was the "Roller Coaster." "I don't know that I wore the label with pride," Jones said for a Detroit Tigers program piece honoring the 2006 World Series team, "but I earned it."

In Jones' first stint with the Tigers, he saved 142 games—topped by a career high 42 in 2000. He was an American League All-Star that year and also won the A.L. Rolaids Relief award. "But I wasn't as good as I thought I was," he said.

When he was traded to the Minnesota Twins in 2001, it ushered tougher times. "Two teams released me," he said.

It wasn't until 2005, when he saved 40 games for the Florida Marlins, that Jones again established himself among the game's premier closers. The Tigers signed him as a free agent after that season, and in the next three years he saved 93 games for them. "I came back a totally different pitcher and a totally different person," he said. "I also came back with a better understanding of what Detroit meant to me."

In other words, Jones returned older and wiser. "In many ways, it felt like I'd never gone," he said. "But I think I was proudest of this: when I pitched bad, I'd just keep chugging along."

There was no better evidence of his persistence than during the Tigers' World Series season of 2006. After struggling early, Jones had a 1.66 ERA and 20 saves in his last 37 appearances of the season. In those appearances the Tigers went 32–5. Riding the "Roller Coaster" was fun that season.

without, and May would be the month in which the dividends of the deal began to pay off. Bergman hit .372 in May, a sizzling stretch that led up to his memorable 13-pitch home run on June 4 against Toronto Blue Jays pitcher Roy Lee Jackson.

For Hernandez, the pendulum of personal momentum finally swung to his side after a dreadful second half of April. The best that can be said of the way Hernandez pitched in his last six April appearances is that it didn't prevent the Tigers from winning five of the six games. But in them he had a 7.45 ERA while allowing 20 base runners (on 14 hits and six walks) in nine and two-third innings.

Fortunately for the Tigers, Aurelio Lopez got the job done when Hernandez didn't.

Despite their hot start, the Tigers needed their ballyhooed bullpen acquisition to start pitching well, which he began to do, oddly enough, after a brush with what would have been another discouraging development

On May 4 in Cleveland, Hernandez was called upon to replace starter Dan Petry in the sixth inning against the Indians. Petry hadn't been particularly sharp. In fact, he said, "I was bad," which seemed harsh because the Tigers had a 5–2 lead. When pinch-hitter Carmelo Castillo, the first batter Hernandez faced, launched a ball to deep right-center field, it looked like the Tigers' three-run lead was about to drop to two. However, Chet Lemon timed his leap at the wall perfectly to take a home run away from Castillo. Relieved to be reprieved, Hernandez went on to earn his only four-inning save as a Tiger.

He still wasn't their primary closer, though. It wouldn't be until the second week of June that Hernandez took over the team lead in saves from Lopez. But the four-inning save was a sign that the worst of his struggles were over. In his last 65 appearances of 1984, Hernandez went 8–3 with 28 saves and a 1.52 ERA. But numbers alone don't convey how important he was to the Tigers. "I said this over and over," Anderson once recalled when comparing the Tigers to the second-place Blue Jays, "if they'd had Hernandez, they would have led us by more than we led them. They had a nice blend of power and speed, but every time I called the bullpen, someone came in to do the job for us. Every time they called, they got a wrong number."

Hernandez won both the American League's Cy Young and Most Valuable Player Awards. Willie's only blown save was caused by a sacrifice fly in the Tigers' 160th game. The run was charged to Bill Scherrer, but Hernandez was saddled with a blown save after he'd been successful in 32 consecutive save situations. Following the game, Anderson openly regretted using Hernandez in a meaningless situation with the pennant already won.

Willie offset that relatively minor setback by finishing the season's three biggest games: the Tigers' East division clincher, their A.L. pennant clincher against the Kansas City Royals, and, finally, the game in which they won the World Series against the San Diego Padres. With the victory against the Padres, Sparky's prediction from the previous year came true. When Anderson watched Hernandez toss three perfect innings against the Baltimore Orioles in Game 5 of the 1983 World Series, he told Lajoie, according to Danny Knobler's book *Numbers Don't Lie* "You get that guy, and we'll win the World Series."

The following spring, Lajoie did get that guy.

It would never get better, though, than that 1984 season for Hernandez. The day before he won the Cy Young Award, he demanded a trade, which was a formality—"more of a request than a demand," said Tigers president Jim Campbell—it made Willie look self-centered.

He eventually signed a five-year contract extension that kept him with the Tigers through 1989, but there were turbulent times ahead. His ERA climbed three years in a row, and he averaged only 11 saves per season during the last three years of his contract as Mike Henneman took over as the Tigers' closer. Opting in 1988 to be known as Guillermo, Hernandez stopped talking to the media at times and achieved additional notoriety one spring by dumping a bucket of water over the head of columnist Mitch Albom. The reality was that Hernandez's first year as a Tiger would remain by far his best.

But when he returned to Detroit in 2009 for the 25th reunion of the 1984 team, he hugged the reporters he once snubbed and had tears in his eyes while reminiscing. Even though he gradually slid from the summit of what he accomplished his first year, that first season still glows in retrospect. "I will always be a Tiger," Hernandez said at the 1984 reunion.

More than that, he'll always be remembered for a trade well worth making—and for a season well worth honoring.

37

BERGMAN'S 13-PITCH HOME RUN

he Tigers were hitting their speed bump. How big would it be? Encountering a hint of trouble in 1984 following their stunning 35-5 start, the Tigers couldn't be sure if they were caught in a momentary ricochet—or the start of a slump. After winning 16 of 17 while grabbing an eight and a half game lead in the American League East—a successful stretch that included a 9-0 roll—the Tigers stubbed their toe by losing six of nine. And nine of 15 before their next winning streak of at least three games.

But just as their start hadn't gone to their heads, spinning their wheels didn't worry the Tigers. They didn't overreact to either. Plus they were too smart, and far too cautious, to think that in June they were already on their way to winning the pennant. If anything, their dominating start put pressure on them. There was still time for a team in their rearview mirror to get hot, make some noise, and to give them a scare.

One team in particular, the Toronto Blue Jays, looked capable of doing just that. While the Tigers were sprinting to 35-5, the Blue Jays had put together a tidy 26-14 start. But both teams knew it was still early enough for the rest of the season to matter far more than the games already played. Such a scenario, in fact, would play out in the league's other division.

The Kansas City Royals were 17-23 in the A.L. West after 40 games but ended up winning the division by three games over the California Angels and Minnesota Twins, both of whom had been 21-19 after 40 games. Moral of the story: as May becomes June, no team is home free.

To make matters even more muddled, the Blue Jays were hot. With a 15-2 streak, they'd taken a chunk out of the Tigers' lead. By the time the Jays arrived at Tiger Stadium for the start of a four-game series on June 4, the two teams were only four and a half games apart.

Tigers first baseman Dave Bergman was on quite a roll, too. Acquired at the end of spring training in the deal that also brought relief pitcher Willie Hernandez from the Philadelphia Phillies to the Tigers, Bergman started slowly in his part-time role, hitting .172 in April.

The Tigers insisted he hadn't been a throw-in, but judging from early returns, that's what he looked like.

As cold as Bergman was in April, however, he was every bit as hot in May, hitting .372.

He hadn't yet hit a home run as a Tiger, but Bergman never needed to hit home runs to contribute offensively. He would not have played 17 years in the majors had he been dependent on his power. "Bergie was the ultimate grinder," Alan Trammell said. "It wasn't always pretty the way he hit, but I mean that as a compliment. He was a guy who showed that if you put your heart and soul into it, you could get something done."

Against the encroaching Blue Jays—"they weren't that far away from us," Trammell said—Bergman would again get something done. Trammell called it "the biggest at-bat of the regular season."

The Tigers and Jays were tied 3–3 in the 10th inning of a Monday night game at Tiger Stadium. With a Toronto win in the series opener, the two teams would have been separated by only three and a half games. Down early but with Bergman's help, the Tigers had bounced back from a 3–0 deficit on Howard Johnson's three-run home run off the right-field foul pole in the seventh. After Chet Lemon was hit by a pitch, Bergman singled him to second. That's when Johnson connected with one out off starter Dave Stieb.

In the eighth inning, Hernandez did a masterful job of dodging damage after the Jays put a runner on third with no outs. But the Tigers would waste a chance, too. After Bergman led off the bottom of the ninth with a walk, the Tigers came away empty from a second-and-third threat, which only stoked the growing tension at Tiger Stadium. "That was the kind of game it was. Everyone was scratching and clawing at each other," Kirk Gibson told George Cantor in his book *Wire to Wire: Inside the 1984 Detroit Tigers' Championship Season.*

Undaunted by not ending the game in the ninth, Lance Parrish led off the bottom of the 10th inning with a single off reliever Jimmy Key, who became a starting pitcher for the Jays the following season.

Parrish advanced to second on a bunt by Darrell Evans, the only sacrifice with which Evans was credited that season.

Jays manager Bobby Cox replaced Key at that point with right-hander Roy Lee Jackson, who'd been having an outstanding season until his last two appearances. Jackson was nearly untouchable in his first 17 games with a 1.17 ERA, not to mention a .156 opponents' batting average. But he had suddenly stumbled by allowing five runs on six hits and four walks in his last three innings. Fortunately for the Jays, his hiccups occurred in two games they won, but they were rough outings all the same.

Facing the Tigers with Parrish on second, Jackson retired the first batter easily enough when Rusty Kuntz tapped a pitch back to the mound. With first base open, Lemon followed with a two-out, four-pitch unintentional walk. Even when a pitcher was inclined to do so, it wasn't entirely easy to walk Lemon, who was an aggressive swinger. The pass from Jackson was Lemon's only walk in a stretch of 11 games.

Going against righty-lefty percentages, it appeared that Jackson preferred his chances with Bergman instead of with Lemon, who came into the game hitting .315 with 10 home runs. But wary of the control problems he had encountered in his previous two appearances, Jackson didn't want to compound one walk with another. Bergman, in other words, would get pitches to swing at, setting the stage for an epic showdown. Tigers coach Dick Tracewski, in fact, would later praise the upcoming at-bat as "the best I've ever seen."

Bergman fouled off the first five offerings from Jackson, miring himself in a two-strike hole right away. On the first 0-2 pitch to him, Bergman had spoiled a good breaking ball. On the second he bounced the ball down the right-field line. On the third he fouled it back into the stands. A strike away from getting out of the inning, Jackson couldn't finish him off. Bergman didn't chase the next pitch, a high fastball, an easy offering to take.

But the next one wasn't easy. The seventh pitch was the closest call of all. Jays catcher Buck Martinez didn't complain when Jackson's 1-2 fastball was called a ball for missing the outside corner. But to this day there are those—many Toronto fans, for instance—who insist the pitch was a strike. Or should have been. Umpire Terry Cooney, though, was not among them.

By this time Jackson had tried everything. In a 2015 interview with *The Detroit News*, he said, "I'm on the mound wondering, *Man, would this guy please strike out—or make an out or something.*" Jackson missed low on 2-2 but caught Bergman off balance with his first full-count pitch. Somehow the Tigers' first baseman got a piece of it. Incredibly, Bergman also fouled off the next two offerings. Of the showdown's first 12 pitches, he spoiled nine of them.

But he put the 13th pitch in play.

Swinging at a slider that was inside and barely off the ground, Bergman golfed it into the air and deep to right. Once the ball was in flight, it became a no-doubter. The battle with Jackson ended with Bergman belting a three-run home run into the upper deck at Tiger Stadium.

And the upshot of it was huge.

Instead of the Tigers' lead being reduced, Bergman's heroics allowed them to minimize the effect of losses in the next two games. Before the end of the month, their lead over the Blue Jays would be up to 10 games. The Tigers would eventually win it all—the division, the pennant, and the World Series—leading wire to wire.

Bergman would suffer from cancer. He fought the disease just as determinedly as he fouled off Jackson's pitches before succumbing on February 2, 2015. "I was really heartbroken," Jackson said after learning of Bergman's death. "I thought really highly of the guy."

So did the Tigers. "He was as fine a teammate as you could have," Trammell said, "a good friend who was always there for you, someone who would give you tough advice, maybe not always what you wanted to hear, but truthful."

That was Dave Bergman—always down to earth, a hardworking, intelligent hitter and individual, he often acknowledged that it was the "thrill of my life to hit that home run." Typically analytical, Bergman told *The New York Times*: "It was a slider about six inches off the ground. Probably ball four. But when you have your good concentration, you can hit a bad pitch. There comes a time when a hitter puts all his mechanics together."

ARMANDO GALARRAGA

AND OTHER

NEAR-PERFECT

GAMES

There have been three of them. Since they joined the American League in 1901, the Tigers have come within an out of throwing a perfect game three times—only to have each of the dreams vanish abruptly and sometimes tearfully. The close-call pitchers were Tommy Bridges in 1932, Milt Wilcox in 1983, and—most excruciatingly—Armando Galarraga in 2010. Their disappointments provided vivid memories for multiple generations of fans.

Galarraga was famously victimized by an incorrect call at first base. The two other bids ended with pinch-hit singles. All three gems shared the dismay of nearing—without crossing—perfection's finish line. The reactions to coming close, however, remain as different as the eras in which the flirtations with fame occurred.

In Bridges' case, for instance, Washington Senators manager Walter Johnson was criticized for using a pinch-hitter for the pitcher with two outs in the ninth inning of a lopsided game. To his credit, Bridges, the slim right-hander who weighed only 155 pounds, never complained. He wanted to earn a perfect game—not be handed it with an easy 27th out.

The way in which Galarraga's bid ended was the cruelest, of course, because he deserved it but was deprived of the prize. The timing also was unfortunate because it occurred when his career was in urgent need of a boost. Galarraga had shown promise as part of the Tigers' starting rotation in 2008, demonstrating an ability to win games at the major league level. Through August he was 12–4 with a 3.05 ERA in 24 starts. Then he slumped in September and didn't win four other games, which had been quality starts.

Despite struggling late the year before, Galarraga went into 2009 with a guaranteed spot in the Tigers' rotation and seemed to pick up where he left off by compiling a 3–0 record with a 1.85 ERA by the end of April. But his next 10 starts, in which he went 0–7 with a 7.48 ERA, were disastrous. Galarraga's consistency utterly vanished—and with it went his effectiveness. It still hadn't returned in 2010 when he went to the mound on June 2 for a Wednesday night start against the Cleveland Indians at Comerica Park.

Coming into the game with a 10–20 record since late April, the Indians were struggling, too. A start against them looked like a good chance for Galarraga to climb out of his rut. The pace of the game was rapid from the outset. Galarraga got through the top of the first with nine pitches. With only 55 more, he cruised through the next six innings, retiring the side in order, out by out, inning by inning.

By the end of the seventh with the Tigers leading 1–0 and the Indians still hitless, the familiar buzz that accompanies a no-hit bid could be heard throughout the crowd of 17,738.

This, however, was more than a chance at a no-hitter. Galarraga hadn't allowed a base runner yet. What's more, he had gone to a three-ball count only once. Not only was the performance a case of Galarraga being at his best, it also was worthy of anyone's best. But could it continue? He had never thrown a complete game in the majors.

In the eighth inning, Galarraga waltzed through Cleveland's 4-5-6 hitters without anything more ominous than Travis Hafner's tricky grounder to shortstop Ramon Santiago.

The Tigers' offense, meanwhile, scored two more runs in the eighth, sending Galarraga out for the ninth with a 3–0 lead instead of the one-run edge he'd been protecting.

Then he got a huge boost from his defense. On Galarraga's first pitch in the ninth, Tigers center fielder Austin Jackson robbed Mark Grudzielanek of extra bases by ranging deep into the left-center-field gap to keep the bid alive. "Oh, my goodness!" broadcaster Mario Impemba gasped when Jackson caught the ball with his back to the plate.

"Jackson! Boy, did he cover some real estate," added a bellowing Rod Allen, Impemba's partner in the booth. "He looked like a young Willie Mays!" He did, indeed. "That's the most fun call I've ever made," Allen said. "I literally jumped out of my seat."

Galarraga was two outs away from throwing the first perfect game in Tigers history before Mike Redmond grounded out to short.

Standing between Galarraga and a permanent place in the Tigers' record books was shortstop Jason Donald and first-base umpire Jim Joyce, it turned out. Swinging at the first pitch, Donald hit a grounder wide of first base, which Miguel Cabrera raced over to field. All Galarraga had to do was catch the throw from Cabrera, which he did, and to step on the bag ahead of Donald, which he also did.

But to everyone's thunderstruck shock, Joyce called Donald safe. It's true that the ball rolled a bit in the webbing of Galarraga's glove,

Tigers pitcher Armando Galarraga beats Jason Donald to the first-base bag, though umpire Jim Joyce would call Donald safe, ruining Galarraga's perfect game. (AP Images)

but that wasn't the deciding factor. It's also true that it was a bang-bang play, but Joyce, a respected umpire, had gotten countless close calls right during his career. "Jim Joyce, no," Impemba groaned, his voice trailing off in disbelief.

The umpire had make a critical mistake. "I missed it," a tearful Joyce said after watching the replay. "The biggest call of my life, and I got it wrong. I took it away from that kid, and I'm totally sorry. Nobody feels worse than I do. If I could get it back for him, I would. When I told him that, he hugged me."

The lasting impression of how Galarraga handled the situation is not one of anger or bitterness but of class and understanding. "When I saw how totally out the runner was, it made me a little bit sad," he said. "But right away the umpire apologized to me. He felt really bad. His eyes were watering. What more could I do than hug him and move on?"

After initially being upset, Tigers manager Jim Leyland took a similar approach. "It wasn't a belligerent mistake. It was an innocent mistake," Leyland said. "That's just the human element of the game."

Galarraga's career went into a tailspin after that. He went 5–16 in the three seasons that followed, which included stints with the Arizona Diamondbacks and Houston Astros. For the grace with which he handled a difficult situation, however, he won't be forgotten.

The other close calls didn't end as emotionally. Wilcox wasn't the victim of a wrong call but of missing his mark by a fraction of an inch. Facing pinch-hitter Jerry Hairston of the White Sox with two outs in the ninth on April 15, 1983, a perfect game was in the offing on a chilly Friday night in Chicago. But Wilcox didn't get his first pitch as far inside as he wanted. "Missed it by about a quarter of an inch," he said. For that, though, he paid the highest of prices when Hairston hit a clean single up the middle. "If I throw that ball where I should have," Wilcox said, "it's a ground ball to second base. It's a perfect game."

Instead, the ball "was hit in a spot where neither I nor Lou [Whitaker] had any chance for it," said shortstop Alan Trammell.

For Hairston, though, a playful comment with a radio producer had become a prophecy.

ANOTHER DISPUTED CALL

To this day, Brandon Inge insists he was hit by the pitch. And based on the replay, it's hard to say he wasn't. But only one opinion, the one that belonged to plate umpire Randy Marsh, counted. In a sense the Tigers were already in the postseason. They were playing their 163rd game of 2009. The score against the Minnesota Twins at the Metrodome was tied at five.

The winner would be champions of the American League Central; the losing team would go home.

After the Twins scored the winning run in the bottom of the 12th, it would be the Tigers going home. Compounding their disappointment, the Tigers had also lost a pivotal dispute, one that, if it had gone their way, would have given them the lead in the top of the 12th inning. With runners at second and third and one out, the Twins opted to intentionally walk Ryan Raburn in the hope that Inge would hit into an inning-ending double play.

But relief pitcher Bobby Keppel, in his only season with the Twins, threw a first-pitch fastball that rode in on Inge, either brushing his uniform or coming close enough to convince Inge it had. If Marsh had agreed that it hit him, the tie-breaking run would have been forced in from third. But Marsh didn't concur, and it had a huge impact on the outcome.

As it turned out, Inge hit into a fielder's choice on a 2-2 pitch, forcing Miguel Cabrera at the plate. Gerald Laird ended the threat by striking out. "It still kind of makes me mad," Inge said on a visit to Comerica Park several years later. "But looking back on it, both teams were done after that game. We could have gotten smacked by the Yankees the same way the Twins did."

Even so, Inge would have enjoyed having that chance. "I had a good relationship with all the umpires, but I told Randy he was dead wrong about the call," Inge said. "I wasn't going to lie to weasel my way on base. It hit my shirt. He wasn't budging, though, so nothing was going to get accomplished."

To Inge, the importance of the game outweighed the call, which was why he didn't put up more of an argument at the time. "No way was I getting kicked out of that game," he said. "It was one of the best I ever played in."

Manager Jim Leyland went out to speak with Marsh, hoping he would ask for a second opinion, but Marsh said he didn't need one. He was adamant about the call. So it stood. Watching the replay the Tigers remained convinced that Marsh missed it, but Leyland didn't want to dwell on it because "It would have sounded like sour grapes."

Marsh later said the replay was inconclusive. The Tigers had no recourse but to move on to their offseason while the Twins moved on to the playoffs.

When he heard in the seventh inning that the postgame show wanted to interview "whoever gets the hit," if there was one, Hairston replied, "Tell him I'll be there." And sure enough, he was.

Bridges' bid took place in Detroit—as did Galarraga's—but 78 years apart. Anticipation of perfection's final out, however, is timeless. En route to winning 20-plus games in three consecutive seasons (1934–36), Bridges was just getting established as a starter in the majors when he went to the mound on August 5, 1932.

Other than a sharp curveball, there'd been little to indicate that he was capable of flirting with a perfect game. In his previous start, for instance, Bridges was knocked out after four innings against the New York Yankees. And although they weren't the first-place Yankees, the Senators—who'd eventually win 93 games that year—were no slouches.

From the outset, the game belonged to the Tigers. With seven runs in the fourth inning and another four in the eighth, they took a 13–0 lead into the top of the ninth. Bridges would face the 7-8-9 hitters in the Senators' lineup, and the first two caused no problems. Ossie Bluege grounded out to third; Howard Maples took a called third strike.

Pitcher Bob Burke was the next scheduled hitter, but the game was well out of reach for the Senators with one out to go. Would Johnson send his pitcher up to hit, as the clamoring crowd at Navin Field obviously wanted? Or would he go to his bench for a pinch-hitter?

Judging by how long he stared at the ground after Maples struck out, Johnson considered both options. Then, from first base where he was coaching, he pointed to Dave Harris to hit for Burke. Unfortunately for Bridges, Harris was an accomplished pinch-hitter.

On the first pitch thrown to him, he lofted a troublesome pop-up over second base. Four Tigers converged on it, but no one could reach it. The ball fell for a single. The perfect game was gone. Speaking later to the *Detroit Free Press*, Harris was matter of fact about his role in spoiling the gem. "He never gives me any breaks," he said of Bridges. "Why should I give him one? I'm getting paid to hit."

But as a former pitcher—and a legendary one at that—Johnson felt badly for Bridges.

"I'm sorry he couldn't get it," he said. "But as a pitcher, I wouldn't want to receive credit for a perfect game if I didn't earn it. I thought Bridges would feel the same way. That's why—and also as a manager, I can never give up—I sent Harris up to bat."

Just like that, it was over. As Charles P. Ward of the *Free Press* wrote, "It was as if someone threw a brick through the Mona Lisa just as da Vinci applied the final brush stroke."

39

THE ALEXANDER/ SMOLTZ TRADE

Through all the years since the deal was done, would you have felt better if the Tigers had traded Steve Searcy—instead of John Smoltz—to the Atlanta Braves for Doyle Alexander?

Of course you would have. And the reality is that they nearly did. The Braves considered both prospects but ended up with a future Hall of Famer instead of a six-game winner.

Searcy was a left-hander from Tennessee who had made steady progress through the Tigers' farm system. When the Braves started doing their homework about which pitcher they'd take in return, Searcy was at Triple A Toledo but would be limited to 10 starts in 1987 because of a knee injury. The Tigers, though, believed the Braves really liked him.

Searcy eventually made it to the majors with the Tigers and Philadelphia Phillies, compiling a 6–13 record with a 5.68 ERA in 70 career appearances, 21 of them starts. His last big league game was in 1992. Smoltz, meanwhile, was a hard-throwing right-hander whose dream was to pitch for the Tigers. He was born in Warren, a suburb of Detroit, but grew up in Lansing, Michigan. Both his father and grandfather worked at Tiger Stadium—his father as an usher, his grandfather (Father John) on the grounds crew.

After being drafted by the Tigers in 1985, Smoltz looked forward to the day he would pitch for them. But it never happened. In a quintessential now-for-later deal, the Tigers dealt Smoltz to the Braves for the well-traveled Alexander on August 12, 1987.

After struggling at Double A in the Tigers' organization, Smoltz flourished with the Braves and was in the majors to stay by July of 1988. Winning 213 games in his career, he was also credited with 154 saves. An eight-time All-Star who won the National League's Cy Young Award for his 24–8 record with the Braves in 1996, Smoltz was inducted into baseball's Hall of Fame in 2015. In a story written for the Hall of Fame, Braves scout John Hagemann said he remembered manager Bobby Cox asking him, "Who the heck is John Smoltz?"

"I told Bobby he had the best arm I'd ever seen on a right-handed pitcher," Hagemann answered.

However, when Smoltz went into the Hall of Fame, Jon Paul Morosi of FOX Sports wrote that the Tigers thought the Braves would select Searcy instead and only included Smoltz on the list of available pitchers as a "throw-in." When the Braves opted for Smoltz, the Tigers were surprised and disappointed but agreed to the deal all the same because they felt Alexander would be a difference maker for them.

And he was.

The Tigers were in second place at the time of the deal, one and a half games out of first. With nearly a third of the season remaining, they needed an experienced starting pitcher who wouldn't wilt during a pennant race. In Smoltz they parted with a pitcher who was more about tomorrow than today. In Alexander they acquired just the opposite. Ultimately the Tigers got exactly what they wanted—an impervious-to-pressure veteran who went 9–0 down the stretch.

It's easy to judge the trade by what Smoltz eventually accomplished. In that respect it will always be lopsided. But consider it from the viewpoint of the late Bill Lajoie, who was the Tigers' general manager. The contending Tigers were three deep in their rotation in 1987 with Jack Morris, Walt Terrell, and Frank Tanana. But they desperately needed a dependable fourth.

Despite going 5–2 as the deadline approached, Dan Petry had struggled with a 7.35 ERA in his last 11 starts. Jeff Robinson was equally inconsistent. Not only that, Robinson was a rookie who was considered too raw for the role. Lajoie wanted a proven pitcher, someone with the mentality of what Alexander said on his first day as a Tiger: "I've been through the wars."

By no means a kid, Alexander had been in the majors since 1971. Within a month of the trade, he turned 37. The Tigers were his eighth team. "I have no loyalty. I win for the team I play for," he told *The Sporting News*.

But he came to the Tigers having gone 1–9 with a 4.71 ERA in his last 10 starts—not exactly on a roll. To some extent, as Alexander claimed, he'd been a victim of inadequate run support. "I wasn't dead in Atlanta," Alexander said. "I just wasn't winning. Obviously someone thinks I can pitch or I wouldn't be here."

Lajoie was an astute baseball executive but was out on a lonely limb in making the deal. He knew that Alexander was historically at his best in the final two months of every season. In August and September of his 19 years in the majors, Alexander won 90 games. From April through July, he won 104. In any case, he now belonged to the Tigers, and there was no turning back.

How'd it go? Not so well in Alexander's first start. The Tigers beat the Kansas City Royals 8–4, but he exited after the sixth inning when the game was tied. The victory went to Mike Henneman in relief. "That wasn't one of my best games," Alexander said of his Detroit debut.

From that point on, though, the Tigers struck gold—a short-term gem compared to how Smoltz would eventually pitch for Atlanta, but gold all the same. In his next 10 starts, Alexander went 9–0 with a 1.20 ERA. He was everything the Tigers hoped he would be—and more. His first win for the Tigers was an 8–0 shutout of the Minnesota Twins. What encouraged him the most was the run support he received. In both of Alexander's starts as a Tiger, they'd scored eight runs, something the Braves hadn't done for him.

In fact, none of his teams had scored more than seven runs in two consecutive starts for him since the Toronto Blue Jays in early June 1984, an early sign that he would thrive in Detroit. The Tigers scored 45 runs in Alexander's first six starts and then just 19 in the next five. But no matter what kind of support they gave him, he didn't lose.

Henneman helped. In Alexander's second consecutive victory against the Twins, for instance, Henneman stranded the tying run at third after entering the game with one out in the eighth. "One of my top moments," Henneman said. "That was the game right there," said Alexander, for whom everything came together after that.

Doyle threw three shutouts in his next four starts and won the other game 11–2. Aware of being traditionally stronger down the stretch, Alexander spoke at one point with rare levity. "I'm thinking about getting a calendar that doesn't show any month except September," he said.

But that was all the humor you were going to get from a laconic pitcher about whom Darrell Evans, after Alexander had been with the Tigers for a month, said, "I've seen him grin once or twice."

Alexander's personality, though, didn't matter. Wins did, and it didn't take long for his impact to become widely noticed. "I figure he's the difference between us being tied for first and being three games out," manager Sparky Anderson said when Alexander picked up his sixth win without a loss.

There were four teams in the American League East that would end up with a better record in 1987 than Minnesota's 85–77, which would win the A.L. West. By mid-September, though, it had become apparent that the Milwaukee Brewers and New York Yankees wouldn't continue to contend. The winner of the division was going to be either Detroit or Toronto. With eight games remaining, the Tigers had dropped to three and a half games out and seemed to be fading. But they were merely "setting the biggest bear trap of all time," as Kirk Gibson said.

What's clear is that the Tigers would not have still been contending if it hadn't been for Alexander. In a 4–0 victory in Boston on September 23, he baffled the Red Sox with his change-up. Said Sox manager John McNamara, "We didn't hit one ball hard."

Alexander, though, couldn't afford to suddenly stumble. None of the Tigers' starters could, including the unsung Terrell, who went 8–0 with a 3.19 ERA in his final 10 starts. And when the pressure was at its highest, none of them did. In a game the Tigers absolutely had to win to avert a four-game sweep in Toronto, Alexander didn't get the victory, but his 10 ⅔ innings—the longest start of his career—kept the Tigers alive long enough to win the game and to creep to within two and a half games of the Jays instead of falling to four and a half out with a week remaining. "Doyle left his heart on the mound," Petry said. "It was beautiful what he did out there."

In his final start of the regular season, Alexander beat the Jays 4–3 to send the two teams into their final two games against each other tied. The Tigers won the first of the two 3–2 in 12 innings on Alan

Trammell's bases-loaded single through the legs of shortstop Manny Lee. The play easily could have been ruled an error, but the official scorer believed the ball was hit too hard for the drawn-in Lee to handle. "It skidded on him," Jays third baseman Rance Mulliniks said after the game. "He had no time to react."

One more win would do it. The Tigers clinched the division with Frank Tanana's dramatic 1–0 victory against the Jays in the final game of the regular season. However, they would lose the American League Championship Series four games to one to the underdog Twins. Strangely enough, Alexander was roughed up and lost both of his ALCS starts, an inglorious conclusion to a wondrous couple of months. He pitched the Tigers to the postseason, fulfilled the intent of the Smoltz trade, and would also pitch well enough to be an All-Star for the Tigers in 1988. Yet from that point on, with Smoltz's path to Cooperstown shining brighter than what Doyle did, the Braves deservedly grew fonder and fonder of the deal. Both teams, sooner or later, got what they wanted. But "later" lasted it longer.

40

GEORGE KELL

In 2001, when he was 79 years old, Hall of Famer George Kell was rescued from his burning house in Swifton, Arkansas, by a volunteer fireman who happened to be driving by at the time. Said Kell's wife Carolyn, "God was on George's shoulder that night. That's what I told him. From his playing days to broadcasting, all his life, God was on his shoulder."

With her husband being a man of faith and forever appreciative of both his life and career, Carolyn's observation could also have been the defining thought Kell took to his final rest in 2009. He'd been blessed. From playing the game he loved at a level to which many aspire but only a few attain; from marrying his high school sweetheart, Charlene, and having her at his side for 50 years; from being fortunate enough to have Carolyn for the last 12 years of his life after he lost Charlene; to a multi-talented career during which he spent 37 years in the broadcast booth after his playing days were over, Kell had been blessed indeed.

He was, of course, every bit a Tiger. But it hadn't started out that way. Connie Mack of the Philadelphia Athletics initially signed him. But just meeting the formal "Mr. Mack" in his straw hat made a lasting impression on George.

In 1943 Kell hit .396 for the Lancaster (Pennsylvania) Red Roses of the Interstate League. The benefit of Lancaster's location was that a prospect could easily travel to Philadelphia if the A's suddenly wanted to see how he would perform in a big league game, which is exactly what happened to the wide-eyed Kell.

He was 21 when he debuted against the St. Louis Browns on September 28. In his first at-bat, Kell tripled off "Happy" Al Milnar, a left-hander who no doubt was happier to have been 18–10 for the Cleveland Indians in 1940 than he was to be facing the A's as his career ingloriously wound down. Kell's triple came in the next-to-last victory of the season for the A's. He wouldn't play in the five consecutive losses they suffered to finish the season with a 49–105 record.

That was part of the problem about playing for the A's, though. They had been seriously bad for 10 years and, despite having a fine young third baseman in their lineup, they continued to lose in both 1944 and 1945. Mack liked Kell—liked him a lot—but he couldn't afford to keep young stars when their salaries began to climb, so the A's traded Kell to the Tigers on May 18, 1946, for outfielder Barney McCosky. The deal worked out well for both teams. Kell loved Detroit, and Detroit loved Kell. McCosky, meanwhile, snapped out of his doldrums and hit .354 in 92 games for the A's that season. Eventually playing the equivalent of three full seasons, McCosky hit .322 for the A's. But the Tigers still got the better of the deal.

It did not take long for Kell to make a good impression. Four days after the deal was made, columnist Malcolm Bingay of the *Detroit Free Press*—posing in print as the folksy "Iffy the Dopester"—wrote, "I am here to remark that little Georgie is about the sweetest thing I have seen hanging around that third-base sack." Not taking the trade at face value, though, Iffy wrote, "I would be willing to retire from all active life and live with the amount that [owner] Walter O. Briggs paid Connie Mack as a bonus for that trade."

It took Kell a couple of weeks to adjust to a new team following the feeling of rejection with which he left the A's, but in his last 81 games of 1946, he hit .348 for the Tigers. After just three seasons in the majors, he already was a reliable hitter—and getting better. Part of what made Kell so efficient throughout his career was that he seldom struck out. Allie Reynolds and Eddie Lopat were two of the better pitchers in the American League at the time. From 1947 to 1952, Reynolds had a record of 105–49 for the New York Yankees. From 1948 to 1953, Lopat was 97–47, also for the Yankees. But in 219 career plate appearances against the two, Kell struck out just once versus each of them.

Despite his innate affability, Kell was a tough out and a hard-nosed player who had grown up rooting for the rough-and-tumble "Gas House Gang" of St. Louis. Much to the delight of 12-year old George, the Gas House Gang beat the Tigers in the 1934 World Series.

For Kell as a player, however, it was a disappointment that the entirety of his career was spent in futile pursuit of a World Series appearance. But he got there twice as a broadcaster. With Kell in the booth, the Tigers won the World Series in 1968 and 1984.

There were two events that best personify the dedication with which he played. The first occurred in 1948, when a line drive off Joe DiMaggio's bat broke Kell's jaw at third base. The second took place in 1949, when he doggedly caught up to and passed Ted Williams of the Boston Red Sox for the A.L. batting title.

The 1948 season was star-crossed almost from beginning to end for Kell. In May, for instance, he suffered a broken right wrist when he was hit by a pitch from New York's Vic Raschi. On the plus side, he missed only 19 games when it could have been much worse. Team doctors, in fact, spoke of Kell's good luck, saying his injury was "the least serious that could occur in an accident like that. He is most fortunate."

After sitting out most of May, there was some thought that Kell returned too soon because he hit a subpar .276 in June. But after July 1, he hit .311. When all seemed right again, another serious injury ended his season early. This time, also against the Yankees, it wasn't a pitch that did the damage but a batted ball. DiMaggio hit a scorcher to third in the bottom of the sixth inning at Yankee Stadium on August 29. He hit the ball so hard, in fact, that Kell did not have enough time to react before it slammed into his face. Despite being in a semi-conscious state while standing at his position with a season-ending broken jaw, Kell managed to record an out on the play.

The other example of how insistent Kell was about playing the game on his terms was the way he won the batting crown in 1949. Knowing he would finish second if he made another out, Kell, though, was still in the on-deck circle in the ninth inning of the season's last game. He was not going to back into a title by sitting on the bench if it came time for him to hit. Heading into the last game, Kell's batting average was .341 to Williams' .344. The Tigers were at home, playing the Indians. The Red Sox were on the road, playing the Yankees.

At the end of August, no one had given Kell a chance of catching Williams, whose batting average was 12 points higher (.356 to .344).

But Kell broke his left thumb on a tag play at third on September 13 in Boston and missed nine of the next 10 games. Williams seemed safely ahead when the injury occurred, but by the time Kell returned to the Tigers' lineup, the gap was down to four points—and closing— as Williams found himself mired in the worst September slump of his career.

It stunned him to be struggling since he usually was a strong finisher. Excluding 1949, Williams was a .367 career hitter in September. But his lackluster .275 batting average in the final month, while trying to fend off Kell, proved costly. One hit in the last game would have clinched the title for Williams, but he went 0-for-2 with two walks. Meanwhile, Kell doubled and singled in his first two at bats against Cleveland's Bob Lemon.

With the tables turned—and with a .3439 to .3437 lead over Williams—Kell could have opted out at that point. But the Tigers were behind in the bottom of the ninth, and skipping an at-bat didn't fit with George's work ethic. With a runner on first and one out, Kell was on deck. The batting title would have been on the line in his next at-bat.

Except the at-bat never happened.

The Tigers' Eddie Lake, who had grounded into just one double play since May 15, hit a bouncer to Ray Boone at short. Boone stepped on second and then threw the ball to Mickey Vernon at first base to end the game, the season, and to give the title to Kell, who had wanted to win it the only way he knew how—the right way. To his lasting credit, he did.

It made sense to start an unknown. It really did. To clinch the American League pennant in 1940—after the irrepressible Bobo Newsom threw two innings of relief, followed by a complete game to win both ends of a doubleheader at home against the Chicago White Sox—the Tigers needed to win just one more game. That's all—just one more victory in a three-game series against the Cleveland Indians. They liked their chances of getting it done—but not their chances of winning the series opener.

After all, the Indians' Bob Feller, who was starting the first game, was the best pitcher in the league. If the Tigers were going to win a game against the Indians in their crucial showdown, they were far more likely to do it in the second or third game in Cleveland instead of in the opener. So with the approval of such star players as Hank Greenberg and Charlie Gehringer, the Tigers started rookie Floyd Giebell, holding their most established, more experienced, and better-known pitchers for another day.

The strategy made sense. Besides, Steve O'Neill, who managed the Tigers' affiliate at Buffalo in 1940 and would eventually manage Detroit to a World Series championship in 1945, thought Giebell was equal to the challenge. "I think he can beat those fellows," O'Neill told Tigers manager Del Baker, which helped Baker take the gamble.

But who the heck was Giebell? And just what was he up against? Compared to Feller, of course, he was an unknown. Then again, compared to almost anyone, Giebell was an unknown.

He had pitched in nine games for the Tigers in 1939—none of them starts—and had won a game in relief. However, he also had allowed 31 baserunners in 15⅓ innings—12 of them on walks—so there was no reason to think he would be a significant contributor at any point in a pennant race.

Even while putting together a 15–17 record at Buffalo of the International League in 1940, Giebell hadn't really done much to get noticed or to be considered worthy of starting a crucial game. But that was the point of the Tigers' strategy. Giebell was a disposable starter if ever there was one. With a complete game, he'd beaten the Philadelphia A's 13–2 in his first start back from the minors, but getting the better of the A's Chubby Dean was one thing. Opposing the vaunted Feller was entirely another.

Unlike their game against Dean, the Tigers couldn't hope to score 13 runs against Rapid Robert. What a fine season Feller had in 1940, starting with the no-hitter he threw against the White Sox on Opening Day. He came into the Giebell game with a 27–10 record for the Indians and was headed for all sorts of honors. But both the Tigers and New York Yankees had beaten him four times that season, so it wasn't as if the high esteem the Tigers had for Feller always translated into losing to him.

The series opener against Detroit, though, still looked like a mismatch in his favor and was regarded as such. Plus the game was being played in Cleveland, where the fans had gotten raucous that season, siding with manager Oscar Vitt in a feud against players who'd become known as "the Crybabies." Not passing up a chance to capitalize on the Indians' reputation for whining, Tigers fans had brought baby bottles to Briggs Stadium when the Indians were in Detroit the previous week. During the series fans serenaded the Tribe with chants sounding like bawling babies.

Despite their stance against the players, Cleveland fans intended to get even. One attempt, though, was badly botched. While trying to hit pitcher Schoolboy Rowe, among others, in the bullpen with tomatoes, a Cleveland fan dumped an entire basket of them, along with some empty beer bottles, on Tigers catcher Birdie Tebbetts, who was dazed and understandably angered by the incident. For "hitting poor little me," Tebbetts accused the clumsy fan of having "control as bad as the Cleveland pitchers." It was also reported—but never proven—that when Tebbetts accompanied security to find the fan who had dumped ancient fruit on his head, the Tigers catcher slugged the culprit.

Meanwhile, the game was still scoreless after three innings. Feller was being Feller. But Giebell wasn't being Giebell. He was pitching better than almost everyone had expected. Giebell walked the first batter he faced, but a one-out line drive to first had been turned into a double play. In the third inning, an error and a single gave the Tribe a first-and-third chance with no outs, but two strikeouts and a fly ball to right kept the game scoreless.

In his prime—a seven-year stretch in which he hit 203 home runs—Rudy York then stunned the Indians and their fans by hitting a fly ball to left that barely stayed fair and also barely made it to the seats, giving the Tigers a two-run lead in the fourth. According to the *Detroit Free Press* account, "Large Rudolph lazily golfed one of Mr. Feller's pitches into the left-field stands, the ball crossing the barrier just inside the foul line."

Suddenly the Giebell-Feller matchup was no laughing matter. Or if it was, Baker had an improving chance of getting the last laugh. As the Tigers' manager, Baker hadn't flaunted the boldness of his decision to match Giebell against Feller. Indeed, he'd kept it a secret as long as he could, prompting some of the Detroit players to ask reporters 15 minutes before game time if they knew who was starting for the Tigers.

But the fact is that from the opening moments, Giebell pitched as if his entire career had been destined for such a center-stage moment. And now that the lanky right-hander had a lead, he was determined to keep it. Returning to obscurity, as he was destined to do, Giebell would never win another game for the Tigers, but he was determined to win this one. As *Free Press* columnist "Iffy the Dopester" put it, Giebell was a "cotton-topped kid from Weirton, W.Va., where they make steel, and it looked as though that's what he was weaned on."

Giebell's biggest hurdle arrived in the bottom of the seventh inning, which featured the pivotal point of the game. Second baseman Ray Mack led off with a single off Giebell's glove. Catcher Rollie Hemsley followed with what was described as an "easy roller bobbled by Gehringer." With a bunt Feller sacrificed the runners to second and third. At that point, the Indians were only a single away from tying the game or giving a lead to Feller, who had allowed the last of the game's three Tigers hits in the fifth inning. In other words, the Indians were a hit away from putting themselves in an excellent position to win.

At the plate was Ben Chapman, the Indians' yappy left fielder, who was already angry that he had struck out twice against Giebell after not striking out twice in the same game against anyone, let alone a no-namer, since May 30. Giebell and Chapman were opposites. For Giebell, a relative novice, the game was the second of only four starts he'd get in the majors. Chapman, meanwhile, was a scrappy speedster who was in his 11th major league season and had led the majors in stolen bases four times.

With an abrasive personality, Chapman would be notoriously known later for the racial abuse that he, as a Philadelphia Phillies manager, shouted at Jackie Robinson after Robinson broke the color barrier with the Brooklyn Dodgers in 1947. But more currently, he was a "Crybaby" ringleader on the Indians against manager Vitt, so one can surmise that Chapman didn't quietly come to the plate for his at-bat in the seventh inning.

Anger also was nothing new for Chapman, who was prone to displays of it. More than once he'd been suspended for hitting an umpire. But for the first time in his career, Chapman had experimented in 1940 with wearing glasses, which hadn't recently helped. He'd hit just .213 in his previous 32 games. So, perhaps, the advantage still belonged to Giebell.

In any case, the unsung Tiger struck out Chapman yet again, the first time in more than six years that Chapman had fanned three times in the same game, let alone against the same pitcher. But for the determined Giebell, there was a huge hurdle remaining. Roy Weatherly, the Indians' center fielder, was a .303 hitter that season and had struck out only three times in his last 20 games. With runners still at second and third, chances were good he would put the ball in play, which he did, but it was just a routine grounder to third. And with that, the Indians' biggest threat ended.

Giebell allowed one hit in the final two innings, a harmless two-out single in the eighth.

When pinch-hitter Jeff Heath grounded out to first base for the game's final out, "large Rudolph" York let out a yell and then tackled Giebell, who was quickly lifted onto the shoulders of teammates. Others pounded the winning pitcher on the back and told him he was "swell."

He was swell, all right. With the game of his life, Floyd Giebell had just pitched the Tigers to a pennant.

NORM CASH

Some ballplayers grow up in cities, some in the suburbs. Norm Cash was from Justiceburg, Texas, a town smaller than small—and as tiny as nowhere. Said to have climbed to a population of 76 in its heyday, Cash wasn't just the favorite son of Justiceburg; he was one of its only sons. From a farm upbringing in a hot country hamlet that not ages ago had only one retail operation—plus an unattended roadside stand selling firewood—to a major league career from which he would retire as one of the most productive hitters in Tigers history, Cash encountered success. "We're just a west Texas desert town," said longtime family friend Mike Burk. "There were a few scrub ranches around here. His family had one of them. The only reason the town existed in the first place was as a place on the tracks for the old steam engines to stop for water."

Norm was driving a tractor by the time he was 10 and, by working the cotton on the ranch with hand tools, he developed strong forearms and wrists. Although he excelled as a running back at Sul Ross State and was drafted by the Chicago Bears, he elected to pursue a baseball career. So instead of playing for the Bears, he signed with the Chicago White Sox.

Eventually he would become "Stormin' Norman," as he was known for the great season he had with the Tigers in 1961. But before his baseball career went anywhere, he fulfilled an obligation. After two years at Waterloo, Iowa, in the old Three-I League, he missed all of the 1957 season because of military service.

Accruing 26 days leave along the way, Cash took them during the spring of 1958, working out with the Sox in Tampa, where he felt he didn't make much of an impression.

Hal Butler wrote in his book, *Stormin' Norman Cash*, that when Cash thanked manager Al Lopez for the opportunity, Lopez replied, "Glad to have you down here, Joe."

"He didn't even know my name," Norm said.

When Cash returned in June of 1958, the White Sox believed he was ready for the majors. Playing left field rather than first base—where he played virtually his entire career in Detroit—he got his first major league hit, a single to center, off the Tigers' Jim Bunning in a 2–1 loss on July 6. By 1959, a World Series season for the White Sox, Cash was in the majors to stay. He hit four home runs that year, three of them against the Tigers, who remembered his power when they traded for him the following spring.

Actually, Cash was traded to the Cleveland Indians first and then to the Tigers for infielder Steve Demeter, who went a quick 0-for-5. Despite 10 more seasons in the minors, Demeter never appeared in another major league game. If you're keeping track, the tally was 3,233 total bases as a Tiger for Cash, zero for Demeter as an Indian. Five days after the Cash trade, the Tigers made another with the Indians—Harvey Kuenn to Cleveland for Rocky Colavito—that dominated the front page. The deal for Cash became a footnote. But in the long run—because Colavito played only four years in Detroit, compared to Cash's 15—the more impactful trade for the Tigers in 1960 proved to be the first one.

And when Cash won the American League batting title in 1961 by hitting .361, it was destined to become one of the Tigers' biggest steals of all time. Though he never again came close to achieving what he did in 1961, Ol' Norman had a heck of a good time as a major leaguer. He loved to play baseball, but he also loved to party. According to *The Detroit Tigers Encyclopedia* by Jim Hawkins and Dan Ewald, Cash once returned to his room on the road in the wee hours, but he threw the evidence of how late it was—namely, his watch—out of the hotel window. Meanwhile, his roommate Jim Price had awakened. Seeing that Cash had thrown a perfectly good watch onto the pavement below, Price went down to get it while dressed only in his pajama bottoms. Standards of appropriate attire were different back then, so Price—because he looked like a half-dressed vagrant—was detained by police while Cash soundly slept upstairs.

To make matters worse, Cash got five hits in a doubleheader the next day while Price went hitless. "True story," said Price, a longtime Tigers broadcaster after his playing career. "The man was amazing."

Other teammates also marveled at him. "We loved Norm because he would play hurt and hungover," Denny McLain said. Added Mickey Lolich: "Sometimes, you weren't quite so sure he'd make it to his locker. Then after some time in the hot tub, plus a couple of showers, he'd perk up, click his heels, and say, 'Let's go get 'em, boys.'"

Cash was immensely popular because he was such a free spirit. He really was a jovial, good ol' boy from west Texas. And sometimes he took his sense of humor onto the field. When he was soon to be the last out of Nolan Ryan's second career no-hitter on July 15, 1973—a game in which Ryan struck out 17—Cash sensed he stood a good chance of becoming No. 18. Having fanned in two other at-bats and acknowledging how overmatched the Tigers were that day, he took a table leg up to the plate in the ninth inning instead of a bat. "Art Kusnyer, who I coached with on the White Sox, was Ryan's catcher that day," Jim Leyland said. "Whenever he talked about that game, he'd laugh about what Cash did. Art didn't know at first it was a table leg. He said he didn't know what the hell it was."

That it wasn't a bat was all umpire Ron Luciano needed to know. He made Cash discard the comical prop and get back to the business of facing Ryan, who finished him off with a pop-up to short. "It wasn't as if I was going to get a hit anyway," Cash said about the prank.

Al Kaline recalled another time when the Tigers were trailing in the rain, and somehow—among the many gadgets fans had sent to him—Cash found a pair of glasses with miniature windshield wipers attached to them. "He went up to the plate wearing them," Kaline said. "That was his way of trying to convince the umpires to call the game." It also wasn't unheard of for Cash to take advantage of a rain delay— or at least try to. More than once he mysteriously advanced a base, reappearing at third when he'd been on second base before. All his attempts, though, were foiled.

What Cash accomplished in his career was impressive—ranking in the top 10 in hits, RBIs, and runs scored on the Tigers' all-time lists, not to mention second in home runs with 373.

But what he did in 1961 was nothing short of spectacular. Applying today's analytics to his accomplishments that year while becoming the only Tiger between 1959 and 2007 to win a batting title, Cash was second in the A.L. to New York's Mickey Mantle in offensive WAR.

That means he finished ahead of Mantle's teammate, Roger Maris, who hit a record-setting 61 home runs that year.

With no explanation other than calling it "a freak season," Cash admitted that he never thought he'd do it again. And he never did, for which the fans never fully forgave him. Cash fell victim to slow starts after that. He hit .355 in the first half of 1961 but wouldn't hit over .300 in the first half of any other season. He had six other second halves in which he hit higher than .300 but just couldn't combine the two. The closest he came to winning another batting title was when he finished seventh in 1966. Even then he hit just .279. Over the long haul, though, he put together a fine career. "A hell of a player," teammate Jim Northrup once said of him. "Better than the media ever gave him credit for."

The world lost Norm Cash in 1986, a month short of his 52nd birthday. He drowned after falling off a dock near his boat in northern Michigan. Those with him earlier said that he'd had a few drinks but was not impaired when he left the bar where he had been with his wife and friends. After some lean years, Cash was getting his life back in order. He'd had a stroke but was coping with that as well. When he went to check his boat on that misty October night, he did not return.

Perhaps the greatest tribute to him came years after his death. Switching to Cash's No. 25 in the final game at Tiger Stadium in 1999, Robert Fick hit a grand slam off the roof in right—the ballpark's last home run. It didn't clear the roof, as Cash had done four times in his career, but came close enough for broadcaster Frank Beckmann to exclaim, "Would Stormin' Norman have loved that!" Indeed he would have.

TRUCKS' TWO NO-HITTERS DESPITE 5–19 RECORD

He had the best of seasons and the worst of seasons—in the same season. Virgil Trucks endured a 5–19 record in 1952 for the last-place Tigers. That same year he threw two no-hitters and a one-hitter. He won another start, though not with a complete game, in which he allowed only two hits. So, indeed, Trucks had some impressive games in 1952. But he either sizzled or froze. There was no in-between for him.

For a position player, the equivalent of a 5–19 record with two no-hitters in the same season would be to hit for the cycle twice with a .180 batting average—something to celebrate but a lot to groan about. Trucks, however, was not a position player. He was an established starting pitcher with a .589 career winning percentage heading into the 1952 season. One of the Tigers' mainstays, he'd won a World Series game for them in 1945. It was the achievement of which he was proudest.

He also threw six shutouts while putting together a 19–11 record for the 1949 Tigers, a far better team than they would be three years later. Then again, there haven't been many teams as bad as the 1952 Tigers. With a storm of losses ahead of him, despite being 103–72 before that year, Trucks was headed for a rough time.

Nearly all the Tigers were. They began by losing their first eight games and would sink to permanent possession of last place after just two weeks. They were shut out 18 times, and when scoring fewer than four runs, which they did in more than half their games, the Tigers went 10–76. Not to be outdone on the pitching side, they had the worst ERA in the American League at 4.25.

To no one's surprise, considering the team's flaws, the Tigers finished in the cellar for the first time ever with a 50–104 record, which pointed to such factors as not enough hitting, not enough pitching, not enough anything. In those offensive categories where the Tigers didn't finish last, they were often next to last.

And their pitching seemed star-crossed. Art Houtteman, for instance, would finish with an 8–20 record, but being able to pitch at all required mental strength. That's because his seven-month-old daughter, Sheryl Lynne, was killed when she was thrown from their convertible that overturned as Houtteman's wife, Shelagh—who was not physically harmed—drove off the road in Tennessee on her way home from spring training.

Overall, it not only was a sad season for the Tigers but a dreadfully bad one. Their woes at the plate, of course, had a lot to do with the weird year Trucks had on the mound, a reversal for him that came out of nowhere. That's not to say Trucks was blameless. He had a 6.24 ERA in his 19 losses, but his record was a shock all the same. A Tiger since 1941, Trucks had encountered just one losing season before 1952.

But instead of letting adversity affect his career after he went 5–19, he shrugged it off.

In fact, he dismissed it so completely that he bounced back to win 20 games in 1953 after being traded by the Tigers. But he didn't come close to throwing a no-hitter that year. In fact, he never threw another one.

Trucks, though, did throw a pair of three-hitters and four four-hitters in 1953 while dividing his time between the St. Louis Browns and Chicago White Sox. After his horrific 1952 record—about which Trucks always was reluctant to talk other than calling it "bittersweet"— the Tigers traded him to the Browns, who shipped him and his 5–4 early-season performance to the White Sox, for whom he pitched superbly and would do so through 1955.

Trucks went 15–6, 19–12, and 13–8 in his nearly three years with the White Sox. Applying today's sabermetrics to how he pitched after the Tigers traded him, his WAR of 6.1 indicated that he was the A.L.'s second-best pitcher in 1953. He would follow that with a fifth best WAR in 1954.

Being a good pitcher both before and after made 1952 even more of an oddity for Trucks. Perhaps the moral to the story is that there's no telling to what depths a good pitcher can sink on a terrible team. Either that or a solid pitcher should not be traded because of one bad year, especially for a borderline package of players. "I thought it was awful," Trucks said of the deal that sent him to St. Louis. "I would have loved to stay in Detroit."

From the three players they received for Trucks (outfielder Bob Nieman, catcher J.W. Porter, and infielder Owen Friend), the Tigers got just one solid season. Not one from each of the three, mind you, but only from one of the three: Nieman, who hit .281 for Detroit in 1953.

As much of a stigma as a 5–19 record could have been, however, and as difficult as it might have been to overcome, Trucks managed to do so without any permanent damage to his career.

As for his no-hitters, the second of the two was bound to make more of an impression than the first because the second was thrown against the New York Yankees, who would again win the World Series that year. As Trucks said, "It always meant more to beat the Yankees."

The second of his two no-hitters, thrown on August 25 at Yankee Stadium, would also be remembered because it hinged on a bout of indecision by official scorer John Drebinger, who twice changed his call on a play in the bottom of the third. Drebinger initially ruled Phil Rizzuto's grounder an error after Rizzuto reached first base safely. The ball had been hit to Tigers shortstop Johnny Pesky, who was slow in throwing it to first. Accordingly, Drebinger called it an E-6. But he deferred to his press box colleagues, who disagreed with him, and changed the ruling to a hit. To settle the matter, Drebinger phoned down to the Tigers' dugout in the fifth inning and spoke directly to Pesky, who said he botched the play by failing to get a good grip on the ball. Speaking honestly, Pesky felt he deserved to be given an error on the play.

Satisfied at last, Drebinger changed it back. The hit that had been an error was an error again—and this time it stuck.

Trucks took it from there, not allowing a hit the rest of the game for his second no-hitter of the season. "When the change was made [back to an error]," Trucks said, "I wanted to go all the way." Catcher Matt Batts helped all he could as well. Before Hank Bauer made the final out for the Yankees, Batts said, "I rubbed the ball up good and kissed it for good luck."

Trucks' first no-hitter was memorable in its own right but for an entirely different reason. He threw it on May 15 at Briggs Stadium against the Washington Senators, and Vic Wertz hit a two-out home run in the bottom of the ninth to hand Virgil a 1–0 victory. (In fact, both of Trucks' no-hitters came in 1–0 victories.) Said Wertz of the fastball he hit, "waist-high, where I'll always dream about it from now on."

What made Trucks' feat of throwing two no-hitters in the same season more surprising was that no Tiger had thrown even one since George Mullin's gem in 1912. And how did the fans react to the weirdness of witnessing the best of games in the worst of seasons? Well, there weren't many on hand for the first of the two, but according to the *Detroit Free Press*, the "small gathering of 2,215 fans made Briggs Stadium rock as though it were jammed."

Less than three weeks earlier, Houtteman had come close to ending the Tigers' no-hitter drought, only to give up a single to Cleveland's Harry (Suitcase) Simpson with two outs in the ninth inning. But with Trucks dealing, there was no late single to ruin it—just a late home run by Wertz to make it real. As the ball headed for the seats in right field on that Thursday afternoon, Washington right fielder Jackie Jensen didn't even bother to watch it land. He knew Wertz had gotten it all.

Giving him a 1–2 record at the time, little did Trucks know just how strange his season would become. In the five games he won in 1952, he allowed only nine hits. But he had to pitch brilliantly or had no hope of winning. On July 22, Trucks was masterful again while throwing a one-hitter in yet another 1–0 victory. He allowed only a first-inning single to Washington's leadoff hitter, Eddie Yost.

That hit and three walks accounted for the Senators' only base runners. Despite being in the midst of a miserable 2–13 stretch, the right-hander from Alabama struck out a season-high 10. Trucks was a hard thrower who was proud of his vaunted velocity. Whenever signing his autograph—until he died in 2013, he responded free of charge to each request—he would write his nickname: Virgil "Fire" Trucks. "It was a natural," he said. "I could throw 100 miles an hour."

And he could pitch with the best of them, which he proved throughout his career, even in 1952.

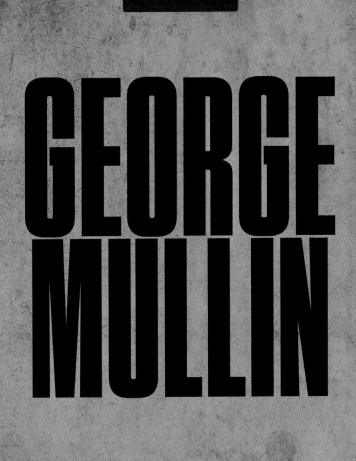

GEORGE MULLIN

George Mullin wasn't just another pitcher from 100 years ago. He once won 29 games for the Tigers. In fact, he averaged 22 wins over six seasons in the middle of his career. Such numbers are impressive, but as a master of the hidden ball trick, a pitcher with distracting gyrations on the mound, and a frequent fugitive from the law, he had an interesting backstory as well.

He also pitched in three consecutive World Series—1907–09. The Tigers lost all three but not because of Mullin. He went 3–3 with a 1.86 ERA as the Tigers lost to the Chicago Cubs, the Chicago Cubs, and the Pittsburgh Pirates, in that order. Three weeks after he was placed on waivers by the Tigers in 1912, Mullin threw the first no-hitter in franchise history.

The Tigers thought Mullin had begun to fade, that all his innings— an average of more than 300 for the 10 previous seasons—had finally caught up to him. But he didn't think so. And he proved his point by no-hitting the St. Louis Browns on July 4, his 32nd birthday. There were some who weren't entirely impressed because the gem was thrown against a team that was 19–48 at the time.

But there were others, such as E. A. Batchelor of the *Detroit Free Press*, who dismissed the doubters. Batchelor wrote, "It might be contended by some that the Browns aren't really a ballclub and therefore the sensational feat is somewhat dimmed." But he quickly added that the Browns "are more than ordinarily liable to smash the sphere to a safe spot now and then."

It was also in 1912 that Mullin won his 200th game as a Tiger, getting the better of the great Walter Johnson in a 2–0 duel against the Washington Senators. And before that, he not only started but won the first game ever played at the rebuilt and newly named Navin Field. Other highlights of Mullin's career were that he was the only pitcher who ever pinch-hit for Ty Cobb, which he did twice; that he proved to be immensely popular when the Tigers played an offseason series in Cuba in 1909, though the fans there didn't like the hidden ball trick in which he participated; and that he also might have been the first Tiger ever to sign a contract with incentive clauses.

It doesn't sound like much of a bonus now—an extra $1,000 for 30 wins and $500 for 20—but keep in mind that when Mullin won 29 games in 1909, $1,000 was worth the equivalent of $28,000 today. So it wasn't chump change. And besides, he nearly did it. He almost won 30.

As for the hidden ball trick, Mullin was a practical jokester who bribed police in Havana to "arrest" his friend and former teammate Herman "Germany" Schaefer for concealing the ball on a play at second base. Playing in Cuba as a touring major leaguer, Schaefer was charged with "winning a game by trickery" and actually spent a night in jail. It was an example of Mullin's pranks but one that backfired when angry fans stormed the field to get at Schaefer for his deception.

There had been no deception on September 17, 1906, however, about Mullin becoming the first pitcher to pinch-hit for Cobb. Mullin batted for him and tripled in the ninth inning of a lackluster 7–2 loss to Boston in which Cobb, nearing the end of his longest stint so far with the Tigers, was 0-for-3 after being 0-for-4 the day before. He'd been hitless, and everyone else had been listless. "No affair of the season seemed slower or sleepier," the *Free Press* said.

The second time Mullin pinch hit for Cobb occurred in the ninth inning of a one-sided 1912 game in which Cobb didn't think he would get another at-bat. So he went up to the clubhouse to take a bath and had fully disrobed when suddenly it was his turn to hit. With Cobb otherwise occupied, Mullin became the logical choice. However, this time he didn't live up to his reputation as a hitter, grounding out to end an 11–3 loss to the Cleveland Indians.

But the at-bat was treated with considerable flair in print by the *Free Press* as the rarity it was. "George," it read, "certainly has the right to throw out his chest and feel proud of himself to be selected as the hitting representative of the greatest ballplayer of all time."

In 12 seasons for the Tigers, Mullin had 372 hits, a club record for pitchers. But it wasn't for his hitting ability that he was valued. A fastball pitcher who tended to lose track of his weight—and was thus known as "Big George"—Mullin had been a highly sought-after right-hander after he pitched for a Fort Wayne, Indiana, team in 1901.

Reacting too eagerly to the interest shown in him, however, he signed with three teams for 1902: the Tigers, the Brooklyn Superbas, and the Fort Wayne team of which he was already a member. But the Fort Wayne team would not exist in 1902. With his choices came down to Detroit and Brooklyn, Mullin selected the Tigers because they played closer to his home in Indiana.

A problem ensued, however, that would test not only his patience, but also threaten to derail his future. It would make Mullin the most harassed Tiger of all time. The owner of the defunct Fort Wayne franchise, Isadore Mautner, felt that Mullin had broken the law by signing with the Tigers after Mautner paid him $25 to stay. In fact, he wanted Mullin arrested for it and pressed the case for an unreasonable amount of time. Although Mautner no longer had a team, it took two years before the matter with Mullin was settled.

Meanwhile, here's what the Tigers and their prized pitcher had to go through. On one occasion Mullin was shaving in his room at the Tigers' hotel in Chicago when detectives hired by Mautner arrived on the scene and began looking for him. With only one side of his face shaven, Mullin was whisked out of the hotel through the ladies' entrance and made his way undetected to the train for St. Louis, where the Tigers were scheduled to play the next day.

He was foiled that time, but Mautner remained insistent on pursuing criminal instead of civil action against Mullin, who had to be on the lookout for detectives whenever traveling through his home state. The wary pitcher was usually one step ahead of them—such as the time a deputy sheriff hid on the Tigers' train from Chicago to Detroit during a September trip in 1902 and began a futile search for Mullin as soon as the train crossed into Indiana. "All members of the team were awakened, and all berths were searched without finding Mullin," the *Free Press* reported the next day. Understandably, many of the Tigers who were awakened threatened to "wipe the car" with the deputy. Such was the feverish extent, however, to which Mautner attempted to prevent Mullin from pitching for the Tigers. At the same time, it's also indicative of how much Mullin was intent on getting the better of him.

On another trip, deputies were successful in hauling Mullin off a train, but the warrant with which Mautner had him arrested was for the incorrect charge of "obtaining money under false pretenses." Upon arraignment, Mullin was released by the judge. Finally—after Mullin's second season with the Tigers—the case was dismissed before going to a jury trial because, as the *Free Press* reported, "Mautner seemed to have forgotten all about the circumstances."

He conveniently forgot about them, it turned out, after Mullin bought all incriminating evidence for $1,000. Mautner got more than his $25 back, and Mullin no longer had to worry about being threatened.

With his two tormented seasons out of the way, the best was yet to come for Mullin, including the day in 1906 when he won both ends of a doubleheader with complete games. Not only that, but his troublesome control would eventually improve. From a career high of 138 walks in 1905, Mullin shaved the number to an acceptable 71 in 1908 followed by 78 in 1909, his best season, when he went 29–8 with a 2.22 ERA.

As a Tiger, Mullin compiled a 209–179 record, winning 20-plus games five times.

By 1913, though—with indications proving correct this time—he was past his prime, which was timely because baseball had begun to clamp down on pitchers known to be "active" on the mound. In Mullin's case, being active meant he was, according to the *Free Press*, "wont to indulge in various gyrations while getting the victim fully under the influence of the hypnotic eye." He was a character all right, the one they called Big George. But hypnotic eye and all, he was a heck of a pitcher in his time. Even when he was being chased.

BASEBALL MAN
JIM CAMPBELL

Jim Campbell was the Calvin Coolidge of baseball. If that doesn't mean much to you, which is likely the case, consider this: it was Coolidge, the 30th president of the United States, who once said, "The business of the American people is business." There were no frills to that belief, just as there were no frills to the way the tradition-bound Campbell viewed baseball. He loved the game he devoted most of his adult life to it, but one can easily describe the personality of the longtime Tigers' executive by paraphrasing Coolidge. If fans were to be entertained, it had to be outcome-oriented. If the Tigers lost, well, it wasn't meant to be a happy day.

For all his front-office skills—of which there were many—Campbell ventured into baseball's Age of Auxiliary Fun kicking, screaming, and grumbling. There were no Ferris wheels in his world of baseball, no carousels. There wasn't much music either other than an organ playing old favorites and "Take Me Out to the Ballgame." That didn't make him a bad person by any means—just sort of stodgy.

When it was mentioned to him once that he might want to branch out a bit, possibly offering Tigers fans an extra menu item or two at the concession stands, he harrumphed—as he often harrumphed. "We serve hot dogs," he replied.

Campbell, though, was totally loyal to the Tigers. He worked for the organization for 43 years, from 1949 to 1992. At the end of his first game as business manager of the Tigers' affiliate in Thomasville, Georgia, the ballpark burned down.

Welcome to your baseball career, Jim.

With a bachelor's degree in commerce from Ohio State, Campbell's initial path of advancement within the Tigers' organization was via the business side. But he recognized talent as well. In 1959 he became a vice president of the team and at the end of the 1962 season, when he was 38 years old, Campbell was named the Tigers' general manager.

He became set in his ways as the years went by, but that didn't mean a barrier separated him from the media. Toward the end of his tenure with the Tigers, he would chastise reporters who didn't call him often enough to chat about baseball. Or just to chat. "I know," he'd say. "You don't have time for ol' Jim anymore."

As their general manager and later as president and chairman of the Tigers, Campbell was an astute executive. Under his leadership, the Tigers won World Series in 1968 and 1984.

He also claimed Denny McLain off waivers from the Chicago White Sox in 1963, a move that paid off handsomely when McLain won 31 games in 1968.

And in 1979, when he realized the Tigers needed a more colorful manager than the solid but silent Les Moss, Campbell hired Sparky Anderson, who would not have remained unemployed for long after his career in Cincinnati ended the season before. In their years together with the Tigers, Campbell and Anderson became best friends.

When it came to entertainment, though, Campbell was a Victrola in a stereo world, a cassette in a world of streaming. He liked what he liked, but what he liked was predictable.

"Which Sousa march do you think we'll be hearing today?" one Tigers beat writer used to say.

Campbell's unchanging taste didn't stop with music either. In 1984 he told popular Herbie Redmond of the Tiger Stadium ground crew to stop doing his dance while dragging the field with a broom in the fifth inning. Fans loved Herbie's dance. But the Tigers called it "distracting."

Then again, the Tigers were considered sticks-in-the-mud. When they introduced the song "Tiger Rag" as a between-innings replacement for John Denver's "Thank God I'm a Country Boy" in 1984, fans booed. "They'd boo anything," Campbell said.

"Tiger Rag" had been meant to accompany Herbie's fifth-inning dance around the bases before he was told to stop, but he didn't like the new song either. No one did. "Tiger Rag" lasted one game. Said Tigers spokesman Dan Ewald, "I'm not saying it will never be played again, but I don't expect it to."

DAVE DOMBROWSKI

One of the reasons Jim Leyland admired Dave Dombrowski as a general manager was for the simple truth that Dave was not afraid. Big deal, small deal, if Dombrowski thought it would help the Tigers, he made it. He would do his homework about the players involved but never backed away because of its magnitude.

According to baseball-reference.com, in fact, Dombrowski made 28 "significant trades" in his 13½ years as Tigers general manager. From acquiring Dmitri Young from the Cincinnati Reds for Juan Encarnacion on December 11, 2001, to sending Yoenis Cespedes to the New York Mets on July 31, 2015, for Michael Fulmer, not a year went by without Dombrowski making a deal that qualified for the website's "significant" list.

Along the way, he acquired an impressive collection of players for the Tigers, including Placido Polanco, Carlos Guillen, Max Scherzer, Anibal Sanchez, David Price, Ian Kinsler, and Cespedes. That's not to mention Young, Fulmer, Carlos Pena, Jeremy Bonderman, Nate Robertson, Sean Casey, Austin Jackson, Jhonny Peralta, Doug Fister, Jose Iglesias, and Joakim Soria.

But, of course, his best, biggest, and brightest trade was for Miguel Cabrera at the winter meetings in 2007. "I just never thought we'd be in position to acquire a player of Miggy's caliber," Dombrowski said. "That has to be No.1 on the list."

Some of his deals didn't click. However, most did. But the common thread through them all, as Leyland said, was that Dombrowski wasn't afraid to make them.

That brought another harrumph from Campbell. Of the possible return of "Country Boy" he remarked, "I'm so sick of that song. I'm a baseball man, not a stage show manager." Amazingly, in the middle of the 1984 season—with the Tigers in first place after a 35–5 start—a ballpark music issue began to steal headlines. The product on the field was being overshadowed.

So it wasn't a surprise when the Tigers became irked. They resented the attention the issue received, instantly copping an attitude about it. As *Detroit Free Press* columnist Mike Downey wrote, "The front office people keep behaving as if everyone is out to get them."

No one was out to get them. It was just a clash of old school vs. new as far as in-game entertainment was concerned. Then again, the Tigers sometimes comically blundered when it came to entertainment such as when the San Diego Chicken came to Tiger Stadium for the first time. Just booking the Chicken for an appearance was a breakthrough for the Tigers. They weren't a team with an energetic mascot, never felt the need for one. Nor were they looking to hire one.

But at least they acknowledged that by bringing one in for a special appearance, mascots could be entertaining. There was a glitch, though. The plan was for the Chicken to be introduced while running in from a gate in center field. He would be waving a pair of Tigers pennants while the soundtrack from the movie *Rocky* played on the stadium loudspeakers.

All went well *initially*. The Chicken raced in, the crowd cheered. There was no introduction necessary, but the Tigers chose to identify their guest all the same. They tried, that is. "Reid Nichols running for Yastrzemski," read the message on the Tiger Stadium scoreboard as the Chicken galloped toward the infield. Oops. The Chicken had just been introduced as a pinch-runner for Red Sox star Carl Yastrzemski.

The mistake wasn't Campbell's, of course. Yet the nature of the blunder underscored the fact that the Tigers were still mired in past generations of entertainment. Not only that, but one blunder invariably led to another, such as whether the Tigers would ever let Herbie dance with his broom again between innings. Redmond was still a fan favorite. In not fully recognizing his popularity, the Tigers had misread a situation that backfired.

In the Tigers' defense there were those who thought Herbie gyrated too strenuously at times, and some African American fans were irritated at the minstrel show appearance of his behavior.

The Tigers eventually relented, allowing Redmond to perform while asking him to gyrate just a little less. He continued to work at Tiger Stadium through the 1989 season before dying of liver disease on Opening Day 1990. In his honor the ground crew dragged the field in the fifth inning that season in a missing broom formation. Like a missing plane formation that is flown after a pilot is killed, the other groundskeepers stayed in formation with one slot vacant before going back and making sure the infield was fully swept.

Before baseball went totally modern on Campbell—with sushi carving out a niche for itself at concession stands—his baseball career ended. He was abruptly relieved of his responsibilities during the ownership transition from Tom Monaghan to Mike Ilitch in 1992.

After retiring to Florida, Campbell died in 1995.

The Tigers were fortunate to have two patriarchal executives guide them through the 20th century. Frank Navin led them from 1902 to 1935—followed by Campbell's many decades of devotion. Both were known for being no-nonsense, thrifty, and dedicated. Both celebrated World Series championships during their eras. And both, for sure, were baseball men. But only one of the two ever proudly proclaimed— or ever had to—that he wasn't a stage manager. Yes sir, Jim Campbell, you likable ol' curmudgeon, you could harrumph with the best of them.

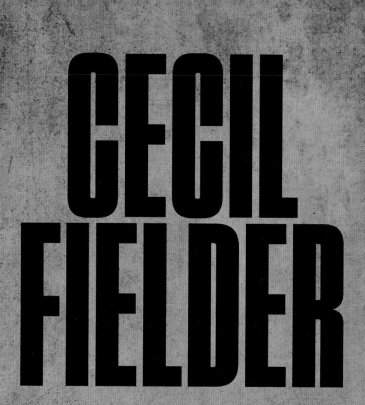

This is a story of power, pride, and of one of the most exciting individual countdowns in Detroit Tigers history—a daily drama that went down to the wire. Cecil Fielder started the 1990 season going 3-for-19 with one RBI—but more notably without any home runs in his first five games. The word of the week, however, was *patience*. After all, here was a slugger coming off an impressive spring, a hitter who'd been a part-time player with the Toronto Blue Jays before signing with Japan's Hanshin Tigers, the only team anywhere that promised to play him every day.

But there was no indication yet if he would live up to expectations—or even what the expectations were. No one, including Tigers general manager Bill Lajoie, disputed that Fielder had power. Playing the equivalent of a full season with the Blue Jays (506 at-bats in four years), he had hit 31 home runs. For Hanshin in 1989 he hit 38. Everywhere Fielder played he had hit home runs.

Keeping their fingers crossed that he would, the Tigers had signed him to fix their power problem. While putting together an embarrassingly bad 59–103 record in 1989, they finished 11th out of 14 American League teams in home runs and 13th in runs scored. They were a team on the skids, one that had to do something drastic to reverse the trend. So while acknowledging that he had never been a regular in the majors, they outbid other interested teams for Fielder, who seemed headed for a big year in spring training when he hit two home runs in three different games.

With the new season about to begin, there was a buzz about the new slugger. Maybe this time the Tigers had actually found themselves a legitimate power hitter. Manager Sparky Anderson went so far as to say Fielder would hit 30 home runs in his first year as a Tiger. "Anything more than that is up to him," Anderson said. "I don't go that far."

After three losses to begin the 1990 season, the Tigers beat the Boston Red Sox 11–7 for their first victory of the season, but Fielder's bat remained quiet. They followed that with a 10–6 victory against the Baltimore Orioles. It looked like the Tigers' offense, which had also added Tony Phillips, suddenly contained some punch—at least to the extent that they hadn't scored 10 runs or more in consecutive April games since 1979. "Big Daddy," as Fielder would eventually be known, hadn't yet contributed.

But that was about to change. After the victory against the Orioles, Fielder chipped in with a booming blast to the upper deck in right field at Tiger Stadium—quite a poke for a right-handed hitter. Four days later, Fielder hit another home run—then two in three days and two more in the same game. His thunder had arrived. By the end of April, Fielder had hit seven home runs.

It was a good trend that would soon get better. When he hit three home runs in Toronto against his former teammates on May 6, Fielder fever was in full force. With seven hits in the next four games, his batting average rose to .305. After an early slump, all was well.

Having Fielder on track didn't mean the Tigers were, however. They had fallen to 9–17 by the end of their visit to Toronto. Making matters more unsettled, Anderson had a blow-up with the Detroit media over the reporting of a team meeting. Some remember it as the worst clash of his 17 years as Tigers manager. Others dismissed it. Team president Bo Schembechler didn't view the incident as being major, for instance saying that "Anytime you get mad at the press, it's justified."

For a while, though, the more home runs Cecil hit, the more games the Tigers lost. They fell to 9–19 as Fielder connected in each of the next two games after the Toronto series. He was up to 13 when they were down to 11–22. As early as it was, Fielder's ability to reach the seats not only became the talk of the Tigers' season, it was also all that mattered.

The newspapers began home-run contests—how many would Cecil hit? But the real measure of how fans caught on to what he was doing is that instead of still calling him Cecil (as in SEE-sil), they began to pronounce his name correctly—as in SESS-il.

By the end of May, Cecil had 18 home runs and was being talked about as an All-Star.

Cecil Fielder bats during 1990, the year he hit 51 home runs in his first season with the Tigers. (USA TODAY Sports Images)

What Fielder did on June 6 at Indians pitcher Greg Swindell's expense in Cleveland, though, had all of baseball talking about him. That's the day he became the first Tiger ever to hit three home runs in a game twice in the same season. Now with 22 home runs—and on a pace to hit 66—Fielder was hitting good pitches, bad pitches, inside, outside, you name it. "I don't understand what's going on," he said. "But I'm basically thrilled."

There hadn't been a 50-home run hitter in the majors since George Foster of the Cincinnati Reds in 1977, the longest such drought since Babe Ruth tossed dirt upon the coffin of the deadball era with 54 home runs in 1920. But by August, Cecil had 50 in his sights. Throughout the summer, Fielder remained graciously quiet about his pace. He continued to say he was trying to knock in runs instead of hitting home runs and that whenever he hit a home run in a defeat, "We all lose."

His son, Prince—a happy six-year-old who seemed born to be around a major league clubhouse—was a frequent presence but not yet reaching the seats himself during batting practice. That wouldn't happen until he was 12. But anyone who remembers Cecil as a Tiger also remembers Prince long before Prince himself became a Tiger.

On August 25 Fielder hit his 40th home run, becoming the first Tiger ever to clear the roof in left at Tiger Stadium. Estimates put the blast at over 500 feet. It was "the longest ever hit off me," claimed Oakland A's pitcher Dave Stewart. "We just sat there in amazement," said Tigers outfielder Chet Lemon.

But Fielder took it in quiet stride. "It's a home run whether it goes over the roof or not," he said. "Give the credit to Bill Lajoie. He's the one who gave me the chance to play here."

Cecil was honorably motivated to live up to Lajoie's trust in him. Immensely proud, Fielder had left the majors for Japan in 1989 to prove he could play every day, but he also enjoyed his time there. "They treated us like kings," he said.

In fact, he would have been happy to spend a second season in Japan, but when several interested major league teams called, he owed it to himself and his family to listen. Although he hadn't met Lajoie face-to-face, Fielder signed with the Tigers because their interest in him did not waver. A signing bonus of $1.5 million—plus

$1.5 million more in salary for both 1990 and 1991—also influenced his decision to return from Japan.

With 10 games remaining, Fielder was sitting at 47 home runs. However, with pressure mounting and his irritation with what he called "constant questions" growing, he had hit only .211 with three

PAW PAW'S SUNDAY PUNCH

Charlie Maxwell was born in Lawton, Michigan, but he was called "ol' Paw Paw" for the nearby town to which he moved after he got married. And he was known for his "Sunday punch" because he hit so many of his home runs on Sunday—40 of his 148, according to one study.

At one point in 1959, Maxwell connected on six of nine Sundays.

Of course, the tradition of playing Sunday doubleheaders helped. A popular Tigers outfielder, Maxwell averaged 24 home runs, 82 RBIs, and a .272 batting average from 1956 to 1960. He was an affable individual who used to run to the dugout after striking out because he thought fans deserved to see the next batter as quickly as possible.

But Maxwell is most remembered for the four home runs he hit in four consecutive at-bats on May 3, 1959 at Briggs Stadium. The four were spread over a doubleheader sweep—the last at-bat of the opener against the New York Yankees, followed by his first three at-bats in the second game. What's more, they were hit off four different pitchers.

Leading off, Maxwell connected off Don Larsen in the seventh inning of the first game.

In the second game, he hit a two-run shot in the first inning off former Tigers pitcher Duke Maas. Then he walked in the second, which, of course, qualified as a plate appearance, not an at-bat.

In the fourth inning, he connected off Johnny Kucks, belting a pitch off the facing of the center-field bleachers with two runners on. In the seventh inning, he hit another solo home run off Zach Monroe. And in the eighth, Maxwell was on deck when Bobo Osborne grounded out to second with the bases loaded to end the inning.

Would Charlie have made it 5-for-5? We'll never know. But 4-for-4 was impressive enough. In fact, it pleased another Paw Paw resident so much that he quickly sent him a telegram. "Look, it's from a barber," Maxwell said. "Free haircuts for life." To the winners, and the sluggers, go the spoils, Charlie.

home runs in his last 16 games. A photo finish seemed certain. The countdown continued.

No. 48 was a grand slam off Mike Moore in Oakland. "I have to keep myself as calm as possible and not think about it," Fielder said about getting closer to 50. "But every time I'm at the plate, someone is yelling 'Hit another one.'"

In his next game, Fielder hit a long fly ball to left against the Seattle Mariners at Tiger Stadium. It looked like it had a chance to become No. 49, but Ken Griffey Sr., also the father of a player who would go on to an All-Star career, caught the ball near the warning track.

Two days later, in a makeup game on September 27, Fielder hit No. 49 against Boston.

He now had one home run to go with six games left, the first five of which proved to be excruciatingly homerless for him—as well as for the fans who so adamantly wanted to see him hit one more. "Who would ever think that 49 home runs would become a horrible cross to bear?" *The Detroit News* columnist Shelby Strother wrote.

In the last series of the season at home, Fielder didn't come close to reaching the seats in three games. "I had a feeling this might happen if 49 and 50 didn't come bang-bang," Anderson said. "I knew the last one might be tough. It's all he's thinking about. He's trying to lift the ball into the air."

Previously approachable, Fielder departed for the Tigers' final series of the season in New York without speaking to reporters. He merely nodded as he left. In the first game at Yankee Stadium, he struck out three times—and twice more the next night. Since hitting his 49th home run, Fielder was 2-for-20.

With one game remaining, the ordeal had consumed almost all hope that he would get it done. Favoring Fielder, however, was the fact that he'd be facing struggling Yankees left-hander Steve Adkins, a rookie who was making his fifth (and final) major league start and desperate to throw strikes because he had walked 25 batters in his first 20 innings. Yankees manager Stump Merrill said, "He has an amazing knuckle-curve. Hitters can't hit him. But too often they don't have to."

With his future possibly on the line, Adkins knew he had to throw strikes to the Detroit hitters he'd be facing. Cecil would be waiting for them. But, of course, he walked in the first inning. In his second at-bat, Fielder lined out to left. Making solid contact, though, he had not been fooled by Adkins' pitch. Nor would he be fooled the next time.

In the top of the fourth—with his good friend Phillips on first base chirping for him to get it done—Fielder got a good pitch to hit. And he hit it well. There was never any doubt that the fly ball had enough distance as it traveled down the left-field line at Yankee Stadium. But it was hooking. "If it had gone foul, I would have been dead," Fielder said.

Would it get to the seats in time? Here is how broadcaster Paul Carey called it: "Here's the stretch by Adkins, the set, the pitch... there's a long fly ball to left down the line. If it stays fair, it's gone... It hits the facing of the upper deck! It's gone! Home run No. 50 for Cecil Fielder—a tremendous belt. You had to hold your breath. Now Cecil is happy. He's waving his hands to the crowd and gets hugs and embraces from his teammates. They're all happy for him."

Four innings later, relaxed and relieved at the plate, he hit his 51st homer. The season ended with Cecil smiling. Fielder would end his career with 319 home runs. Forced to retire in 2016 because of repeated neck surgeries, his son, Prince, also finished with 319 home runs, making it a fitting end to a terrific baseball story.

47

LES MUELLER'S 19²/₃ INNING EFFORT

The most enduring stories in baseball are sometimes about players whose hopes were dashed at the next-to-last moment—if not at the very last moment. What happened to Tigers pitcher Les Mueller will forever rank as one of the harshest roster cuts ever.

But through the years, there have been some dandies. For instance, there were two young Tigers leaving spring training with the big league club in 1985. At least they thought they were.

Mike Laga, a first baseman, and Doug Baker, a shortstop, packed their bags at the team hotel in Lakeland, Florida, and took the short bus ride to pick up the other players at Joker Marchant Stadium—all the while hoping they wouldn't be taken off the bus. But, alas, their names were called. They had not made the team. Their excitement about being on the brink of making the Tigers' roster became the disappointment of finding out they were headed back to the minors.

At the time, it seemed hard-hearted. That's because at the time it was. But in the case of both Laga and Baker, they eventually made it back to the majors.

Jack Morris said the same thing happened to him in 1979, but he obviously made it back, too. "I was taken off the bus before it left for the airport," he said. "My bags were packed. I was so angry. But I went down to the minors where Jim Leyland helped me get it out of my system. He showed me tough love. After two really good games at Triple A, I got called up and never looked back."

In 1991 pitcher Mark Leiter actually left Florida with the Tigers—only to be optioned to the minors on the morning of the home opener, so that the team could make roster room for newly signed outfielder Pete Incaviglia. Leiter would eventually pitch another nine seasons in the majors, but even his was not the cruelest case of a player being sent down at the last moment.

Years before—back in 1946—there was a Tigers' player who was told even later than the morning of a day-game opener that he hadn't made the team. Mueller was that player.

What he had done as a Tiger the year before—one grueling contribution in particular—not only made the move more surprising, but also the demotion far more difficult to take. In Jim Sargent's biography of Mueller for the Society of American Baseball Research, the right-hander from Illinois said he was in the dugout at Briggs Stadium waiting for the Tigers' 1946 home opener to begin. He wasn't the scheduled starter, but after being relied upon by the Tigers down the stretch in 1945 and responding with some big wins, it was reasonable for Mueller to think that his spot on the pitching staff was secure.

But it wasn't. "You're wanted in the office," Mueller was told as game time approached.

The message was more odd than ominous. Nobody already in the dugout waiting for the first pitch on Opening Day gets sent to the minors. But Mueller had been summoned to general manager George Trautman's office to be told the bad news.

It can't get much more shattering than that for a ballplayer, especially for one who had helped the year before in a way we will never see again. Getting the starting assignment on July 21, 1945, against the Philadelphia Athletics during a season in which the Tigers would eventually win the World Series, Mueller, according to his estimates, threw 370 pitches in one game. The way the game has evolved, a pitcher who throws 120 pitches in a game in today's world is praised for his durability. If a pitcher throws more than 100 pitches on a consistent basis, he's called a "horse."

But the Tigers didn't have a deep bullpen available to them that July day at Shibe Park in Philadelphia. They were coming off two doubleheaders in three days in Washington, so it was up to Mueller to pitch as deep into the game as he could, which he proceeded to do. With the score tied 1–1, he worked the first nine innings. But he didn't stop there.

With his team needing him to, could Mueller possibly go 10? Sure, he could go 10.

Could he go 11? Sure, he could go 11. Could he maybe even go 14 innings? Whether or not he could, he did, cruising through uncharted outs. As crazy as it sounds, Mueller was asked if he could pitch 17 innings if needed. What the heck? He was feeling good, throwing well, so on he went. The 18th inning went by. So did the 19th.

Finally in the 20th inning, Tigers manager Steve O'Neill replaced Mueller, who had just issued his second walk of the inning with two outs. The Tigers dodged the trouble, and the game continued—only to have it be called because of darkness in the 24th inning while the two teams were still tied. All those outs led to a no-decision.

But the Tigers were indebted to Mueller. They had to be. He had just pitched 19 ⅔ innings for them. He had faced 74 batters before tiring. No starting pitcher since Mueller has pitched into the 20th inning. No pitcher before Mueller had done it since 1929, and no pitcher probably will ever again. It's lucky his arm didn't fall off. Even in the 20th inning, however, Mueller didn't want to be replaced. When O'Neill arrived at the mound to make the move, Mueller responded by saying, "Gee, the game isn't over yet."

Growing up in the St. Louis area, Mueller had attracted the attention of several scouts as a teenager but signed with the Tigers because they gave him a bonus of $5,000. As it did with many other players, World War II interrupted his career. Mueller pitched in four games in 1941 and then left for military service. It wasn't until 1945 that he returned to the big leagues with the Tigers.

During his comeback season, Mueller blanked the New York Yankees in his first start with a two-hitter on May 31, but he was both good and erratic after that. For instance, in the best four of his first eight starts that season, Mueller allowed five earned runs in 32 ⅔ innings. In the worst four, he allowed 22 earned runs in 18 ⅔ innings. He was either hittable and wild—or extremely effective.

Then along came the historic July 21 game against the Athletics on such a sweltering Saturday afternoon that a crowd of only 4,526 was on hand. Of course, it also didn't boost their attendance that the

A's were 28–51 at the time and firmly in last place with a team that had a hard time scoring runs. It took the two not to tango, though. The game reached the 24th inning because the Tigers' offense mustered nothing more than Mueller had allowed. And the one run off him had been unearned.

The Tigers didn't end up with any of their hitters going 0-for-10 during the ordeal, as future Hall of Famer George Kell did for the A's, but Detroit's Eddie Mayo and Bob Swift both went 0-for-9. Along with the lack of runs, there was another problem: the game took forever to play—four hours and 48 minutes, to be exact. Shibe Park had lights, but in those days, the rules were that stadium lights could only be used for night games. They could not be turned on for extra-inning day games. So, by the time the 24th inning rolled around for the Tigers and A's, it was getting dark. A run for either team would have decided the outcome, but the umpires eventually had to suspend play. Mueller had thrown 19 ⅔ innings of a 24-inning tie.

After that, understandably, he didn't pitch again for two weeks. His next appearance was August 5. Mueller never said his arm ached after his epic start, but it had to be tired. Any arm would be after 370 pitches. He made other important appearances down the stretch in 1945, going 3–4 with a 3.48 ERA in nine starts, following the marathon in July. But he also ran into some bad luck.

For instance, in his first start back from the 24-inning game, Mueller took a six-hit shutout into the bottom of the ninth against the Chicago White Sox, only to have the Sox eke out a 3–2 victory with the help of an unearned run. To balance that, Mueller was the winning pitcher in a 1–0 game against the A's that was called because of rain after five innings.

The Tigers, though, won the American League pennant in 1945 and then the World Series against the Chicago Cubs. In his only appearance of the series, Mueller pitched two scoreless innings. Following the series, he went home to contemplate his future, which looked bright during the winter of 1945–46. After all, he was only 26.

Throughout spring training and as the season approached, it was reasonable to think that the Tigers valued him as a pitcher and that he'd make the team in 1946. But along came those words dreaded by any player: "You're wanted in the office." That was the end of Mueller's time as a Tiger. Sadly—and also unfairly, it would seem—he never pitched in the majors again.

RON LeFLORE

"I don't want you around me ever again. You are no friend of mine."
—Tigers president and general manager Jim Campbell
to Ron LeFlore, March 12, 1981

In the beginning, when they signed him out of prison, the saga of Ron LeFlore and the Detroit Tigers was a joyous one, a shining example of redemption, an illustration of a life no longer errant—until that day in spring training when an angry Campbell walked away from LeFlore and all the warmth between the two was gone. Biting the hand that had fed him—with comments that his former boss correctly construed as insulting—LeFlore burned the bridge connecting the world of crime he once knew to his new life as a major league star. "That's the first time I've ever told a player to stay away from me," Campbell said. "But I meant it. Ronnie opened his mouth too many times."

How had such a strong bond between LeFlore and the team that rescued him been broken? It happened in part because LeFlore so successfully left his past behind that he eventually viewed life only through the lens of being a highly paid ballplayer, not as a felon reclaimed. But it also was broken because LeFlore simply could not help himself. He seldom stopped short of going too far. Consequently, he eventually became persona non grata to all three major league teams for which he played—the Tigers, Montreal Expos, and Chicago White Sox. From being the toast of baseball to his career becoming toast long before it should have, LeFlore experienced a mercurial rise but a rapid fall as well. Years later he would become a broken man far removed from the game that once embraced him. What a story he was in his time, though.

Maybe you read the book that was written about LeFlore or saw the movie made about him. Or perhaps you just remember him as a lightning bolt on the bases in the 1970s. He was an outfielder the

DETROIT TIGERS

Tigers signed out of Jackson State Prison in Michigan, an athlete who had never played baseball and never even knew he could be good at it until he started playing the game in what he called "the institution." That's where LeFlore's talent was first noticed. That's where his potential attracted attention. Not only was he fast, but he also was strong. He also had natural ability. Said Ralph Houk, LeFlore's first major league manager, "Nobody has taught this kid. He just has that instinct."

But he was raw. At one of his first tryouts with the Tigers, LeFlore took some swings and then was told to run to second base. So that's what he did. The story goes that LeFlore ran straight from home plate to second over the pitcher's mound.

But the workout resulted in a signed contract all the same, and as soon as LeFlore was paroled, not only was he on his way to Clinton, Iowa, his first stop in professional baseball, but also to a life no longer dependent on crime. To understand LeFlore, though, and to fully comprehend the degree to which his well-being was salvaged, one must understand the four major chapters of his life:

1) Before signing with the Tigers
2) After signing
3) After the Tigers traded him
4) After ending his baseball career

Some of the twists benefited him. Many of the turns did not. But at the summit of his career, he felt that he had become a superstar. "Although there is some speculation by others that I don't fit the label," he said after being traded to Montreal, "I'd have to say 'Yes, I'm a superstar.'"

At LeFlore's lowest professional point, however, the man who made it all possible for him said he never wanted to speak to him again—and never did. LeFlore's offense was to say that the Tigers were only pretending when claiming they wanted to win. Basically, he called them liars. "I've always been able to kid with him," LeFlore said of Campbell that day in 1981. "But this time he would have none of it. I guess he's getting sensitive. It doesn't bother me if that's the way he wants it. He's not my boss anymore."

Because of where LeFlore came from and eventually got to—serving a sentence for armed robbery before carving out an impactful baseball career—he ranks as one of the most iconic Tigers. His story started on the streets of Detroit. The exact year in which he was born—1948, 1950, or 1952—has never been accurately ascertained, but for sure he was headed for trouble as a teenager. "I fell in with the wrong people," he said. "My parents told me to stay away from 'those guys,' but I didn't listen. I was hardheaded. I was too busy trying to be slick."

LeFlore preferred being out of school to being in and, according to his own description, he was "a flashy guy." But to possess the clothes and whatever else qualifies one as "flashy," money was needed. When the amount he had ran out, more was needed. One night LeFlore and two others robbed a check-cashing agency in Detroit. After fleeing the scene, the three called for a taxi—only to have a police car arrive at the same time the taxi did. LeFlore was caught holding the gun. He was convicted of armed robbery and sentenced to five to 15 years.

In the fourth year of LeFlore's sentence, he caught a break. Tigers manager Billy Martin learned of a wondrous talent playing baseball in prison, a player to whom he should grant a tryout. "I was crazy about him," Martin told *The Sporting News'* Jim Hawkins, who chronicled LeFlore's career in the book *Breakout.* "Someone [in the front office] said, 'but Billy, he's in jail,' and I replied, 'where did you get Gates Brown—out of kindergarten?'"

Brown, the Tigers' pinch-hitter extraordinaire, served time for burglary in Ohio before signing with the Tigers. He would prove to be invaluable in giving LeFlore advice. "You're going to hear it all from the people in the stands," Brown told him. "With me, it was 'Con' and 'Jailbird.' It was pretty vicious at first in the minors, but it made me try harder and do better. By the end of the year, I led the team in hitting and all the fans were on my side."

LeFlore signed with the Tigers on July 2, 1973. Before leaving prison, he told his fellow inmates that by the following year "you guys are going to see me playing on television."

They scoffed. But he was determined. At Clinton, Jim Leyland was LeFlore's first professional manager. He was also one of the first victims of how hard LeFlore could hit a ball.

"I brought him out early one day to throw him batting practice," Leyland said, "and he nailed a ball on about my fifth pitch that hit me right in the kidney. It hurt so bad that, to be honest with you, I wanted to cry. But I didn't. I thought to myself, *I can't let this guy know I'm not tough.*"

Leyland recalls that "NBC sent a reporter to cover LeFlore's first game, and on his first at-bat, a routine ground ball to the shortstop, he beat the throw to first. I'd never seen anything like it. That's how fast he ran. He was a real talent."

LeFlore's prediction about how soon he'd be in the majors came true. Although feeling down deep that he wasn't ready and sensing the Tigers were promoting him only to boost attendance, he played in his first big league game on August 1, 1974. Houk said the move was "a good gamble. He's no baby. I doubt this can hurt him." Besides, Houk was eager to utilize LeFlore's vaunted speed. "I don't think I've ever seen anyone run faster or get into high gear faster," the manager they called "the Major" said.

Looking out of place for only his first seven games, LeFlore hit .280 in the final 200 at-bats of his rookie season. But he soon found out there was more than speed to stealing bases.

After setting a goal of 60 stolen bases in 1975, he came up far short at 28. But with an improved technique and better timing, he averaged 61 steals and a .310 batting average for his next four seasons. In 1976, LeFlore's only All-Star season, he began the year with a 30-game hitting streak, during which he hit .392. He even got three hits the day his brother, Gerald, was shot and killed. "I don't know how I played that day," he said. "I don't know how I was able to hold back the tears."

Thirty was a rare feat, one to be fully appreciated. Tigers great Al Kaline never hit safely in 30 straight games. Neither did Ted Williams, Mickey Mantle, Lou Gehrig, Babe Ruth, nor Hank Aaron. And LeFlore was still a relative newcomer.

Always in the background, but not always heeded, was advice from Brown, LeFlore's mentor, who told columnist Joe Falls: "You never have anything made. You can make it for two weeks, two months or two years, but you have to keep working and hold yourself together."

Somewhere along the way—maybe because of all the attention surrounding *One in a Million: the Ron LeFlore Story*, the 1977 movie about LeFlore in which LeVar Burton played the lead role—bad habits reappeared. Nothing that got him in trouble with the law (until later), but it was enough to land him in a doghouse or two. Four whiskey bottles were thrown at LeFlore on Opening Day at Tiger Stadium in 1979 because he played so badly. "I've overcome more than this," he said.

Looking for a better contract than the Tigers were offering as free agency began, LeFlore was traded to Montreal for pitcher Dan Schatzeder after the 1979 season. The Tigers later let it be known that LeFlore had been fined four times that year for being late to batting practice—not the way to get on Sparky Anderson's good side.

Making matters worse, if there was a lesson to be learned, LeFlore didn't learn it. The Expos opted not to bring back LeFlore, despite his 97 stolen bases in 1980, because another manager was fed up with his behavior. Said John McHale Sr., the Expos' president, "Dick Williams had a major say in not offering him a contract." In a story by Ian MacDonald for *The Sporting News*, McHale said, "Williams was very clear. He told me he did not want LeFlore on the team. He said it was impossible to control him."

LeFlore landed on his feet when he signed a four-year, $3 million contract with the White Sox that same offseason, but in his second year with the Sox, he fell out of favor with manager Tony La Russa for being late to a July game after "oversleeping." He seldom started after that.

In October of 1982, LeFlore was arrested on two counts of unregistered weapons as well as for possession of a controlled substance. He never played in another major league game. After his career LeFlore ricocheted from one personal crisis to another.

He was charged at least twice for non-payment of child support, including when he returned to Detroit in 1999 for the last game at Tiger Stadium. He lost his right leg from the knee down in 2011 to a disease he said was caused by his many years of smoking. Tragically, he also lost his seven-week-old son to Sudden Infant Death Syndrome.

With baseball as his guiding light, LeFlore had once grabbed the world by the tail, but success slipped away until none remained. Brown's words of wisdom had been painfully correct all along, and they echo through canyons of sadness to this day. As much as you might think otherwise, "You never have anything made."

COMING CLOSE IN 1909

Game 6 of the 1909 World Series ended with a Pirates player unsuccessfully attempting to steal third base with his team down by only a run. Can you imagine how many times such a bonehead play would be replayed and critiqued if it were to happen today? Twitter would light up—and stay lit. Well, it was a blunder that carried the Tigers to the threshold of glory for the first time but not quite through the door. The year was 1909. The Tigers and the Pittsburgh Pirates were in the World Series.

It was the third World Series in a row for the Tigers, but nothing had gone right for them in the first two. In fact, when they lost the opener against the Pirates in 1909, combined with what had taken place the two previous years, the Tigers had failed to win 10 of their first 11 World Series games. Would they ever get over the hurdle, the mental block, or whatever was preventing them from looking like they were capable of winning a championship?

They would, but it would take a gift from the Pirates—a daring, but dumb play that backfired—for the Tigers to force their first Game 7. Despite reaching their third consecutive World Series, the Tigers hadn't exactly made a name for themselves as a postseason powerhouse.

Not only were they swept by the Chicago Cubs in 1907, but after also scoring three runs in the opener of that series, the Tigers added only three more the rest of the way.

In 1908 the Tigers won Game 3 against the Cubs, but either the shock or the joy of actually winning a game dealt them such a setback that they were blanked in the next two. Bottom line, they were embarrassed—again.

So when the Pirates opened the 1909 World Series with a 4–1 victory, it looked like the Tigers might suffer a similar fate. This team, though, had more spunk than its predecessors. After losing the opener, it won Game 2. It also won Game 4—a shutout in which the Pirates made six errors. But to win it all in 1909, a hint of hope had to come first, which it did with a Game 6 victory that served as the Tigers' most celebrated triumph for the next quarter of a century.

However, it also set them up for more disappointment.

Baseball was played in faster fashion back then. It was rare for an individual game to last two hours—even in a World Series. The first five games of the 1909 Series had flown by—all of them finishing in less than two hours. That meant the Tigers had rapidly advanced to Game 6, where they found themselves in the familiar position of staring at elimination. For them to have a hope of winning the World Series, or even convincing anyone that they weren't going to be pushovers again, they had to win Game 6—any way they could—to tie the series at three games each. Or any way the baseball gods would allow.

The game at Bennett Park in Detroit began badly for the Tigers, however, with the first four Pittsburgh batters bunching hits to take a 3–0 lead against the Tigers' best starting pitcher, George Mullin. Was it happening again? Would the Tigers go through three World Series in three years without giving themselves a chance to win any of them?

It looked like it.

A Detroit run in the bottom of the first inning helped, however. Not only did it quickly cut the Pirates' lead from three to two runs, but it also interrupted Pittsburgh's early momentum. This time the Tigers were not going to go away quietly. Mullin settled down. Then again, he had to or there wouldn't be a Game 7.

A tough right-hander who'd been 29–8 during the season— heights he would never come close to reaching again—Mullin got out of a second-and-third jam with a strikeout in the third inning before the Tigers tied the score with two runs in the bottom of the fourth. Was a comeback taking place? Indeed, it was, and the extent of it was carrying the Tigers from three runs down to two runs in front.

With runs in the fifth and sixth innings, they took a 5–3 lead. Having a lackluster series—his second in three years—even Ty Cobb contributed. But the drama was just beginning. Mullin was still in the game for the Tigers when the game moved to the top of the ninth. That wasn't surprising. With 29 complete games that season, he was their horse. There were no closers back then—not as we know the role now—plus Mullin had kept the visiting Pirates off the scoreboard since the first inning. The game was his to finish if he could. And oh, how Mullin wanted to prove to the fans that he could. Not trusting their team after miserable conclusions to the World Series in 1907 and 1908, Detroiters didn't fill Bennett Park for Game 6.

Part of their skepticism could have been because the responsibility for keeping the Tigers alive had been placed on Mullin—with just one day's rest. But it was a challenge he embraced. Hall of Fame baseball writer Fred Lieb described it in his book, *The Detroit Tigers*. "How do you feel," manager Hughie Jennings asked Mullin the morning of Game 6. "I want to start you if you are right." He responded: "I think I can tie that series up for you."

When Pittsburgh came up to hit in the ninth, trailing by two, it set the stage for an inning that Lieb said "was another classic in Detroit history. Conversation on both sides was sulphuric, and spikes rode high."

After a quick run, it came down to this: with nobody out and runners on first and third, the Pirates needed another score to tie the game. But it looked like they might get two. In the course of the rough-and-tumble ninth inning, Chief Wilson of the Pirates had knocked Tom Jones of the Tigers out of the game with a heavy collision at first base. Jones had to be taken off on a stretcher. Everything pointed to the Pirates suddenly having the advantage, but they quickly relinquished it.

On a grounder to Sam Crawford at first base, Pittsburgh's Bill Abstein—"despite his coach's advice," wrote Lieb—tried to score. With his slide, Abstein badly cut Tigers' catcher Boss Schmidt, but he was called out. The usually aggressive Wilson had not taken third on the play, however. He had settled for second—a blunder for which he would soon try to make amends.

With pinch-hitter Batty Abbaticchio at the plate, what happened next became the Tigers' most memorable World Series moment of a generation. Mullin, wrote Lieb, "blazed a third strike over on [Abbaticchio], giving it everything he had. On the pitch, Wilson tried to steal third but was called out on a close play in which [Tigers' third baseman George Moriarity] was spiked."

Tempers erupted on the field. Fights threatened to break out on numerous fronts.

"The end of the game," Lieb wrote, "was almost a Donnybrook Fair," referring to a riotous event in Ireland.

But the Tigers had won. With Mullin throwing a complete game, they'd finally given themselves the chance at their elusive first World Series victory. That was all it proved to be, however—just a chance.

Not able to get loose on a cold and windy day, Wild Bill Donovan of the Tigers lived up to his nickname in Game 7. He walked six and hit a batter in the first three innings. By the time Mullin—yes, Mullin again—replaced him in the fourth, Pittsburgh had taken charge. Clearly overworked, Mullin was ineffective in relief, and the Pirates would win 8–0.

Another Detroit player was spiked and removed on a stretcher in Game 7, but the bigger impact of the loss was that the Tigers and their fans would have to wait another 26 years for their first championship. They would not win a World Series until their fifth try in 1935. But what the Pirates did in the ninth inning of Game 6 in 1909 enabled the Tigers to get as close to winning as they would get before finally ending their drought. The glimpse of glory had been fun while it lasted.

50
MAYO'S GAMBLE

Mayo Smith isn't remembered because he was wildly charismatic—which, incidentally, he wasn't. Nor, of course, is he remembered because he enjoyed golf so much that he retired to his Florida home at age 55 to play more of it. Nor because he became known as "America's Guest" for the many hours he spent talking baseball in various press rooms around the major leagues. As the manager of the 1968 World Series champion Detroit Tigers, Smith is remembered for two related reasons—the big decision and the courage required to make it.

Heading into the World Series against the St. Louis Cardinals, Smith faced what looked like a can't-win situation. Who was going to be his shortstop? Because that question hadn't yet been answered, the Tigers also weren't sure who would be starting in center or right field either. As soon as the Tigers clinched the American League pennant on September 17—which came about when Don Wert drove in Al Kaline with a walk-off single, as Ernie Harwell memorably described to his radio listeners, "Let's listen to the bedlam"—Smith knew he had a dilemma on his hands.

Ray Oyler was his best defensive shortstop, but Oyler could not hit. Seriously, the man simply could not hit. Oyler had reached new heights—such as they were—with a .207 batting average in 1967, but a year later, the Tigers had no recourse then to give up on him. In mid-July he was hitting .162 (even had a little three-game streak in the works), but at that point, Oyler just shut down offensively. From July 14 to the end of the 1968 season, he went 0-for-36 with two walks. No matter how slick Oyler was with the glove, the Tigers could not start a shortstop in the World Series with a .053 on-base percentage in his last 33 games.

But before Smith could turn to Plan B, he had to devise one. At the same time, the Tigers had four outfielders for three positions—

actually three for two because Willie Horton was such a mainstay in left that he would not be part of a musical chairs game if there was to be one. The luxurious complication was created when Kaline had fully recovered from the broken left arm he suffered when hit by a Lew Krausse pitch on May 25. Since returning from the injury on July 1, however, Kaline had been a part-time player for the Tigers, hitting .305 while starting about half the games—many of them at first base—throughout the summer.

Mickey Stanley, meanwhile, had played errorless ball in center, and Jim Northrup, while taking over in right, had made a mark for himself offensively by hitting four grand slams by the end of June. With the World Series approaching, all three outfielders deserved to play. Stanley and Northrup deserved it because of how they contributed during the regular season, and Kaline merited it because of who he was and for how he had always contributed.

But the designated hitter era was five years away from beginning, so Mayo had to come up with a way of getting all three into the same lineup. It was first thought that Kaline might bump third baseman Wert to shortstop—or out of the lineup entirely. Wert began to worry he'd be left out. "I can see why they want Al in the lineup," he said. "But I want to be in there, too. I don't think I'd have any trouble [at short] if they let me play a few games before the series."

Such a move meant two players would be playing out of position, though, so it wasn't practical. Smith also felt that because of the bunting ability of the Cardinals' Lou Brock and Curt Flood that they could have taken advantage of Kaline at third. "We have to keep Wert at third," the manager concluded, "just for that reason."

Another thought was that rookie Tom Matchick might replace Oyler at short, but that would not solve the problem of the outfield. There seemed to be many options but no solutions. Columnist Joe Falls liked Smith and once wrote that Mayo's most frequent saying was "Aw, to hell with it."

But taking that approach wouldn't have been a problem solver either. Then suddenly, without even saying he was about to begin experimenting, Smith started Stanley at shortstop in the first game after the Tigers clinched. Stanley had only three fielding chances in the 6–2 victory against the New York Yankees, which garnered bigger headlines for being Denny McLain's 31st victory. But after the game, Smith said he would "probably" play Stanley again at short before the World Series.

To make matters even more complex—substantially so, in fact—the selfless Kaline already had told Smith that he didn't "deserve" to play in the World Series. Those were his words to Smith before the game in which the Tigers clinched the pennant. The future Hall of Famer felt that the players who'd been more instrumental in getting the Tigers to the World Series deserved to keep playing. "It's killing me, but I know what Mayo is up against," Kaline said. "I've waited all my life to get into the World Series, but he has to go with the kids [Stanley and Northrup]."

Falls went so far as to write that Kaline had lately been "a forlorn figure—working out at first and third, throwing batting practice and hitting with the scrubs." There had to be a way to get him into the lineup, but it wasn't with Kaline playing third base or at first base, where Norm Cash had hit .324 for a month before the Tigers clinched.

Fortunately for Smith, he had time to mull over the situation. It was going to be either a blessing or a curse that the Tigers had nine games remaining until the regular season ended. It would have been a blessing, for sure, if Smith knew what he was going to do. And while nothing can be called a curse for a manager when his team is headed to the World Series, this was close to being one.

Three games later, with six left, the solution began to play out. Stanley got another start at short, then another. "I think he can do the job," Smith said. "At least I want to see for myself."

In reality, the Tigers' manager had no idea how it was going to turn out, saying that Stanley's chances of starting the World Series at his new position were "about 50-50." Two days later, Falls wrote in the *Detroit Free Press* that it "is doubtful Smith is serious about starting Stanley at short, especially after the way Mick looked the other night against the Baltimore Orioles. He made the tough plays, but flubbed the easy ones, and generally looked like a player out of position."

There was this to keep in mind about Smith, though: "In his two seasons here," wrote beat writer George Cantor, "he's been an incredible gambler when it comes to using and switching around his personnel." But it was always done within the parameters of what players could do. "Mayo attempted to not overmanage," outfielder Northrup once said.

Still, Smith had come a long way from how he initially had been viewed by the local writers: "A bland man without imagination," Jerry Green of *The Detroit News* had described him. Smith might have been bland, but he didn't lack imagination. "He just never got the credit he deserved," McLain said.

With one regular season series remaining, Smith needed to see more from Stanley at short—where he had improved to the point of playing "fairly well," according to Cantor.

But Stanley hadn't yet turned a double play and still looked "uncertain." So it came down to the final three games—during the first of which Stanley made several good plays and looked "relaxed." It was enough to convince some that Stanley would start the World Series as the Tigers' shortstop. But after that Friday night game against the Washington Senators, Smith said, "I don't know. I just don't know. I'll let you know Saturday."

Then he quickly changed his mind. "I'll let you know Sunday," Smith said. "I just want to put the best team on the field that I can." But there was still no announcement before Sunday's game, the last of the regular season. That's because Smith said he made up his mind during the game, not before. After the final out of a 3-2 loss, he called reporters into his office. "All you vultures get in here," he said. "Let's get everybody in here."

Falls wrote that Mayo had the look of a man "under extreme pressure." There was a decision to be made, though Stanley would start at short, Kaline in right, and Northrup in center. "We're out to win this thing," Smith said. "By putting an extra bat in the lineup, we think we can do it. Maybe it won't work out that way, but that's the way we'll go."

It did work out that way, though. With Stanley making only two errors—despite years later admitting nervousness "because of so much pressure"—the Tigers beat the Cardinals in seven games.

Would they have done so without the decision to play Stanley at short, a sports decision ESPN called the third "gutsiest" decision in sports history? Who can tell? But the bottom line is Mayo gambled, and Mayo won. Forever more, he'll be known for his big decision—and the daring needed to make it.

[Acknowledgments]

This book has been a labor of love—while demanding a love of labor since it goes back to 1901, the year the Tigers joined the American League. I welcomed the challenge, though, because the Tigers—as most of you know—have been a fascinating franchise encompassing gladness, sadness, tragedy, and triumph.

I became enthralled with them and the game early on. Arrival day for baseball cards was golden. *Hey, I got a George Zuverink.* And imagine a late evening edition of a daily newspaper. The *Detroit Free Press* had one. It was delivered after dinner. I could check the box scores before going to bed.

But I'm already doing what I told myself I would not do in this acknowledgement section. I didn't want to spend a lot of time acknowledging my own love of the game, which, of course, has led to writing this book. So before the gentle reminder music starts and I'm escorted off the stage, I'd like to say thank you to...

Lisa, my wife, my love—you know I couldn't have done this without you.

JT, my son, and Melinda, my daughter-in-law, for as much help as they could be...from Dallas.

Claudia and Baba—for being supportive sisters.

Bill, my brother-in-law—for saying I should write a book, long before I wrote a book.

Dan Marowski, editor, friend—for his hard work, his diligence, and good advice.

Dan Marowski's family—for allowing Dan's time to be shared.

Chuck Klonke—for his incredible collection, a veritable library of books, newspapers, magazines, yearbooks, programs, guides, much of which he can sort of, sometimes, easily find.

Chuck Klonke's basement—for being big enough to house his incredible collection.

Chuck Klonke's understanding wife, Barb—who said good-bye to her basement years ago.

Jeff Fedotin and Tom Bast at Triumph Books—Jeff for helping a novice learn the ropes of a project lasting beyond a day's deadline; Tom for persistently knocking on my door.

Jim Hawkins, the one, the only "Hawk"—a great friend who kept telling me what to expect, always was right, and always answers his phone—except when he is watching *Judge Judy*.

Rob Parker—without whose support my life would not have changed the way it did.

My friends and colleagues in the Comerica Park press box—who kept saying, "That's one I'm going to read." Hopefully they do. I value their feedback.

Dan Ewald—a true friend and a heck of a writer

Jerry Green—the opposite, a heck of a writer and true friend.

In no particular order—Al Kaline, Willie Horton, Jim Leyland, Alan Trammell, Kirk Gibson, Mickey Lolich, John Hiller, Lou Whitaker, Denny McLain, Jack Morris, Frank Tanana, Robert Fick, the late Paul Carey, Dan Dickerson, Mario Impemba, Brandon Inge, Chet Lemon, Todd Jones, Brad Ausmus, Dave Dombrowski, Justin Verlander, Joel Zumaya, Ivan Rodriguez, Craig Monroe, Jim Price, Juan Berenguer, Bert Blyleven, Buck Martinez, and John Wockenfuss—for their time.

Danny Knobler—the most readable writer I know. If you haven't read *Numbers Don't Lie*, go out and buy it. Now.

The digitized archives of the *Detroit Free Press* at newspapers.com. Unequaled, they facilitated research.

The memory of Joe Falls—whose writing was the reason I didn't go to law school.

My *Monday Night Football* crew—we talk more than watch, eat more than drink, and solve the world's problems.

The National Baseball Hall of Fame and Museum—for helping me on trips back to 1909 and 1987.

Rusty, Chuck, and Sandy—all of whom helped with their interest.

My friends at N.A.T.E—National Association of Tiger Enthusiasts—for making suggestions on the porch in Lakeland.

Karen Bush—for the Eddie Lake Society, and whose love of baseball is unsurpassed.

Don Keko—for his help with the big list.

Ron C—for your help, too, and...your attempts to help.

Ed Devine—who would have been proud.

Scott Ferkovich—my SABR coach who opened the world of *The Sporting News* archives to me.

Our kitchen's granite slab—where I spent countless hours.

The many talented Detroit baseball writers who preceded me by decades, not years. Their style was different because the times were. What fun they had with their words, though.

And to 36 years on the road for *The Detroit News*—how fast they flew by.

[Bibliography]

Wire Services
Associated Press
United Press International

Periodicals
Detroit Free Press
The Detroit News
The Kansas City Star
Los Angeles Times
The New York Times
New York World-Telegram
The Sporting News
Toronto Sun

Writers
Bill Dow
Paul Gallico
Ian McDonald
Grantland Rice

SABR/Bio Project Writers
Ralph Berger—Bobo Newsom
Charlie Bevis—Mickey Cochrane
Matt Bohn—George Kell
David Cicotello—George Mullin
Dan D'Addona—Harry Heilmann

Scott Ferkovich—Hank Greenberg
David Ginsberg—Ty Cobb
Maxwell Kates—Norm Cash
Bill Lamberty—Sam Crawford
Rob Neyer—Tommy Bridges
Bill Nowlin—Marty McManus
Marc O'Konen and David Jones—Frank Navin
Bob O'Leary—Hooks Dauss and Bobby Veach
Ruth Sadler—Charlie Gehringer
Jim Sargent—Charlie Maxwell, Les Mueller
Terry Simpkins—Kid Elberfeld
Mark Stewart—Hal Newhouser
Cort Vitty—Goose Goslin
Nick Waddell—Al Kaline
Phil Williams—Boss Schmidt
Gregory H. Wolf—Virgil Trucks

Websites

baseball-almanac.com
baseball-reference.com
bleacherreport.com
blessyouboys.com
dailyfungo.com
detroitathletic.com
fangraphs.com
mlb.com
momsteam.com
newspapers.com
sabr.org/bio project
seamheads.com
thisgreatgame.com
youtube.com
wikipedia.org

Books

Auker, Elden and Keegan, Tom. *Sleeper Cars and Flannel Uniforms.* Triumph Books (2001).

Bak, Richard. *Cobb Would Have Caught It.* Wayne State University Press (1991).

Butler, Hal. *Stormin' Norman Cash.* Julian Messner (1968).

Cantor, George. *The Good, The Bad, & The Ugly.* Triumph Books (2008).

Cantor, George. *Wire to Wire.* Triumph Books (2004).

Cava, Pete. *Indiana-Born Major League Baseball Players.* McFarland & Company (2015).

Cohen, Robert W. *The 50 Greatest Players in Detroit Tigers History.* Taylor Trade (2016).

D'Addona, Dan. *In Cobb's Shadow.* McFarland & Company (2015).

Foster, Terry. *100 Things Tigers Fans Should Know Before They Die.* Triumph Books (2009).

Freedman, Lew. *The 50 Greatest Tigers Every Fan Should Know.* Blue River Press (2014).

Freehan, Bill. *Behind the Mask.* The World Publishing Company. (1970)

Green, Jerry. *Year of the Tiger.* Coward-McCann, Inc. (1969).

Hawkins, Jim and Ewald, Dan. *The Detroit Tigers Encyclopedia.* Sports Publishing L.L.C. (2003).

James, Bill. *The New Bill James Historical Baseball Abstract.* The Free Press (2001).

Knobler, Danny. *Numbers Don't Lie—Detroit Tigers.* Triumph Books (2015).

Leerhsen, Charles. *Ty Cobb—A Terrible Beauty.* Simon & Schuster (2015).

LeFlore, Ron and Hawkins, Jim. *Breakout—From Prison to the Big Leagues.* Harper & Row (1978).

Lieb, Frederick G. *The Detroit Tigers.* G.P. Putnam's Sons (1946).

McLain, Denny and Zaret, Eli. *I Told You I Wasn't Perfect.* Triumph Books (2007).

Moffi, Larry. *This Side of Cooperstown.* Courier Corporation (2013).

Nash, Bruce and Zullo, Allan. *The Baseball Hall of Shame.* Rowman and Littlefield. (2012).

Ritter, Lawrence. *The Glory of Their Times.* The Macmillan Company (1966).

Smith, Curt. *Voices of the Game.* Diamond Communications Inc. (1987).

Smith, Ira L. *Baseball's Famous Outfielders.* A.S. Barnes and Company (1954).

Smith, Ira L. *Baseball's Famous Pitchers.* A.S. Barnes and Company (1954).

[About the Author]

Tom Gage is a Hall of Fame baseball writer who covered the Detroit Tigers for *The Detroit News* as a traveling beat writer for 36 years (1979–2014). He also assisted with the coverage of the team for *The News* in 1976 (Mark Fidrych's breakout year), wrote columns for FOXSportsDetroit.com in 2015, and was a longtime correspondent for *The Sporting News*.

Taking into account spring training and postseason games, plus the regular season, he has covered more than 5,000 Tigers games.

In 2015 he was honored on Induction Weekend in Cooperstown, New York, by the National Baseball Hall of Fame and Museum for winning the J.G. Taylor Spink Award, the highest honor of the Baseball Writers Association of America (BBWAA). A winner of multiple Sportswriter of the Year Awards for Michigan, he was elected into the Michigan Sports Hall of Fame in 2016. He is the longtime chairman of the BBWAA's Detroit chapter.

Among his other honors are a Lifetime Achievement Award (2015), presented by the Detroit chapter of the Society of Professional Journalists, and the Dick Schaap Memorial Award for Excellence in Media, presented in 2016 by the Michigan Jewish Sports Foundation. In his final full year with *The News* (2014), his entry was judged "Best Sports Column" by the Michigan Associated Press Media Editors.

Married to Lisa with one son, J.T., he is a 1970 graduate of Washington & Lee University in Lexington, Virginia—where he was inducted, as an honorary member, into the national leadership honor society, Omicron Delta Kappa (ODK), in 2016.